The Adventurous Future

The Adventurous Future

A compilation of addresses, papers, statements, and messages associated with the celebration of the two-hundred-fiftieth anniversary of the Church of the Brethren

COMPILED
AND EDITED BY
PAUL H. BOWMAN
Chairman, 250th Anniversary Committee

An Anniversary Volume

1708 - 1958

THE BRETHREN PRESS
ELGIN, ILLINOIS

Copyright 1959
by
The Brethren Press

Book Design by Paul Dailey

Printed in the United States of America

"If any one comes to me and does not hate his own father and mother and wife and children and brothers and sisters, yes, and even his own life, he cannot be my disciple. Whoever does not bear his own cross and come after me, cannot be my disciple. For which of you, desiring to build a tower, does not first sit down and count the cost, whether he has enough to complete it? Otherwise, when he has laid a foundation, and is not able to finish, all who see it begin to mock him, saying, 'This man began to build, and was not able to finish.' Or what king, going to encounter another king in war, will not sit down first and take counsel whether he is able with ten thousand to meet him who comes against him with twenty thousand? And if not, while the other is yet a great way off, he sends an embassy and asks terms of peace. So therefore, whoever of you does not renounce all that he has cannot be my disciple." — *Luke 14: 26-33.*

CONTENTS

1. Foreword 11
2. The Anniversary Theme 15
3. Anniversary Objectives 16

Part One
ANNIVERSARY MESSAGES

4. Greetings to Fellow Christians in the United States 19
5. Greetings to Fellow Christians in All Lands 24

Part Two
THE GERMANTOWN CELEBRATION

6. The Germantown Program 33
7. The Brethren and Germantown 35
8. The Mind of Christ Revealed 38
      Vernon F. Schwalm
9. The Mind of Christ in Judgment 52
      Harper S. Will

10. The Mind of Christ Symbolized 61
    MORLEY J. MAYS
11. The Litany of Self-Examination 67
12. The Anniversary Litany 70
13. The Mack Memorial Service 72

PART THREE
THE DES MOINES CELEBRATION

14. The Des Moines Program of Special Anniversary Addresses .. 77
15. "And How Shall the Brethren Be Recognized?" 79
    DESMOND W. BITTINGER
16. The Brethren and the Adventurous Future 92
    HARRY K. ZELLER, JR.
17. The Brethren and the Book of Books 103
    CHALMER E. FAW
18. The Brethren and the Modern State 117
    DAN WEST
19. The Brethren and Biblical Ethics 132
    W. HAROLD ROW
20. The Brethren and Their Culture 142
    KERMIT EBY
21. The Brethren and Biblical Reconciliation 154
    T. WAYNE RIEMAN
22. The Brethren and the Ecumenical Church 172
    KURTIS F. NAYLOR
23. The Brethren and Their Interpretation of History 183
    WARREN F. GROFF
24. The Brethren and Biblical Proclamation 194
    JOHN B. GRIMLEY
25. The Brethren Under the Lordship of Christ 206
    PAUL M. ROBINSON
26. The Brethren and Destiny 220
    CALVERT N. ELLIS

Part Four
THE EUROPEAN CELEBRATION

27. The Schwarzenau Program 233
28. Editorial Introduction 235
29. The Church Living Her Lord's Vision 237
    NORMAN J. BAUGHER
30. Let Brotherly Love Continue 243
31. The Brethren and Schwarzenau 248
    DESMOND W. BITTINGER
32. Changeless Principles in a Changing World 256
    PAUL H. BOWMAN
33. The Litany of Dedication 267

Part Five
GREETINGS, RESOLUTIONS, AND MISCELLANEOUS MATERIALS

34. Greetings From the President of the United States 277
35. Greetings From the National Council of Churches 278
36. A Statement From Church World Service 281
37. Greetings From the Evangelical Church in Austria 283
38. Greetings and Welcome From Schwarzenau 286
39. The Schwarzenau Resolutions 287
40. In Memoriam 289
41. God of All Nations 291
42. At the End of Our Two-Hundred-Fiftieth Year 292

1. FOREWORD

The committee on the two-hundred-fiftieth anniversary of the founding of the Church of the Brethren anticipated from the beginning the publication of two special anniversary volumes. The first of these was based on the research of Donald F. Durnbaugh and bears the title, *European Origins of the Brethren*. This volume, released at the Des Moines Conference of 1958, is now in the channels of our church life.

The second volume was to consist of sermons, addresses, papers, messages, and materials directly connected with the anniversary celebration. This volume, it was hoped, could be released at the Annual Conference of 1959, at Ocean Grove, New Jersey. This expectation being fulfilled, the committee is pleased to present to the church this second anniversary volume under the title, *The Adventurous Future*. It is our hope that countless generations may find inspiration and blessing in the messages of this publication and that the church may be stimulated to a continuing triumphant ministry in the dramatic future which is now unfolding.

The anniversary celebration by the Brotherhood centered mainly around the inaugural convocation at the mother church in America, Germantown, Pennsylvania, on January 1, 1958; the 1958 Annual Conference at Des Moines, Iowa, June 17-22; and the anniversary convocation of Brethren at Schwarzenau, Germany, on August 6, 1958. This latter gathering was preceded on August 3-5 by the European Annual Conference of Brethren workers at Kassel and followed the next day, August 7, by the participation of Brethren in the seven-hundredth anniversary of the founding of the city of Berleburg, ending the same day in the unforgettable love feast and holy communion at Brethren House, Kassel. These inspiring peaks of spiritual uplift and vision have suggested the plan followed in this volume.

The Annual Conference Standing Committee assigned to the Anniversary Committee the responsibility for the major addresses at the Des Moines Conference. These were considered special anniversary features, although the Conference program throughout carried anniversary emphases. Many other stimulating and worthy addresses were made by able Brethren. Most of these have been printed in the *Gospel Messenger* and other Brethren publications. It has seemed necessary, therefore, to confine this volume rather rigidly to those materials which were directly and officially a part of the anniversary celebration itself.

Many materials of anniversary character were published during the anniversary year as significant contributions to the total anniversary observance. These included the special devotional booklet entitled *Meditations on Brethren Life,* edited by DeWitt L. and Mary Hartsough Miller of Hagerstown, Maryland, for use in home and family, where, it was hoped, the celebration would first take root. This was followed by special curricula materials for the church school, which were used in the second quarter of the year.

The Anniversary Committee encouraged the writing of *The Story of the Brethren* by Virginia Fisher, the publication of *Studies in Christian Belief* by William M. Beahm, and the printing of a revised edition of J. E. Miller's *The Story of Our Church*.

Other materials included the special love feast order of service; the art volume of Brethren history and mission presented to the community of Schwarzenau; the anniversary pageant entitled *Brethren in the Court of History;* the chancel play, *The Time So Urgent;* the anniversary hymn, *God of All Nations;* the anniversary anthem, *O Church of Christ, Count Well Your Charge;* and numerous other helps and materials.

No effort has been made in this volume to write the history of the Brethren. The purpose of the Anniversary Committee in the several programs of the year was rather to express the witness of the Brethren in great areas of Christian faith and to undergird the ministry of the church more adequately with Biblical and doctrinal foundations.

The addresses and sermons published in this volume are presented as nearly as possible in the form in which they were presented by the speakers. True to the Brethren pattern of a free pulpit, each message must stand on its own merit. The Brethren have spoken their own messages in their own words. No attempt has been made to reconcile conflicting ideas or otherwise to censor the materials. Publication here does not imply official endorsement by the committee or by the church. It is hoped that from the exchange of thoughts and ideas in the arena of debate and discussion, and out of the crucible of study and prayer, the church may come to a common mind which at least is progressively nearer the truth of God.

The Anniversary Committee was eager to include in this volume the addresses delivered by European churchmen at Kassel and Schwarzenau. The task, however, of securing copies and translations from German into English proved to be very difficult without considerable delay in publication. This is a matter of disappointment and regret.

The church, magnificent in its response to the anniversary celebration, is now responding to the Anniversary Call with equal devotion and loyalty. That our study of the past has awakened within us a fresh love for Christ and the church is being evidenced in new commitments of life and of resources to the Kingdom of our Lord. It is not too much to hope that the spiritual tides released among the Brethren in 1958 will sweep on into the centuries of an adventurous future.

Brethren generally have honored the past realizing that the roots of the present are embedded in the soil of history. We have striven in this anniversary year to resist the mere lure of what has gone before. We have endeavored to quicken our sensitivity to the mind of Christ, to preserve the living elements of our heritage, and to pierce the obscurity of human vision in the interest of a ministry which is continually relevant to the hungers and needs of the sons of men.

Anniversary Committee
Paul H. Bowman, Chairman
Norman J. Baugher
DeWitt L. Miller
Donald E. Rowe
B. F. Waltz
William G. Willoughby
Nevin H. Zuck

January 1, 1959

2. THE ANNIVERSARY THEME

Whoever confesses that Jesus is the Son of God, God abides in him, and he in God (1 John 4:15).

"You call me Teacher and Lord; and you are right, for so I am. . . . I have given you an example, that you also should do as I have done . . ." (John 13:13, 15).

The Church of the Brethren, founded at Schwarzenau, Germany, in 1708, sought to unite in faith and practice the streams of spiritual idealism of that day. The founders believed that men were justified by faith but insisted that faith was not genuine unless expressed in the good life.

The genius of the Brethren consists in relating religion to life, belief to action, and theology to ethics. The church, therefore, extends a ministry to the world which offers redemption to sinners, relief to the needy, assurance to the hungry of heart, joy and harmony to the home and family, love and brotherhood to the church, and peace, justice, and neighborliness to the world.

The Brethren witness begins with a humble confession of sin. It continues with an unceasing prayer for purity of heart, for clearness of spiritual vision, and for grace to bend the human will to the will of God. It seeks to touch all of life, and to build under the Lordship of Christ a redeemed world of personal excellence and of social righteousness.

In this two-hundred-fiftieth anniversary year, under the guidance of the Holy Spirit, we commit our lives and our total resources to a fuller realization of our opportunities and a more faithful discharge of our responsibilities as Christians.

— Annual Conference Minutes, 1957

3. ANNIVERSARY OBJECTIVES

1. To reappraise Brethren history with a view of conserving the living values of our past for the times in which we live.

2. To explore anew the New Testament message and the mind of Christ in our quest for the further revelation of God's will for ourselves and for our turbulent world.

3. To strengthen the spiritual foundations of the Brethren way of life and to demonstrate its relevance to our modern world, which we believe to be in desperate need of spiritual renewal.

4. To face the dramatic future under the Lordship of Jesus Christ with the adventurous spirit of the early Christians to the end that the sons of men may be continually redeemed from sin and the Kingdom of God may be an expanding reality among men.

5. To confront and challenge our Brethren people with our priceless religious heritage in such manner as to quicken our sensitivity to the will of God and to encourage complete and continuous dedication among our people to Christ and to peace, justice, truth, and right.

— Adapted from the Annual Conference Minutes, 1957

PART ONE

Anniversary Messages

4. GREETINGS TO FELLOW CHRISTIANS IN THE UNITED STATES

These greetings were presented to the General Board of the National Council of the Churches of Christ in the United States of America by Norman J. Baugher on June 5, 1958.

The Church of the Brethren, founded at Schwarzenau, Germany, in 1708, and now celebrating the two-hundred-fiftieth anniversary of its founding, desires to extend greetings to fellow Christians in the United States. On this occasion we greet in particular the National Council of Churches of Christ in the United States of America and its affiliated communions with whom we labor in the common tasks of the Kingdom of God. We are grateful for this privilege and look forward to the further opportunity in August of extending greetings through the Central Committee of the World Council of Churches to our fellow Christians of the world.

The Brethren, sometimes called Dunkers, formerly known as the German Baptist Brethren, came to America in 1719 as refugees from persecution in central Europe. Led by Peter Becker, twenty families crossed the Atlantic and settled at Germantown, now a part of Philadelphia, Pennsylvania. Four years later, in 1723, the Germantown congregation was organized, selecting Becker as the first ordained elder of the Brethren in the New World. These German immigrants were joined one year later by others from Germany, among whom were Christopher Sauer and his young son, Christopher, Jr. In 1729, led by Alexander Mack, the founder of the church, about thirty additional families joined the Germantown congregation. The Brethren arose out of the

Pietist movement of Germany. However, they largely rejected Pietism and adopted Anabaptist views. They joined these and other minority groups in protest against what they considered the abuses and the formalism of the state churches of that period. Declared heretical by the ecclesiastical authorities, they were suppressed by both church and state. Excommunicated by the one and banished by the other, they left Europe almost en masse in quest of the freedom which the New World promised them.

Organizing an independent religious community, the Brethren rejected the prevailing creeds and dogma of the established church and declared the New Testament to be their only guide in matters of faith and practice. They rejected the civil oath as contrary to the teachings of the New Testament and as an affront to their integrity. They refused to participate in war or in preparation for war. They disavowed compulsion in religion and tended to exclusiveness in their position of nonconformity to the world. They later developed a measure of literalism in their interpretation of the Scriptures. They contended for freedom of worship and the right of conscience. They subscribed to the great common body of Christian doctrine but were nontechnical in theology. They accepted Christ, the Son of God, as Lord and Savior and were committed to obedience to His commands. They seriously undertook to practice in daily life the teachings of the New Testament.

The Brethren were especially given to the spirit of neighborliness and to the relief of suffering, distress, and human need.

The Germantown Brethren were aggressive in good works. Their best known ministry was through the printing operations of the Sauer press. The first printing of the Bible in America in a European tongue is credited to these enterprising pioneers. Their publication included the first hymnbook for German colonists, the first religious magazine in America, one of the earliest and most successful German newspapers in the colonial period, an almanac which was published for many years and circulated widely among the German settlements along the eastern seaboard, and numerous pamphlets, leaflets, and books covering a wide range of subjects.

The Sunday afternoon meeting for the unmarried, in operation in 1738, was an early venture by the Brethren in religious education. Its materials were supplied by the Sauer press. Their charities included a "Good Samaritan" ministry to the arriving immigrants at the port of Philadelphia, and care for the aged, the orphans, the widows, and the poor.

The Brethren joined the Germantown citizens in establishing a community school which gave rise to the Germantown Academy, an institution which still enjoys academic distinction.

The Brethren moved on from these beginnings to a broader service in the name of Christ. They have expanded their membership to most parts of the country, with heavy concentrations in Pennsylvania, Maryland, Virginia, West Virginia, Ohio, Indiana, Illinois, Iowa, Kansas, and the Pacific Coast area. They have established six colleges and a graduate seminary. The over-all work of the denomination is administered by the General Brotherhood Board from offices at Elgin, Illinois.

During the last three quarters of a century the Brethren have sponsored the establishment of the church in India, China, Nigeria, and Ecuador. They have expanded to five continents of the world their ministry of relief, material aid, and rehabilitation to war victims, refugees, displaced persons, and others in distress. The Heifer Project, which owes its origin to the Brethren, has been a conspicuous example of this ministry. These services, carried on in the name of Christ, rest on the assumption that concrete expressions of love and human sympathy are in the will of God for His children and that such a ministry is calculated to break down fear and suspicion among the peoples of the world and create a world atmosphere favorable to the establishment of abiding peace among classes, races, and nations.

The Church of the Brethren is a body of two hundred ten thousand communicants. Membership in the church is restricted to those who are of sufficient maturity to "count the cost" and to enter into the Christian life with an intelligent comprehension of the Christian faith and its obligations.

We are humbly grateful for our past. We are persuaded that God has spoken to us in our history and that the principles advocated by our fathers apply still in this restless, changing, and vindictive world. We seek, not to idolize our past, but to recognize ourselves as debtors to that which has preceded us and to those Christians in all lands and in all ages who have helped preserve and enrich the religious heritage to which all of us are heirs. We confess our proneness to unfaithfulness and stand penitent for our tendency toward religious exclusiveness.

We seek to discover in this anniversary year the living elements of our history and to undergird them, so that we too, as members of the body of Christ, may contribute our full share to the continuing and expanding universal church of Christ. It is to this end that we seek the fellowship and prayers of our fellow Christians in the United States of America. We recognize the diverse history of our Christian communions, but we rejoice in the manifest unity and reconciliation which we are finding in Christ.

We pledge to our Christian brethren in different traditions, and with different commitments, our prayers and our striving to transcend the boundaries and dimensions of our own traditions to the end that we may find unity in Christ and that the church may be delivered from the tragedy of dividedness.

We further desire in our anniversary year to recommit ourselves in an increasing witness:

— To the saving power of the gospel of Christ and to the more complete acceptance of His Lordship in all areas of life.

— To the right of men everywhere to worship and serve God in the light of their own inner faith and conscience without the restraint or coercion of any human authority.

— To belief in the sinfulness of violence and bloodshed among the children of men, and to the right of believers under God to refuse to participate in war or preparation for war in violation of their religious convictions.

— To personal integrity in speech and in conduct, and to simple honesty in all of life's transactions, both public and private.

— To the sanctity of home and family and the enduring bonds of marriage and chastity as a bulwark of society.

— To love, neighborliness, and justice among individuals, classes, races, and nations and to the peaceful and orderly settlement of disputes and grievances among all men.

— To the relief of human need and distress without distinction or discrimination, in recognition of the principle that we cannot as Christians consistently claim excessive convenience and comfort for ourselves so long as our advantages are assessed to others in terms of hunger, want, and suffering.

In this year of our Lord nineteen hundred fifty-eight, we greet our fellow Christians in America in the name of our Lord and Savior Jesus Christ.

Desmond W. Bittinger, Moderator
    Annual Conference, Church of the Brethren

Norman J. Baugher, General Secretary
    General Brotherhood Board — Church of the Brethren

5. GREETINGS TO FELLOW CHRISTIANS IN ALL LANDS

These greetings were presented by Desmond W. Bittinger to the Central Committee of the World Council of Churches at its meeting in Nyborg, Denmark, on August 22, 1958.

The Church of the Brethren, prior to 1908 known as the German Baptist Brethren, is celebrating in the year 1958 the two-hundred-fiftieth anniversary of its founding. In this our anniversary year, we desire to extend greetings to our fellow Christians throughout the world, particularly to those communions in the membership of the World Council of Churches.

The Brethren had their beginning at Schwarzenau, Wittgenstein, Germany, in the year 1708. Alexander Mack, the founder, was originally a follower of John Calvin. He subsequently was identified with the Pietistic movement which developed in Europe during the latter part of the seventeenth century. Finally renouncing Pietism as it became more extreme in its opposition to organized Christianity, and despairing of correcting from within what he considered the abuses, the formalism, and the cold intellectualism of the established churches of that day, Mack determined to organize an independent religious fellowship. He proposed the establishment of a religious movement based on the teachings of the New Testament as final authority in faith and practice. When the Scriptures were silent or uncertain, he relied upon new light emerging from prayer, study, the open mind, and the guidance of the Holy Spirit. Membership in the new body was restricted to repentant adult believers who committed themselves to the acceptance and practice of the rites and ordinances of the New Testament.

The Brethren experienced rapid growth at first and several congregations were established in Germany. They, of course, were declared heretical and both church and state were arrayed against them. Excommunicated by the one, banished and their property confiscated by the other, they finally left Germany almost en masse. Small groups migrated to Holland and Switzerland, but the main body faced the perils of the Atlantic and of the New World known as America. Under the leadership of Peter Becker they left Europe in 1719. They settled at Germantown, now part of Philadelphia, Pennsylvania, and four years later, in 1723, organized their first congregation on the new continent. They were later joined by Alexander Mack and others who in considerable numbers found their way across the sea.

The Brethren made a substantial contribution to the political and social life of colonial America, particularly to the German immigrants who entered the country. Their ministry was especially significant through the press of Christopher Sauer and his son, Christopher, Jr., the latter becoming a minister and elder in the Germantown congregation. They contended for freedom of worship and the free exercise of conscience. They conceded to no earthly power authority over the human spirit. They believed in reconciliation between man and man and in the peaceful arbitration of disputes between nation and nation. They renounced war and the taking of human life. On the basis of religious conviction they refused military training and service. They rejected the civil oath as contrary to New Testament teaching and as an affront to their integrity. They were Biblical Christians and sought to demonstrate in daily life the teachings of the gospel.

The Brethren accepted the Lordship of Christ as a cardinal tenet of their faith. They looked to Him as their Leader and Savior. Rejecting as they did creeds and dogma, they became theologically nontechnical and exercised broader latitude in matters of doctrine than they did in what they considered the practical and more urgent issues of daily living. The Lordship of Christ implied for them absolute obedience to Him who was to them the Master of every life and of all life. On this premise they considered man's life here as temporary and transient and all life precious in the sight of God. They could, therefore, do violence to no human being. Man, in their view, was of infinite worth and possessed rights as a child of God which could not be denied him.

The Brethren were not ascetic. They did, however, develop a doctrine of nonworldliness and accepted disciplines austere and removed from the immediate ends of life. The Brethren were less involved in the physical comforts and the accumulation of wealth than they were in the deeper meanings and the final fulfillment of life.

The Lordship of Christ also undergirded their doctrine of peace and nonretaliation. They strove for harmony among themselves and with their neighbors. They deplored conflict in the social order and sought to alleviate passion and violent conflict between races and nations. They regarded all war as sin. Every war for them was civil war inasmuch as it involved hate, bitterness, and destruction within the family of God and among His children.

The Church of the Brethren, now a body of two hundred ten thousand members, has sponsored the church of Christ in India, Nigeria, and China. We have lately established the church in Ecuador, South America, as a ministry to the Calderon Indians of that country. Our ministry of relief, material aid, refugee resettlement, and rehabilitation has been extended to five continents of the world.

We are committed in America and other countries both in theory and in practice when possible to the policy of comity and visible unity. We have no intention or desire to establish congregational units in areas where we carry on relief work except when clear need for such a ministry is demonstrated by indigenous groups and when it can be done in a prevailing pattern of Christian co-operation. We desire to serve in the spirit of ecumenicity and in the name of our Lord Jesus Christ, to the end that human distress may be relieved, communities and individuals rehabilitated, and the gospel proclaimed in areas of spiritual retardation.

The Church of the Brethren, a co-operating communion of the World Council, is also a member of the National Council of the Churches of Christ in the United States of America. We are affiliated with Church World Service and with numerous other intercommunion movements such as the National Service Board for Religious Objectors in the United States of America, the American Bible Society, and the Heifer Project which owes its origin to the Brethren.

On this two-hundred-fiftieth anniversary of our beginning, we humbly acknowledge our indebtedness to the past. We have been the recipient of contributions from the total church and from the centuries of Christian thought and worship which had already preceded our beginning. Except for the continuing witness of the apostles and martyrs, and generations of devout men and women, we could never have known Christ. We recognize in gratitude "the clouds of witnesses" through whom the word of life has been made available to us.

We acknowledge ourselves debtors to those pioneers of Protestant Christianity who contended for the purity of the church and for the rediscovery of the mind of Christ, and who in their quest for truth demonstrated the adventurous spirit of the disciples and the early apostles. They have contributed to our belief in the centrality of the Scriptures, to our concern for practical piety, and to our reliance upon internal rather than external authority. We confess our excesses in emphasizing the danger of creeds, and our failure to contribute more positively to the undergirding of the Christian faith in its doctrinal and theological structure. This we do, however, without surrendering our conviction that there is an inner witness of the Holy Spirit which now and always has relevance to religious thought and experience.

We desire the fellowship of the universal church in searching out the bases of unity in Christ and in sharing the variableness of the Christian faith with which God has endowed the members of His body. We, too, stand under the Lordship of Christ, our common Leader and Savior, confessing our fealty to Him in all areas of life, admitting our proneness to unfaithfulness, and penitent for our tendency toward religious exclusiveness.

We seek openness of mind and heart that we may perceive what God, who has spoken to us in our history, is saying to us in our own day. It is our prayer that in so doing we may be drawn closer to the God who loves us, to the Christ who is our Lord, and to fellow members of the community of faith who are our brothers.

We could not be true to the light which we believe has been shed abroad in our hearts without at least sharing with our fellow Christians the following concerns:

FIRST: We urge the Universal Church of Christ, in this time of supreme need in the life of the world and of dramatic possibilities for the Kingdom of God, to recognize the relevancy of goodwill and resolute love in the affairs of men and of nations. Let us as Christians demonstrate throughout the world our concern and compassion for distressed and disadvantaged peoples of all races that a climate of trust and brotherhood may emerge in which peace among nations, races, and peoples may have positive promise of success.

SECOND: Realizing how desperately urgent it is that nations turn from the suicidal madness of war and preparation for war to the settlement of disagreements in the spirit of reconciliation and also recognizing that the convictions concerning the establishment of peace, and justice, and liberty which have been elaborated in the ecumenical movement have not yet penetrated the wider membership of the churches, we urge the consideration of a world assembly of churches in a special and concerted effort to undergird every sincere approach to peace among the nations to the end that they may be persuaded to seek security, not on the basis of fear and preponderance of arms, but on the basis of reason, understanding, and goodwill.

THIRD: We beseech our fellow Christian bodies through the common voice of the World Council of Churches to seek, on the part of the governments of the world, recognition of the right of conscience and religious conviction in regard to participation in war and military service. We seek for men everywhere freedom to follow unrestricted and unafraid the inner light of love and the divine will. We implore for all such persons the privilege to serve mankind as positive, constructive, and creative citizens of their respective governments.

That there may come to pass among the Christians of the world genuine unity grounded in Christ our Lord; that the church of Christ may be the instrument of unity for the total life of the children of men; and that races and peoples and classes may be drawn more closely together by the One whom we worship and serve, we pledge our ceaseless prayers and our continuing effort, and beseech for our fellowship the prayers of the Church Universal.

PART TWO
The Germantown Celebration

6. THE GERMANTOWN PROGRAM

MORNING SESSION
11 A.M.
Desmond W. Bittinger, Presiding

ORGAN PRELUDE — — — — — — — *Stanley Dotterer*

CALL TO WORSHIP

HYMN — — — — — — — — — — No. 321
    God of Grace and God of Glory

THE SCRIPTURE
    Romans 5:1-2; Matthew 5:13-16; 5:20; 7:20; Philippians 3:7-11

VOCAL SOLO — — — — — — — — *Nevin W. Fisher*
    God Is Love, by James G. Ellis

MORNING PRAYER

STATEMENT OF PURPOSE — — — — — *Paul H. Bowman*
    Schwarzenau, Germantown, and Beyond

HYMN: God of All Nations

ANNIVERSARY LITANY

ADDRESS — — — — — — — — — *V. F. Schwalm*
    The Mind of Christ Revealed

BENEDICTION

POSTLUDE

LUNCHEON
Second Baptist Church
12:30 P.M.
DeWitt L. Miller, Presiding

AFTERNOON SESSION
2 P.M.
Nevin H. Zuck, Presiding

ORGAN PRELUDE	*Stanley Dotterer*
CALL TO WORSHIP	
HYMN	No. 22
From All That Dwell Below the Skies	
THE INVOCATION	
ADDRESS	*Harper S. Will*
The Mind of Christ in Judgment	
HYMN	No. 24
Holy and Reverend Is the Name	
ADDRESS	*Morley J. Mays*
The Mind of Christ Symbolized	
SERVICE OF SELF-EXAMINATION	
HYMN	No. 232
Spirit of God, Descend Upon My Heart	
BENEDICTION	
POSTLUDE	

EVENING SERVICE
6 P.M.
ANNIVERSARY LOVE FEAST AND HOLY COMMUNION
Edward K. Ziegler, Officiating Minister

7. THE BRETHREN AND GERMANTOWN

The Anniversary Committee chose to inaugurate the celebration of the two-hundred-fiftieth anniversary of the founding of the church at Germantown because it symbolizes a new beginning for the Brethren. The following excerpts quoted from the introductory statement by Paul H. Bowman, chairman of the 250th Anniversary Committee, at the Germantown convocation emphasize the importance and the significance of Germantown for the Church of the Brethren.

It was at Germantown that the Brethren faith had its first rootage in the New World. The Germantown church is known among the Brethren as the mother church of the Brethren in America. Here the Brethren first worshiped God in the freedom which in vain they had sought in Europe and for which they had paid a heavy price in hardship and suffering. It is here that the body of Alexander Mack, and those of others of our early leaders, rest in peace.

The official beginning of the church in America took place here on Christmas Day, 1723. On that day, two hundred thirty-five years ago, the Brethren held their first council meeting in the New World. Here on that day they elected their first minister and established their first congregation in America. Here they administered their first baptism, perhaps the first baptism by trine immersion on American soil. On that same day, in emulation of their Master, they poured water into a basin, girded themselves with a towel, and washed their brothers' feet. They observed the agapé, the feast of love, likely the first religious ceremony of its kind in America. They concluded that day in the sacrament of the holy communion in remembrance of their Master's supreme sacrifice, and in recognition of New Testament ordinances as instruments of God's grace to the sons of men.

The Brethren experienced their first Pentecostal awakening in America here at Germantown in 1724. They resolved to send missionaries and evangelists on horseback and on foot into those sections of Pennsylvania then remote to Germantown. It was then that the home mission enterprise of the church was first inaugurated and resulted in the establishment of other congregations of Brethren in the eastern part of the state.

It was here from the press of Christopher Sauer that the Scriptures were first produced in America for the colonists of German lineage in their native tongue. This was the first printing of the Bible in America except for an earlier edition in one of the Indian languages.

Here in 1739 the Brethren produced the first book to be printed in German type in America. It was in the form of a book of hymns, many of which were written by Brethren. Some of them provoked theological controversy which led to a revision of the hymnal in 1762, edited by Christopher Sauer himself, under the title, *A Compilation of Beautiful, Instructive, and Devotional Hymns.* This book was in great demand and is believed to have been the first hymnal printed in this country.

There came also from the Sauer print shop the first printing in America of a religious magazine, the first publication of a newspaper for the colonies, the first printing in America of Martin Luther's shorter catechism, and many other publications both religious and secular.

It was here in the Sauer residence, especially constructed to accommodate religious gatherings, that the Brethren conducted their Sunday afternoon meeting for the "unmarried." This service was in operation in 1740, which is nearly a half-century earlier than the study classes organized in London by Robert Raikes and generally considered the beginning of the modern Sunday-school movement.

Here the Brethren constructed their first house of worship in

1770, a section of which remains as a remnant of their handiwork.

It was at Germantown that the Brethren first expressed their interest in public education. They joined their neighbors in the establishment of the famous Germantown Academy, which is still in operation.

It was here that the Brethren fathers first rejected the civil oath in the New World as contrary to the teaching of Jesus and as inconsistent with their religious principles. Then, as now, they considered the oath as an affront to their integrity and wholly unnecessary for men whose simple *yes* or *no* was abundantly supported by the force of their own character.

It was at Germantown that the Brethren first voiced their opposition to war and refused to serve in the military forces of the colonial government on the basis of Christian belief and freedom of conscience. They paid the price of such refusal in the coin of persecution, personal abuse, and confiscation of property. But they chose to be regarded as traitors to their new government rather than violate their pledge of nonviolence made in loyalty to their Lord, the Prince of Peace.

It was here in the new land of Penn's Forest, to which they had come by invitation, that they failed to find the millennium of which they had dreamed, but where they did contribute to the establishment of a new government founded upon principles which they advocated.

8. THE MIND OF CHRIST REVEALED

Vernon F. Schwalm

President emeritus of Manchester College; minister; lecturer; writer; home, North Manchester, Indiana. Formerly: president of McPherson College (1927-41); president of Manchester College (1941-53); visiting professor, Indiana Central College, Huntington College, Indiana Technical College; member, General Educational Board; member, General Mission Board; member, General Brotherhood Board; Annual Conference moderator, 1938 and 1953.

We are privileged today to attend and participate in one of the historic events in the life of the Church of the Brethren. It is perhaps the most significant of its kind that many of us will ever attend. As we roam about among these historic spots, a bit of imagination will people them with the personages who made them memorable: Alexander Mack, Christopher Sauer, Peter Becker, John Naas, and others. May God grant us to be worthy descendants of these devoted and courageous spiritual ancestors.

It is inevitable at an anniversary that we look backwards. But it is important how we look backwards. Not with strong nostalgia for the good old days; not with hero worship, as if all good had been interred with their bones; and not with a critical attitude that makes all the past look ridiculous. But with such insight and discernment as to discover in their lives and activities some principles which have relevance for our times, that from "these honored dead we may take increased devotion to that cause for which they gave their last full measure of devotion."

The Christian church is the oldest institution in our culture. It is more than ten times as old as our national government. If we think of the changes in our manner of life and in our institutions since Washington's time, we can understand better why the church has changed again and again through the centuries.

But there are threads of continuity that reach from century to century, and no important movement in the church can be fully understood apart from its historic setting. To understand the origins of the Brethren we must know something of the major movements in central Europe from the Reformation to 1708.

The Great Reformation led by Luther, Zwingli, and Calvin took place in the half-century following 1517, and had its beginnings in Germany and Switzerland. Up to that time all of western Europe was under the control of the Roman Catholic Church. Everyone was baptized into it in infancy and remained a member until death, unless excommunicated. The Middle Ages was an age of faith. Religion played an important part in the life of men. Only an age steeped in religion could have produced the *Divine Comedy,* the *Sistine Madonna,* and the great cathedrals. The church was everywhere present and the clergy dominated the life of the people.

Salvation was by grace mediated through the sacramental channels of the church. Man's part consisted in the performance of the "works" which the church required of him and the proper use of the sacramental means of grace. Through these sacramental channels, actual grace-substantial Divine help would come into man and work the miracle of salvation.[1]

But the sacraments were under the control of the clergy. By withholding the sacraments from refractory men, they could bring kings and emperors to their knees. The mere threat of it made common sinners quake with fear. Such power tends to corrupt, we are told, and it did corrupt the clergy. They used the power to extract vast sums of money from the masses and to keep everyone subject to their wills.

Martin Luther was especially prepared to meet this evil. After a long spiritual struggle to find his own peace of soul and divine acceptance, he finally found peace and serenity in the

---

[1] Rufus M. Jones, *Spiritual Reformers of the 16th and 17th Centuries* (New York: Macmillan, 1914), page 75.

doctrine of justification by faith. Henceforth he had a platform on which to stand in his battle with the Pope, and a weapon to use against the Roman clergy.

He began his attack when he saw churchmen sell indulgences — the forgiveness of the temporal penalties for sin — without any evidence of repentance on the part of the purchaser. From this point on he was led to attack other practices of the church, the inevitable outcome of which was papal excommunication and the imperial ban.

In the meantime, Zwingli and Calvin were leading similar movements at Zürich and Geneva. These combined strands of the Reformation, along with economic, political, and moral factors, brought about the Protestant Reformation. Together they threatened the very existence of the papacy. Large areas of northern and central Europe followed the Reformers out of the church.

For approximately one hundred years after Luther's death there were heated arguments, theological discussions, and church councils trying to settle the issues between Protestants and Catholics. By 1555 Lutherans and Catholics were recognized in the empire. Finally these ecclesiastical matters became entangled with political and international issues and the terrible Thirty Years War broke out, during which the armies of many nations marched and countermarched across Germany. The country was devastated; one third of the population and two thirds of the property were destroyed.

By the Treaty of Westphalia (1648) it was determined that the Catholic, Lutheran, and Reformed churches should be recognized, and that the ruler of any political division should determine which religion should prevail. All other forms of group worship were forbidden. Since Germany was divided into about three hundred political divisions, with occasional changes of rulers, one can readily see the terrible confusion which followed. The Rhenish Palatinate changed religion six times between 1546 and 1648.[2]

---

[2] Donald F. Durnbaugh, *Brethren Adult Quarterly*, April-June 1958.

Since our interest lies chiefly in Germany, let us note some developments there. Luther had stressed justification by faith alone so much that some of his later followers seemed to think that, since they were saved by faith, what they did made no difference, for grace determined their salvation. To some, believing that it had a magical effect in the invisible realm, it seemed that an intellectual acceptance of the doctrine was sufficient. "The momentous shift was not in the personal character of the individual but the way the individual was regarded in the Heavenly estimates."[3]

Furthermore, Luther held to the principle that whatever was not forbidden should be left in the churches. Thus much of the ritual, the statuary, the organs, and other accretions of the past were left in the churches. Many sincere people in Germany and Switzerland wanted the Reformation to go further and to sweep out of the church the remnants of medievalism.

Donald Durnbaugh said of the German church as of about 1700:

Church life had become cold and sterile. The intense religious fervor of the Reformation and of the Catholic Counter Reformation had hardened into lifeless crusts of dogma and doctrine. The Protestants jealously guarded the "purity" of the "true doctrine" — the creeds and the theological statements of the sixteenth century. Orthodoxy was the aim of the church. Sermons were either violent attacks against other faiths or involved treatises on obscure points of dogma. Particularly offensive to the devout were the worldly lives of many priests and pastors. Protestant and Catholic clergy were political appointees and often were not well fitted for their positions. Open drunkenness at weddings and funerals, and immorality were the most common complaints.[4]

One can understand then why Elder James Quinter[5] in 1860 wrote that the Lutheran Reformation was incomplete, why Dr. T. T. Meyers[6], speaking at Des Moines at the Bicentennial Con-

---

[3] Jones, *op. cit.*, page 75.
[4] Durnbaugh, *op. cit.*
[5] See the introduction to Mack's *Rites and Ordinances* (Ashland, Ohio: Brethren Publishing Company, 1939), page 6.
[6] *Two Centuries of the Church of the Brethren* (Elgin, Illinois: Brethren Publishing House, 1908), page 27.

ference in 1908, said that the Lutheran Reformation had made for the pacification of conscience but not for the sanctification of life, and why John T. McNeill[7], veteran church historian, says, "The departure from Babylon took place but the city was not yet built."

So one is not surprised that during the sixteenth century there sprang up in central Europe a large number of earnest Christian groups who were not content with the Reformation and wanted to carry it further. They were stimulated by the Reformers, but, being more radical, they wanted to go further than the Reformers were willing to go.

These groups appeared at various places: at Zürich, at Wittenberg, at Münster, at Bern, at Basel, at Strassburg, at Augsburg, in Württemberg, at Nuremberg, and elsewhere. At Zürich were the Swiss Brethren; at Wittenberg appeared the Zwickau prophets; in Holland were the Mennonites; and in Moravia were the Hutterites. Because most of the groups were opposed to infant baptism they were all often referred to as Anabaptists.

In general they all contended for regenerate adult church membership, voluntarily associated in a church fellowship. They rejected infant baptism since children could not repent or exercise Christian faith. They believed in rigid discipline in the church with power of excommunication. They insisted on separation of church and state. They were opposed to all force in religion, which included taking the oath, engaging in military training, and going to war. Many of them also opposed capital punishment and declined official positions in the state. They believed in complete discipleship to Christ and in a sincere practice of Christian brotherhood and love, some groups — notably the Hutterites — going into some sort of communal organization.

Basic to the Anabaptists is the idea that the church is a voluntary association of Christians patterned after the New Testament. For them the new life in Christ through the Spirit,

---

[7] McNeill, *Modern Christian Movements* (Philadelphia: Westminster Press, 1954), page 54.

rather than justification by faith, is the center of New Testament faith and therefore of the church. In some localities these groups went to extremes. Some discarded the Bible and depended on the Spirit to speak directly to them. In some cases they felt they should revolt against their masters, as in the Peasants Revolt. In some cases they turned into iconoclasts, destroying images and statuary in the churches. In one community they practiced polygamy, and a few went off into immorality. This purely subjective religion, with no objective criteria for guidance, not infrequently runs off into such abberations.

The great Reformers and the leaders of the established churches were bitter against the Anabaptists. First, because they discredited the whole Reform movement, for the public held the Reform movement responsible for the fanaticism of the extremists. Further, by denying the efficacy of infant baptism, the Anabaptists unchristianized the entire Christian world and completed the rupture with the historic church. In most countries it was a crime to baptize anyone who had been baptized as an infant.[8]

As a result, the Lutheran and the Reformed were as severe on the Anabaptists as were the Catholics. Ernst Troeltsch says:

> First of all leaders of the movement were taken and put to death. Some were burned to death, some slain with the sword, others drowned. Some were exiled and some sent to the galleys. Then came the turn of the masses, who were decimated with savage cruelty.[9]

There were not just a few cases. Hundreds and thousands were slain. State and church combined to wipe out the danger and the disgrace of having radical heretics in their midst.

The Diet of Spires in 1529 decreed that every Anabaptist and rebaptized person of either sex should be put to death by sword or fire or otherwise. At Gorz the house in which the Anabaptists were assembled for worship was set on fire. In Gorz and Tyrol the executions in 1531 already numbered one thousand; at Linz

---

[8] Schaff, *History of the Christian Church* (New York: Macmillan, 1910 and 1911), Volume VI, page 691.
[9] Ernst Troeltsch, *The Social Teachings of the Christian Church* (New York: Macmillan, 1931), Volume II, page 704.

seventy-three were killed in six weeks. Throughout the greater part of upper Germany, persecution raged like a wild chase.[10]

So severe was the persecution that Anabaptism as a movement was nearly destroyed in Europe in the latter part of the sixteenth century.[11] But the blood of martyrs is never shed in vain. While the movement was defeated in Germany it was not destroyed. It was revived in Holland, in England, in America, and later in isolated congregations on the Continent.

The first half of the seventeenth century must have been a drab and dreary time for the churches of central Europe, especially those in Germany. The formalism, the dry-as-dust theological controversies, and the religious anemia of the post-Reformation days continued. Then came the Thirty Years War, from 1618 to 1648, which decimated the population, ravaged the country, and set German culture back for decades.

Soon thereafter, however, a new religious movement began to develop which brought new faith and new fervor to the Christian life of Germany. It is called the Pietist movement. Philip Spener is credited with being the father of the movement. He in turn, however, got his inspiration from the well-known work, *Wahres Christenthum,* by Johann Arndt.

Spener started the movement while he was a pastor at Frankfurt. The religious indifference, the absorption with scholastic theology, and the immorality around him led him to set up within his church a program to counteract these tendencies. He did this by making his preaching more practical, by increasing his pastoral labors, by holding meetings in his home for devotional study of the Bible and for prayer and edification. Spener wanted to replace the emphasis on doctrine with an emphasis on life. In a booklet called *Pia desideria* he set forth a program to bring about these ends. First, the study of the Bible by all classes of Christians in *Collegia Pietatis* — little groups not unlike Wesley's

---

[10] Schaff, *op. cit.,* Volume VII, page 84.
[11] Robert Friedmann, *Mennonite Piety Through the Centuries* (Goshen, Indiana: Mennonite Historical Society, 1949).

midweek meetings or our modern cell groups. Second, the priesthood of all believers — everyone to be responsible for instruction, inspiration, and reproof. Third, emphasis on conduct, especially on love and service. Fourth, an emphasis on the evil of controversy. Fifth, the importance of piety as well as learning in candidates for the ministry.

Spener felt that one of the causes of the low spiritual condition of the church was a misunderstanding of the nature of saving faith, leading to an unfortunate divorce between justification and sanctification, between belief and life. He emphasized the doctrine of regeneration, and insisted that the all-important thing was the transformation of character through vital union with Christ. Only when life is actually changed and the spirit and motive of Christ control one's conduct does one have any right to think that he has been born again and is to be counted in the number who are saved.

McNeill says, "A Pietist is a man who studies the word of God and taking it for his rule of faith and conduct leads an exemplary life."[12] And Floyd Mallott says, "One could not claim conversion without showing ethical character, no matter how orthodox his opinions."[13]

The influence of the Pietist movement was greatly extended through the work at the University of Halle, where August Herman Francke labored. From here went out Pietist missionaries to all parts of the world, and here were trained six thousand clergymen for the church of Germany. McNeill says, "Pietism did stir the German people, and, so to speak, awakened them out of moral and religious sleep."[14]

Pietism was not an effort to found a new church, but to bring new spiritual life into groups within the state churches in the hope that it would leaven the whole lump. It was not doctrinal, not a new sect, but an emphasis to bring new inner

---

[12] McNeill, *op. cit.*, page 58.
[13] Floyd E. Mallott, *Studies in Brethren History* (Elgin, Illinois: Brethren Publishing House, 1954), pages 13 and 14.
[14] McNeill, *op. cit.*, page 73.

spiritual life to the individual Christian. It was subjective in nature with emphasis on emotion and will rather than on intelligence.

In his book, *Mennonite Piety Through the Centuries,* Robert Friedmann contrasts the Anabaptist and Pietist movements. The Anabaptists — among whom he classifies the Mennonites and the Brethren — emphasized many of the same points as did the Pietists, but they were separatists who withdrew from the state churches, set up their own churches, became sects, and stood against many of the things in the world around them, even things in the churches. They were in tension with the world and consequently were persecuted by it.

Friedmann believes the Pietists to have been quietists, who remained in the church, subjectively cultivated the inner life, tolerated the world around them, and often later compromised with the world. He believes that the Pietists had an unfortunate effect on the Mennonites, making them into passive, withdrawing quietists rather than an aggressive sect which challenged the evils in the world.

To sum up this picture: Mack and his associates inherited Luther's emphasis on justification; the church had lived through a long barren period of theological controversy, of cold sterile religious formalism, and religious wars. In its heritage were vestiges of Waldensian influence, and here and there Swiss Brethren, Anabaptist, Moravian, Mennonite, Hutterite, and Pietist influence, not to speak of the influence of the Catholic, Lutheran, and Reformed churches. One is amazed at the tangled threads of influences which surrounded them. And one is surprised to find how the leaders of these movements traveled all over central Europe and were in constant touch with one another.

In most of central Europe, religious dissenters were sought out, persecuted, and destroyed. But here and there were a few islands of tolerance where refuge was to be found. Such were Holland, Wittgenstein, and, strange to say, Prussia.

Heinrich Albert was the prince in that part of Wittgenstein

where Schwarzenau is located. His four sisters were Pietists and he was sympathetic toward dissenters. He offered an asylum to all kinds of religious refugees and leased to each who desired it a bit of land and a place to build a hut in the woods. On the road from Schwarzenau to Berleburg there grew up a village of huts, Hüttental, where these refugees lived.

To this village of huts there came Huguenots from France, Pietists from Germany and Switzerland, Inspirationists who did not believe in any formal organization of religion, and separatists who were ready to leave their old church homes and found new ones.

Here, too, came Alexander Mack from the Palatinate, Luke Vetter from Hesse, Andrew Boni from Basel in Switzerland, and John Kipping from Württemberg — all members of the well-known first eight.

Alexander Mack was born near Schriesheim, not far from Heidelberg, in 1679, the son of a fairly wealthy miller who was an officer of the local Reformed church and a member of the town council. He had the advantage of the local schools, but we have no evidence of college training. There is no indication of extraordinary brilliance, but he was an intelligent man, of good practical judgment and some wisdom. He reveals that he had read widely in the field of religion, and we know of his spiritual sensitivity and discriminating insights.

A member of the Reformed Church, Alexander Mack was dissatisfied with that church and withdrew from it. It is probable that his religious awakening came about through his association with Ernest Hochmann of Hochenau, one of the most forceful evangelists and spiritual leaders of his time. Hochmann himself was a member of a noble and wealthy family, but gave up business and privilege to become an itinerate evangelist. Everywhere he went he stirred up the people and got into trouble with the authorities. He was imprisoned thirty times, once for over a year at Nuremberg. Friedmann, the Mennonite church historian, tells of Hochmann's coming to Krefeld, where he preached in the

Mennonite church and won some of the brethren to his following. He says that Hochmann was a German mystic, a man of unusually powerful spirituality, who deeply influenced everyone with whom he came in touch. Then he adds, "He was opposed to 'forming sects' but his activity nevertheless eventually prompted one of the strong and aggressive religious movements of the time, that of the Dompelaars, or Dunkers."[15] It was Hochmann's written confession of faith of which M. G. Brumbaugh says, "It expresses more nearly than any other contemporary document the views of the Brethren at Schwarzenau."[16]

He and Mack became fast friends and Mack accompanied him on evangelistic tours. We even know of one trip to Switzerland together.

Mack was married to Anna Margaret Kling in 1701. Because of the threat of prosecution for holding religious meetings in his old mill, he moved to Schwarzenau in 1706 and lived in the village of huts, along with other refugees.

Here lived a strange admixture of questing religionists, seekers for a spiritual home for their unhappy souls. One can imagine the endless discussions and heated arguments as for many months they sought a solution to their problem. Some were Inspirationists who wanted no church organization; some were Pietists and would remain in their old church homes; others wanted to form a new church. Included in the latter group were Mack and some of his associates.

As early as 1703 it had already been urged by some brethren at Schwarzenau that "we must be baptized according to the teaching of the apostles and found a new church." In 1706 two foreign brethren — probably English Baptists or Dutch Collegiants, a contemporary immersionist group[17] — visited them and spoke of the necessity of baptism.

Mack and others traveled in various parts of Germany to

---

[15] Friedmann, *op. cit.*, page 63.
[16] Brumbaugh, *A History of the Brethren* (Elgin, Illinois: Brethren Publishing House, 1899), page 83.
[17] Durnbaugh, *op. cit.*

find a church that followed apostolic practices. They wrote to the famous church historian, Gottfried Arnold, and to Jeremiah Felbinger, a contemporary theologian, and then went into an intensive study of the New Testament to determine the nature of the apostolic church and her practices.

Mallott says that there is no clearer statement of their purpose than the one drawn up at the Germantown church in 1761: "We have vowed to die and to live according to the doctrine of Jesus Christ and to follow in everything the manner and institution of the Apostolic congregation of the first Christians."[18]

And Mack says, "We have indeed no new church, nor any new laws but in simplicity and true faith we desire to remain with the old church which Christ instituted through his blood, and to follow the commandment which was from the beginning."[19]

Apparently there had been much discussion about whether to form a new church or not. It is quite well known in Brethren circles that Mack and his associates decided the issue on the basis of Matthew 18. How could they "tell it to the church" if there was no organized church? And how then could they keep the ordinances without an organized church?

Since the issue of baptism had been a matter regarding which many people had lost their lives in the last one hundred fifty years, it was inevitable that it should be a matter that received a great deal of attention in founding a new church — just as the issue regarding peace and the conscientious objector has received a great deal of attention for the last forty years. Having written to Arnold and learning from him that there had been no infant baptism for the first two hundred years of Christian history and that the early form of baptism was immersion, they followed the pattern of immersion for adults.

They wrote Hochmann about it and he gave them this advice: They should use caution lest they baptize with water those who had not been baptized with the Spirit and who had not

---

[18] Mallott, *op. cit.*, page 14.
[19] Mack, *op. cit.*, page 91.

experienced the new birth; and they should not become too sectarian and insist that everyone be baptized in the same manner.[20] This latter advice they did not take. It would appear from the discussions at the 1957 Annual Conference at Richmond that there are many in the church who regret that Hochmann's advice as to the form of baptism was not taken.

A superficial reading of Alexander Mack's writings would lead one to conclude that he believed in regeneration through the physical act of baptism. Asked whether he thought water baptism and regeneration were inseparably connected, Mack replied that "genuine regeneration is nothing else than real and genuine obedience toward God and all his commandments."[21]

In answer to one of the basic questions asked by Eberhard Gruber — whether they had assurance of their acceptance — Mack said:

> Surely the acceptance must be before God as Paul describes in Romans 5, "Therefore being justified by faith we have peace with God through our Lord Jesus Christ, by whom also we have access by faith into the grace wherein we stand, and rejoice in the hope of the glory of God." But this assurance is no longer promised even to the apostles than they would abide in him and his words abide in them. Then they would be his true disciples and they should ask what they will and it should be done unto them.[22]

This audience knows the story of the eight who were baptized down in the beautiful winding Eder River — how they formed a church, which spread rapidly for a few years, and how they were persecuted until they fled to Krefeld, then to Friesland, and finally to America.

It is not difficult to see that they made some mistakes; and we have made many since their time. We need not deify them, extol all they did, and follow them blindly. Perhaps they were too literalistic. Perhaps they let their differences divide them too often. But one cannot read the record without feeling the sincerity and the courage of the group.

---

[20] Durnbaugh, *op. cit.*
[21] Mack, *op. cit.*, page 881.
[22] *Ibid.*, page 92.

A Methodist minister, who appreciates the fine work our church has done in recent years, asked me some days ago why our church has not grown larger. Somewhat embarrassed, I gave him a stumbling answer. I am not fully certain now. But if we are small because we have taken a position on certain social issues, such as war and temperance, and this has put tension between us and the world, then I have no apology for being small. If, on the other hand, we have been too contentious regarding matters that have little relevance for individual salvation, for the welfare of others, or for the welfare of humanity at large — for this I would be sorry.

Alexander Mack and his associates could say to Luther, "Yes, we believe in justification by faith, but we think a reformation of doctrine is not enough; a new life in Christ must follow a reform in doctrine."

To the Anabaptist he and his associates could say, "We follow in your train, but we do not go along with those of you who are iconoclasts, or who would resort to violence to reform the world."

To the Pietists they could say, "We believe in your emphasis on regeneration and the inner life, but we do not follow those of your number who would withdraw from the world into passive quietness. We would set up a church that keeps tension between us and the unchristian practices of the world."

To the subjective Inspirationists they could say, "We too believe in the inspiration of the Spirit, but we would test the spirits by the Word of God whether they be good or evil."

I would not recommend that we should, even if we could, reproduce and duplicate their eighteenth-century church in the twentieth century. But I am convinced that there were certain qualities of life in them which our generation seriously needs — their reverence, their devotion to the Scriptures, their courage, and their willingness to suffer for the cause of Christ as they saw it.

9. THE MIND OF CHRIST IN JUDGMENT

HARPER S. WILL

Pastor, Lincolnshire Church of the Brethren, Fort Wayne, Indiana. Formerly: pastor, Wenatchee, Washington; Chicago (First), Illinois; South Bend (First), Indiana; member, General Brotherhood Board; alternate moderator and acting moderator of Annual Conference, 1950.

The suggested title for our meditation this hour, "The Mind of Christ in Judgment," gears closely into the over-all theme of our two-hundred-fiftieth anniversary year, *Brethren Under the Lordship of Christ.* The sequence of the gospel call is to look to Christ as Savior, to make Him Lord, and to accept the discipline of His judgment.

Questions freely arise as we begin our two-hundred-fiftieth anniversary observance on this New Year's Day with a love feast. Are Christian liberty and the use of forms compatible? Can a form be taught and practiced without making its participants legalists? Is it necessary to partake of the communion to be a follower of Jesus? Is a rite such as feet-washing relevant to the Christian way for our time?

Judgment is one of the major concepts of Christianity. Truth revealed is to be accepted and obeyed; but it may be disregarded, distorted, or even denied. When men respond to truth, they are as Jesus suggested, like a wise man who built his house upon a rock. But when we hesitate in the presence of truth, or disregard or defy it, we are like a foolish man who built his house upon the sand. Inevitably judgment follows our responses in approval or in disaster. Man is free to choose the better or the worse; but once his choice is made and his action taken, he reaps what he sows. Man's freedom to select comes to an end with his choice. It never extends to the consequences. A wise Providence has kept judgment within His own hands. Man is a subject, not a monarch. His dominion has bounds.

Further, judgment is not only certain and final, but also continuous. Most textbooks on theology deal with judgment near the end, but in a true sense every moment is a moment of destiny and judgment. Every day is Judgment Day. The day the foolish man selected his foundation of sand, cut the first timbers, and drove the first wooden peg, he moved step by step nearer an approaching doom. God, it appears, has two hands — a right hand and a left hand. In His right hand He extends to the children of men His love and grace — all the daily providences of life, plus a crucified and resurrected Teacher and Savior. If we accept the offered gifts of God's right hand, we experience the goodness of life. But if in our blindness and willfulness we refuse the gifts of His right hand, we become acquainted with the left hand of God's judgment.

Heaven and hell are not afterthoughts of God. God has attached heaven or hell to every thought we think, every word we speak, every deed we do. Men are not victims of circumstance, and we are not living in a world ruled by blind fate. There is a divine order in our world and day by day our lives are measured before this order of justice. The ethical escalators of our universe operate on regular schedule, and men of every race and clime move up and down hourly in accordance with their deeds. The record is very plainly written that judgment at the end of the way will be as simple as the act of a Syrian shepherd at the day's close separating the sheep and the goats of his flock.

The significant feature of judgment, however, is in its basis. The same Christ to whom we look for salvation, whom we choose to be Lord, is also our Judge. He incarnated the truth of God; "the Word became flesh and dwelt among us, full of grace and truth." And it is His mind and His character that stand as the eternal measure of men's thoughts and deeds and lives. Christ is inescapable, and, whether we will to have it so or not, we live out our days under the judgment of His mind, and all history moves steadily onward to a throne of judgment upon which He is seated. Individually, we will learn the way of love, or lose our lives in frustration and emptiness. "For whoever would save his life will lose it, and whoever loses his life for my sake will find it."

Economically, we will share, or the treasures we cherish will be torn from us by an outraged humanity. "No one can serve two masters. . . . You cannot serve God and mammon." Racially, we will learn the ways of brotherhood, or we will plague our future with bitterness and strife. "You shall love your neighbor as yourself." Internationally, we will learn to live peaceably with all peoples, or we will bring down the house of our civilization with a terrifying crash. "Every one who hears these words of mine and does not do them will be like a foolish man who built his house upon the sand; and the rain fell, and the floods came, and the winds blew and beat against that house, and it fell; and great was the fall of it." The mind of Christ has been revealed. The handwriting of God is on the wall.

When we enter the Upper Room with Jesus and His disciples we find that His judgment became pinpointed. The Upper Room was a now-or-never moment in human history. It demanded decisive action. Words alone were inadequate. For months Jesus had toiled with His disciples, struggling most of the time with their hesitant humanity, only to discover as the end of His fellowship with them approached that they were far from the goal of the Kingdom which He had held constantly before them. Immersed as we all are in ourselves, we tend to underestimate the price required to lift a soul from servitude to self into an understanding of the truth that sets us free.

Observe the Master as events unfolded in that Upper Room. To begin with, when they entered not one volunteered the common courtesy of the basin and the towel to cleanse their dust-stained feet. In utter self-disregard, Jesus silently rebuked their irresponsiveness by accepting the role of the servant. "Knowing that the Father had given all things into His hands, and that He had come from God and was going to God, he girded himself with a towel" and washed their feet. The judgment was sharp and telling, and, to Peter's credit, he protested vehemently. In clear accent the Master stated this to be a price of participation with Him in His Kingdom: "If I do not wash you, you have no part in me." And in thoughtful exhortation He counseled that His followers should do as He had done.

Then, in quiet but with thunderous impact, He announced that one of those who sat at the table would betray Him. There were surprise and hope in the responses of the disciples under this rapier-like thrust of judgment. It would be expected that they might have questioned, "Is it Judas?" or, knowing Peter as they did, "Is it Simon?" As the record discloses, it was not so, but with one accord they asked, "Is it I?" This response is revealing as to what happens to people as they come into intimate fellowship with the Master. They see not others, but themselves, in the searching light of His mind and character.

After Judas had taken his leave, there followed the bread and the cup, the final word in self-giving which they failed utterly at the moment to comprehend but which subsequent happenings etched indelibly upon their minds. Henceforth, the Upper Room would be to them, and still is to those who find the Master's fellowship, the Holy of Holies, and that bread and that cup, which are a memorial of His suffering and death on the cross, stand as the ultimate judgment of the passing generations. The witness of His words and that of His deeds became parallel — to find life we must pour it out for the redemption of others.

It is the goal of Christendom that the whole of humanity be brought under judgment to Christ. The final order of the departing Master was: "Go therefore and make disciples of all nations, baptizing them in the name of the Father, and of the Son and of the Holy Spirit, teaching them to observe all that I have commanded you."

The obvious place always for the judgment of Christ to begin is at the house of God, as is suggested by the author of the Book of Hebrews. But who among us can stand in the presence of the Christ of the Upper Room? Is not our righteousness at its best, in the light of His self-giving, "but as filthy rags," as the prophet Isaiah expressed it long ago? The Brethren are to be commended for the exacting importance they have attached to self-examination in preparation for participation in the love feast. Historically, each member was visited to check whether he was still in the faith and in Christian fellowship with all the Brethren. At times in pioneer communities they tarried for days in self-examination before gathering about the table of the Lord. There is much to commend in the Brethren observance of the Lord's supper, but often our preparation and reasoning have been superficial in the true light of the judgment of the Christ of the Upper Room.

We Brethren, with our eagerness to do all that Jesus taught, have been at times a contentious and proud people. Our mood has often been that of debate, with the consequence that about the only thing demonstrated was our forensic skill. We have prided ourselves that we are different, that we have taken the whole gospel, that the New Testament only is our rule of faith and practice. There have been times when we have almost adopted the Hebrew role of "the chosen" and have seriously wondered if any except the Brethren would be among the elect.

I can hear a Brethren elder saying, "I have been baptized by trine immersion. I have washed my brother's feet. I have kept all the ordinances the Master taught." He then drew some conclusions. It led me to think of the boasting of a man whom the Master once quoted: "'I thank thee that I am not like other men, extortioners, unjust, adulterers, or even like this tax collector.'" There is no word more despicable in religious circles than the term *Pharisee*. Yet, at times, we Brethren have dangerously approached a spiritual kinship with the Pharisee. We too have reasoned with ourselves, commending ourselves that we were not like other followers of the Master. It has never been very easy for the Brethren to repent. We have not been skilled in the art of penitence; and yet penitence is the needed mood as we approach the Upper Room.

The twenty-third chapter of Matthew's Gospel has not been very popular in recent years among the Brethren. If Jesus stood with us today, as we inaugurate our anniversary observance, what would He say? Could it be that He would be constrained to say as once He did — paraphrasing a bit: "Woe unto you, Brethren, hypocrites, for you shut up the Kingdom of heaven against men; for you neither go in yourselves nor do you allow them that are entering to go in"; or "Woe unto you, Brethren, hypocrites! You make clean the outside of the cup and the platter, but within they are full of extortion and excess"? An outward imitation of the Master is never sufficient. The distance between washing someone's feet and feeling genuine humility may be wide. The distance between taking the loaf and the cup and giving one's self in sacrificial love may be wider. Always beyond the form is the spirit. The letter can kill. It can sink into a dull legalism. "It is the spirit that gives life," the Master taught.

Is there any place then for the use of rites in the church? Why not by-pass all outward expressions and think only of the mind and the spirit of Jesus? Why concern ourselves with the externals of a loaf and a cup, or a basin and a towel? A few would go so far as to say that we should forget about the church and concentrate on the Kingdom.

We meet here an age-old struggle. It involves the nature of man and our universe. What is matter? What is spirit? Some have concluded that they are inimical, that we live in a dualistic world, and that there is a constant warfare between the two. Paul came close to this position in his analysis of man's struggle between the flesh and the spirit.

Jesus, on the other hand, held a sacramental view of the material world within us and about us. To Him it was good, as was stated in the creation story in Genesis. To Jesus, the visible was a gateway into the invisible. Through an earthly father He saw beyond to the Eternal Father. In a new patch sewed on an old garment, He saw a likeness to His Kingdom. And in a piece of bread He memorialized His death and His living presence. Jesus freely used the material to unveil the truth He taught. The material is a ladder by which we climb upward to the mind and the spirit of the Master. It seems there is no other way.

We argue as to the value and the place of forms in Christianity. But would it not be as impossible to express Christianity without rites as it would be to fashion a garment without materials? A formless religion is an impossibility. Gratitude, penitence, and love can be expressed only as we say or do something. It takes a word, a song, a pilgrimage, a lifted head, a bended knee, or some action to express the emotions of the heart. How does a lover express his love? If it is genuine it will be incarnated into some expression — a look, a whisper, a touch, a kiss, a rose, a letter, or some other symbol. A Christianity that is genuine will evoke the cry, "What must I do?" When the grace of God in Christ breaks into a life, or is operative in a life, something is going to happen, something is going to be done, something must be done. It is not a question as to what rites will be employed. Discontinue all rites and churches would close. Man is not a disembodied spirit. He dwells in a house of clay, and until this mortality puts on immortality he will be compelled to reach upward through ritual observances for the Eternal Christ.

This sacramental view of our universe is glimpsed in writings of many of our leading scientists and poets. To Whitehead, Eddington, and Jeans, matter is energy and the vehicle of mind and spirit. Henry Drummond, in his *Natural Law in the Spiritual World,* envisioned the seen as the scaffolding that reaches up into the unseen. Elizabeth Barrett Browning could write:

> Earth's crammed with heaven,
> And every common bush is afire with God.

Alfred Tennyson wrote:
> Flower in the crannied wall,
> I pluck you out of the crannies,
> I hold you here, root and all, in my hand,
> Little flower — but if I could understand
> What you are, root and all, and all in all,
> I should know what God and man is.

A religious rite might be likened to an iceberg afloat on the ocean. We are told that one eighth of it is visible, that the great mass of it is hidden beneath the surface of the water. Always it is the hidden aspect of any rite that gives it primary significance. In the communion we see and handle a piece of unleavened bread and a cup. It is the vast reality beyond the bread and the cup, what they symbolize, namely, channels to convey to the communicants the re-assuring touch of the real presence of Christ, that makes them genuine means of grace. Participating in a Christian rite is following a trail that leads upward into infinity.

A rite can be a channel of grace, but we dare not forget that it may become a rut. There is nothing that human hands touch that cannot be degraded. Think of what has been done times without number to the cross. What was a supreme act of devotion to Jesus, and a passion in the early days of the church, has been time and again casually reduced to an ornament and a wayside fetish. Likewise with the ordinances of the New Testament — with them means and ends have often been confused, and frequently our faith has been reduced to a rigid set of rules. Always we will need to be vigilant to safeguard our ordinances for the purpose for which they were intended.

Two assumptions undergird these reflections, namely, that to be a Christian here and now it is a necessity that we live out our days under the constant discipline of the judgment of Christ, and that the use of rites is a necessity in expressing the Christian faith. Caught as we are in our pride and willfulness, in our greed and sin, we need every means of grace available through the example and teaching of Jesus. Jesus intended His way to be a venture second to none. His Kingdom was to be like a treasure hid in a field; when a man found it, with joy he sold all that he had and then bought that field. It is easy to permit one's religion to sink into a hollow and drab affair. A Christian, like the mountain climber, sets out for the glimpse of the higher vista. He seeks to discover those relationships that admit him to the circle of the Burning Heart. No Christian pilgrim journeys far along the steep ascents of commitment, forgiveness, and love until he encounters the need for the presence of the living Christ. Is it not logical to conclude that a fertile trail for finding that Presence is along that pathway where the footsteps of Jesus led during His brief earthly pilgrimage? Are we not presumptuous to assume that we can find His way and attain His standards without accepting the discipline of His judgments!

The fruits of the Spirit — such as love, joy, peace, and patience — are not found by casual seekers. Only those who accept Christ's yoke and the daily discipline of His judgment find the pearl of great price. Spiritual enrichment is not attained through minimum practices. Leslie Weatherhead tells of a conversation within a small circle in a university club. The talk had become deeply personal, with each participant sharing his inmost desires. After others had commented, one of the circle spoke in these revealing words: "You are going to smile, perhaps, and think me queer, but if I understand aright my inmost being what I really desire above all else is to be a saint." Intuitively, we sense the truth in this insight; and we make little headway in answering the question, "How?" until first we have found the answer to the questions, "What?" and "Whom?"

When we gather in our Upper Room it is a voluntary submission of ourselves to the corrective judgment of the self-effacing and self-giving Christ of the Upper Room, to the end that He may be truly born in us and that we may be truly born in Him.

10. THE MIND OF CHRIST SYMBOLIZED

MORLEY J. MAYS

Dean of the college and professor of philosophy, Juniata College; writer; minister; lecturer; member, board of directors, Bethany Biblical Seminary. Formerly: associate professor of English, Bridgewater College.

As the Christian sees it, all of life is rooted in mystery. Christianity has no other starting point than the mystery which we sense in our experience of the universe about us. He who has no awareness of mystery is not fit for the Kingdom; he is not even ready to accept with any degree of meaningfulness the claims of the church for his love and loyalty. Take away mystery, and you take away the primary reason the Christian faith has for being.

I make these broad assertions knowing full well how much I lay myself open to the criticism and the scorn of my fellow men. Ever since the dawn of the modern age, roughly three and a half centuries ago, modern man has ridden to the crest of his major enterprises on the simple assumption that everything is fully knowable. I am quite ready to admit that without this confidence we would never have achieved so amazingly in science and technology. Now we are literally ready for new worlds to conquer, in a way that would have made the tears of Alexander a childish whimpering, wholly confident that these other worlds are within our grasp. We may falter now and then, but in the end the sure conquest is ours.

As a consequence modern man has largely abandoned any sober respect for the proposal that there is mystery to be reckoned with. Science is out to discredit mystery as anything other than the unprobed residue of nature's secrets. The only kind of mystery which modern man can allow is the kind that simply represents ignorance and that will yield to his persistent entreaties at the right time.

Likewise in his less learnéd undertakings, in his role as the common man, modern man has largely scorned the idea of mystery. No such nonsense for him — let's get on with the hard facts. He lives at the level of sensuous pleasure, full of desires and appetites, searching for the thrilling and the titillating, restless, tense, active, concerned about his personal security. And so he rejects mystery for practical purposes, as the scientist rejects it for theoretical purposes.

May I add that this prevailing impatience with mystery has crept into certain religious postures. There are those Christians who appear to believe that it is their responsibility to flatten out every mystery. Faith for them means having assuredly all the answers. They have poked into all of God's plans for the future; they know the why and the wherefore of every event; they have reduced everything to barren literalism. They make no admission that the glories of God are far richer than their poor minds can comprehend.

Nevertheless, we must say that there is reality which lies at the edge of our lives, just beyond the bounds of time and space, and this is where religious experience begins. Amos N. Wilder has said, "To deny or minimize the abiding element of mystery and awe in the religious life is to forfeit that life itself."

The Christian tradition not only teaches that there is an abyss of mystery at the boundaries of our experience (poets and seers have also witnessed to mystery); it believes also that meaningful resources for the living out of our days are to be found in that mystery. In this mystery, says the Christian, man can find the answers to his perplexities, his mixed and sometimes contradictory motives, his craven appetites, his ambiguous morality, his tragic sufferings. It is in relation to this mystery, in short, that he can find the source and destiny of his existence.

Still further, the Christian tradition teaches that man of himself and with his natural bent cannot penetrate the mystery. If man is to establish any kind of meaningful contact with the mystery, the initiative must come from the side of the mystery itself. So profound is the mystery that, when it comes through, man realizes that the advance was not with him. He strives to find, but when he finds he discovers that really he has been found. If he projects himself in love, he discovers that it has been because he was first loved. If he cries out, "How long, O Lord, how long?" he hears a voice which says, "Lo, I am with you always." If he tries to find some solid anchoring for his life, some mooring post, something beyond the transient, he hears the measured words from the depths of mystery, "Before Abraham was, I am."

Only now do we come to the critical part of our inquiry. It is necessary to concede the reality of mystery, but that is not sufficient. It is necessary that we concede the self-disclosure of the meaning of that mystery, but even that is not sufficient. We must address ourselves to the language of the self-disclosure. To borrow a phrase from business practice, we must ask about the letter of transmittal.

The mystery is not silent, the Christian insists; it is only unheard. But neither does the mystery speak to us in the language of human speech. We do not receive the message of the mystery in the language of everyday discourse; nor do we hear it in the syllables of scientific discourse. Our reception of the mystery is different from our reception of everything which we come to know of the world of things about us. This means that our knowledge of the mystery is different from our common habits of thinking and knowing. What we can know about the mystery will not neatly and without remainder fit into the pigeonholes which we have contrived for ordinary and even extraordinary use. "His ways are not our ways; his thoughts are not our thoughts."

This adds up to something startling and rewarding: our knowledge of the mystery is symbolic knowledge, and our language is the language of symbol. Recent studies have reminded us afresh of the peculiarities of Biblical language. The Bible is full of symbolic language from beginning to end, ranging from the single detail or metaphor through the parable, the allegory, and the legend to the mythical narrative. This is no accident of composition; nor is it only a mark of the literary excellence of the Bible. If all we have in the symbolism of the Bible is literary flourish, mark it up as a gratuity and let it go at that. Symbols are of the essence in the communication of the message. They are the bearers of the mystery, bringing it within our grasp.

What is a symbol? It is similar to a sign, and we are all familiar with signs; they are all around us. Their purpose is to point to something beyond themselves. Some signs indicate danger or need for caution: the buoy on the water channel, the beacon on the mountain crest. All signs are alike in that once their pointing or indicating function is over they have no further value. What is more, save for the temporary inconvenience, which might be considerable, there is no reason why we could not agree on other signs.

But symbols are also unlike signs. They too point beyond themselves, but in pointing beyond themselves they also partake of the character of that to which they point. Our most immediate and familiar examples of symbolisms are to be found in the secular order. The flag, for example, not only "stands for" our country; in itself it is worthy of our respect, and so we handle it with care and honor it in ceremonial custom.

In our time perhaps the most impressive instance of symbolism is the reigning monarch of Great Britain. Although the queen may have little or no governing power, the crown possesses tremendous symbolic power. In their monarch the British people find all their personal and national ideals symbolized. Accordingly they grant to her an unusual degree of ceremonial recognition, generally unappreciated elsewhere in this matter-of-fact modern world.

Our principal concern today is with the mind of Christ and

the part symbols played in His thinking and His teaching. In Him the mystery hidden for ages broke through to us in ways which we can best comprehend through symbols. He taught us that God comes to us not in mystical detachment, but in wrestling with events, in being unwilling to let them go until their blessing comes upon us. He taught us that the revelation comes through circumstance and event and not apart from it, that in everything we confront we can see the dimension which runs inward to the heart of the universe. If we will let Him, God will take up the frayed ends of our lives, the rents and tatters, and in the eternities of His presence bring pattern and purpose to them. He will bring the completion of the fragmentary, the restoration of the broken.

This redemptive possibility Jesus Christ opened to us by symbols, symbols of language and also symbols drawn from the intimacies of His own experience. Taking familiar acts — the cleansing of feet, the breaking of bread — He gave them the power to represent symbolically the loving care and the embracing fellowship which on every hand reach out to us from the heart of God. He gave the vitalities of His person — His body and His blood — as the symbols by which to seal God's forgiveness of our sins and confirm the redemptive act which God in Him undertook in our behalf.

But Christian symbolism is complete only when we accept Jesus Christ as Himself the supreme symbol. Like other symbols, He pointed to the reality beyond Him, to the mysterious grace of God's purposes for us. Certain things, He said, were known only in the bosom of the Father. Moreover, "though he was in the form of God, [he] did not count equality with God a thing to be grasped." Again, like other symbols, He embodied the reality to which He pointed. In Him all the fullness of God was pleased to dwell; "God was in Christ reconciling the world to himself." He was indeed the symbol above all symbols.

Every Christian must reckon with the symbols by which the realities of his faith are mediated to him. Paul reminded us that we are to be stewards of the mysteries, which incidentally tells us something about the nature of Christian stewardship too easily overlooked. As stewards of the mysteries we cannot be casual about the symbols of the mysteries, as though they had no power in themselves. Nor can we take them to be ultimate; that way lies idolatry. To recognize and appreciate the symbolic character of our faith is to find the way of interpreting spiritual truth by spiritual means.

11. THE LITANY OF SELF-EXAMINATION

Used as preparatory to the love feast and holy communion service, at which Edward K. Ziegler, who had prepared the litany, officiated. Mr. Ziegler is pastor of the Williamson Road Church of the Brethren, Roanoke, Virginia; lecturer; writer; member, General Brotherhood Board. Formerly: missionary to India; pastor, Johnson City, Tennessee; pastor, York (First), Pennsylvania; pastor, Bridgewater, Virginia; professor of religion, Manchester College; director of evangelism, Brotherhood staff.

THE SCRIPTURES — 1 Corinthians 11:23-34 and the following:

"The Lord is nigh unto all that call upon him, to all that call upon him in truth. He will fulfill the desire of them that fear him; he also will hear their cry, and will save them.

"Seek the Lord while he may be found, call upon him while he is near:

"Let the wicked forsake his way, and the unrighteous man his thoughts; and let him return unto the Lord, and he will have mercy upon him; and to our God for he will abundantly pardon.

"He was wounded for our transgressions, he was bruised for our iniquities; the chastisement of our peace was upon him; and with his stripes we are healed.

"All we, like sheep, have gone astray: we have turned every one to his own way; and the Lord hath laid on him the iniquity of us all."

THE LITANY OF REPENTANCE

MINISTER: Almighty God, Spirit of Purity and Grace, whose dwelling is with the humble and contrite heart, hear Thy children's confession of sin and grant us Thy mercy. For all that has been evil in our lives, for unholy thoughts, and impure motives, for any scorn of goodness, trifling with truth, and indifference to beauty; for all our wanderings from the better way —

CONGREGATION: Forgive us, O Lord.

MINISTER: For lack of love toward those whose love has never failed; for doubt of Thy goodness, and unbelief in Thy providence, for ingratitude for blessings received and unwillingness to give of that which Thou hast given, for any dullness of insight which has kept us unaware of Thy glory, and for disobedience unto such heavenly visions as we have been able to see —

CONGREGATION: Forgive us, O Lord, and may we henceforth love Thee as we ought.

MINISTER: For all the wrong we have done our fellow men: for unkind words and untruthful speech; for loss of temper and irritating conduct; for neglect of charity and failure in justice; for arrogant pride and contempt of the lowly; for forgetfulness of other's pain and for advantage taken of another's weakness; for whatever any person may rightfully hold against us —

CONGREGATION: Forgive us, O Lord, and help us to love our neighbor as ourselves.

MINISTER: For our faulty following of the Master, our slow faith in His power to save, our timid, hesitant answers to His call for service, our insensibility to the meaning of the Cross; for all that mars our discipleship, and makes it difficult for others to believe in Him;

CONGREGATION: Forgive us, O Lord, and give us grace to follow Jesus more steadfastly.

THE PRAYERS, AND THE HYMN RESPONSES

MINISTER: Help us, Thy people, O Lord, to be truly penitent; empower us to overcome all temptations, enable us faithfully to love according to Thy will; create in us a growing likeness to Jesus —

CONGREGATION: Hear our prayer, and answer us, O Lord, our God.

MINISTER: O God, who didst send Thy Son into the world for our salvation, as we plan to gather about the communion table, spread with its holy emblems, to remember Him who never forgets us, we thank Thee that here we may sense the unity of our fellowship with our Brethren and with Christians of every land. Remember in mercy Thy children as they gather about the Lord's Table, and as they shall gather together in their separate places of worship.

Congregation Singing:
>   Blest be the tie that binds
>   Our hearts in Christian love;
>   The fellowship of kindred minds
>   Is like to that above.

Minister: We pray for Thy Church. Bestow upon her a greater responsiveness to duty, a swifter compassion for the needy everywhere. Teach her how to save her own life by losing it in courageous unselfish service to all humanity. Unite her scattered people in an unbreakable fellowship ever to bear witness to Thy love and power in Christ, our Lord.

Congregation Singing:
>   In Christ there is no East or West,
>   In Him no South or North;
>   But one great fellowship of love
>   Throughout the whole wide earth.

Minister: Lord Jesus Christ, who biddest Thy Church to bring all men to Thyself and to make all mankind one family in Thee, make clear to each one of us his part in the task. Fire our minds with a vision of a world under the Lordship of Christ, in which justice and right, peace and brotherhood shall reign according to Thy will; and help us each one, O Lord, to do our part that Thy will may be done on earth as it is in heaven.

Congregation Singing:
>   In Him shall true hearts everywhere
>   Their high communion find;
>   His service is the golden cord
>   Close-binding all mankind.

12. THE ANNIVERSARY LITANY

Prepared by Edward K. Ziegler of Roanoke, Virginia.

MINISTER: In the name of the Father, and of the Son, and of the Holy Spirit:
PEOPLE: Amen.
MINISTER: For the light of Eternal Truth which has witnessed to the redeeming love and power of God in every age:
PEOPLE: We give Thee thanks, O Lord.
MINISTER: For that of God in every man which has responded to God's revelation of His will and purpose in every time and place:
PEOPLE: We give Thee thanks, O Lord.
MINISTER: For Alexander Mack, Peter Becker, Christopher Sauer, and all others who have followed in their train, who in obedience to a heavenly vision have upheld the New Testament as a sufficient rule of faith and practice, the New Testament ordinances as a means of grace, and the principle of brotherly love as the Golden Rule of life:
PEOPLE: Accept the gratitude of our hearts, we pray Thee, O God.
MINISTER: For this two hundred fiftieth anniversary year in which we can examine again the spiritual foundations of the church, bring ourselves more fully under the Lordship of Christ, and commit our lives more fully to the will of God in the pursuit of truth and right, of justice and peace:
PEOPLE: Accept the gratitude of our hearts, we pray Thee, O God.
MINISTER: From any bowing at old altars that would keep us from building new ones, from any satisfaction in past achievements which would keep us from seeing new opportunities, and from any identification with the glories of our fathers

which would keep us from serving our generation as they served theirs:

People: O God, deliver us.

Minister: From any pride in our past that would blind us to our imperfections or from any exultation with regard to the insights with which God has blessed us but which would in turn keep us from learning from others:

People: O God, save and redeem us.

Minister: From any sectarianism that would deny our oneness in Christ or that would keep us from joining in fellowship, worship, and service with all who love the Lord:

People: Gracious Lord, in Thy mercy, deliver us.

Minister: For a fresh outpouring of Thy Spirit upon the church, for a new revelation of Thy will and purpose for our time, for a greater sensitivity to the will of God, for greater courage in denouncing evil and for a more adventurous spirit in witnessing to the way of goodness and love:

People: We pray Thee, O God.

Minister: For a greater devotion to God's Word, for a more faithful cultivation of the tie that binds our hearts in Christian love, for a more sacrificial stewardship of our time, our ability, and our resources:

People: We beseech Thee, O God.

Minister: For an unreserved commitment, for an unfaltering faith, for an undimmed hope and for an unfailing love:

People: We pray and beseech Thee, O Lord.

Minister: For a church that is true to the best in its heritage, for a church that loses its life in the service of human need: for a church that presses on toward the mark of its high calling; for a church committed to live under the Lordship of Christ:

People: We consecrate our lives, dedicate the activities of our church and earnestly seek Thy guidance, Thy grace, and Thy mercy, in the name of Him who loved us and gave Himself for us, even Jesus Christ our Lord. Amen.

13. THE MACK MEMORIAL SERVICE

TRIBUTE

Alexander Mack once said to his family, "Now when I am gone, don't mark my grave, or they might sometime want to erect a monument over it." The family protested against an unmarked grave and finally got his consent to place his initials on a small stone slab. After his death in 1735, a quite unpretentious blue slate stone, bearing the initials *A. M.*, was erected at the place of burial in Axe's burying ground. Here his body rested for one hundred fifty-nine years. Later it was desirable that his remains should be removed from this unkept cemetery. On November 13, 1894, twenty-five descendants of Alexander Mack of the fifth, sixth, seventh, and eighth generations were present at a service and erected a plain white marble headstone in the Germantown church cemetery. On this stone are the words, "The first minister and organizer of the Church of the Brethren in the year 1708, born at Schriesheim, Germany, 1679, came to Germantown 1729, died 1735. Removed from Axe's Burying Ground."

On this first day of January 1958 we stood in the cemetery near the grave of Alexander Mack and waited in silence, with profound emotions, while the chairman of the 250th Anniversary Committee, Paul H. Bowman, gave tribute to the founder of the church as follows:

"Spirit of Alexander Mack:

"You lost your mills and your fortune in a land of tyranny and found a resting place for your body in a land of freedom.

"You lost your battle to purify the church from within but your quest to discover more fully the pure mind of Christ continues still.

"You failed in your crusade to abolish war and bloodshed in your own generation, but the instruments of peace which you forged abide and the Prince of Peace is our Lord."

PRAYER

"O God, have mercy upon us gathered here. Help us to seek first the Kingdom which is everlasting. Amen."

PART THREE

The Des Moines Celebration

PART THREE

III. The Soviet Civilisation

14. THE DES MOINES PROGRAM OF SPECIAL ANNIVERSARY ADDRESSES

Sunday, June 15

Standing Committee, opening session of praise and worship. Sermon: The Adventurous Future — *Harry K. Zeller, Jr.*

Tuesday, June 17

Opening session of the Conference. The Brethren and the Modern State — *Dan West*

Wednesday, June 18

8:30 A.M. Bible Hour. The Brethren and the Book of Books — *Chalmer E. Faw*

8:15 P.M. Moderator's Address: "And How Shall the Brethren Be Recognized?" — *Desmond W. Bittinger*

Thursday, June 19

8:30 A.M. Bible Hour. The Brethren and Biblical Ethics — *W. Harold Row*

8:10 P.M. The Brethren and Their Culture — *Kermit Eby*

Friday, June 20

8:30 A.M. Bible Hour. The Brethren and Biblical Reconciliation — *T. Wayne Rieman*

8:10 P.M. The Brethren and the Ecumenical Church — *Kurtis F. Naylor*

Saturday, June 21

8:30 A.M. Bible Hour. The Brethren and Their Interpretation of History — *Warren F. Groff*

SUNDAY, JUNE 22

9:00 A.M. Bible Hour. The Brethren and Biblical Proclamation — *John B. Grimley*

11:00 A.M. The Anniversary Sermon: The Brethren Under the Lordship of Christ — *Paul M. Robinson*

8:30 P.M. The Church Convocation: The Brethren and Destiny — *Calvert N. Ellis*

15. "AND HOW SHALL THE BRETHREN BE RECOGNIZED?"

Desmond W. Bittinger

President of McPherson College; president, Kansas Foundation for Private Colleges; minister; writer; lecturer; member, General Brotherhood Board. Formerly: pastor, Lima, Ohio; missionary to Nigeria; member, General Mission Board; editor, the Gospel Messenger; member, constituting committee of the World Council of Churches; moderator of Annual Conference, 1951 and 1958.

"By this all men will know that you are my disciples, if you have love for one another" (John 13:35).

A story comes down to us out of the past that after Alexander Mack had founded the church by baptism in the Eder River two hundred fifty years ago, one of his neighbors asked him, "And how shall your members be recognized?" It was natural that such a question should be asked if denominational groups were to be distinguished one from the other, for on all sides new religious orders and new denominations were coming into being.

Indeed, religious divisions are as old as religion itself. They had occurred among the Hebrews: some were Sadducees, some were Pharisees, and some were Essenes. They had occurred in the early Christian church: some inclined to follow Paul, some Apollos. They had occurred down through the history of the developing Catholic Church: some were Greek Orthodox, some Roman Catholics; within these various larger groupings many orders had sprung up, each stressing some differing emphasis that seemed to them significant. Protestantism has continued these divisions into scores, and later into hundreds, of bodies.

These various religious divisions were distinguished by clearly discernible characteristics. The various friar orders were recognized by their dress, the manner of cutting the hair, the type of shoes, and whether the cross was worn around the waist, on the chest, or on the back. The various denominations and orders could be distinguished, also, by their published statements of belief, by their hymns, by their orders of prayer.

Protestants are still amazed to discover, particularly among the sisterhood of Catholics, what seem to be scores of distinguishing items of dress: the cut of the sister's headdress varies sharply from order to order; the looping of the belt at the waist is not the same. The Catholics find themselves similarly amazed at the variety of creedal statements which distinguish the Protestants. They are interested in our varied construction of the altar, the arrangement of the chancel, and the placement of the baptistry, as well as in the great variety of organizational patterns which characterize Protestants. Frequently, Catholics and Protestants ask each other today the question which was asked of Alexander Mack, "And how shall your members be recognized? How is your order distinguished?" Identifying markings are much older than Hebrewism or Christianity. Indeed, they are as old as man himself.

The necessity of having some mark to distinguish an order of worshipers, a clan, or a tribe is exceedingly important among aboriginal people who do not know how to write creeds. Apparently, the necessity for men to be distinguished, one from another, has always seemed of urgent importance.

Recently, I reread Paul's words, "I bear on my body the marks of Jesus." As I closed the Book and meditated, there came into my mind, vividly, a picture background out of which he might well have written those words. This background focuses vivid attention upon the question, "And what are the distinguishing marks of a Brethren, or of a Christian?"

I shall present the background to you.

One day in an aboriginal Nigerian setting there came rushing up the hill to our house, which was located on a shelf of the hill, twenty or more panting young men. They were not members of the tribe among whom we lived, but had crossed the tribal boundary and come hurrying to call upon us, from a neighboring tribe. Some of them, however, spoke the language we knew.

After they had followed the required proprieties of greeting us, their excitement caused them to rush into an urgent invitation: "Teacher, get your horse with three legs and quickly follow us! We have a great surprise for you." As we turned to comply, they added with just as much excitement, "And don't forget to bring the Book that has in it the mind of God."

We got the horse with three legs — a motorcycle with a sidecar — and they ran before us, showing us the way. When we came to the end of the existing road, part of their surprise for us became apparent. With their own hands they had extended the road for many miles. Though it twisted and turned and was exceedingly bumpy, the horse with three legs followed as they ran ahead, showing us the way. Presently, at the end of some bouncing and wearisome miles, we drove into the center of their village. The second part of the surprise now became evident. At the one side of their spreading council tree, with much labor they had built a church.

Their chief was waiting. Many of the villagers had gathered. They said with dignity and pride, "We have dug this house of God from the earth; we have laid it up handful by handful of adobe construction; we have crowned it with a roof of grass. We have invited you to come to place within it the Book which has in it the mind of God. Now together we shall present the house to God, for it is God's house. It is the biggest and best house in the village; that is the kind of house God should have."

But before we turned to go into the house, we looked across the open space to the other side of the spreading council tree where we saw in operation an ancient aboriginal practice such as Paul must also have seen. We walked over to watch it; the crowd hushed and followed. A young girl, comely and beautiful, approaching the age for marriage, was kneeling in the sand. Crouching above her was a priestess, so intent upon her responsibility that she had not stopped, even amidst all the excitement of the coming of the motorcycle and the shouting of the multitude.

Before this young woman could be married it was necessary that the marks which distinguished her tribe be carefully cut into her body. With a knife shaped like a fishhook, the inside of it sharpened as a cutting edge, this priestess was digging into the body of the girl, cutting from side to side and from shoulder to hip, making forever sharp and clear the marks which would reveal the tribe to which she belonged. Blood from the cutting stained the ground. The priestess rubbed ashes into the cuts so that they would heal in a raised condition. Henceforth, anyone seeing this woman even at a long distance could know her tribe by the marks which she bore cut into her body. The young girl accepted this as necessary. It was important that all people know the group to which she belonged.

We looked with increased interest upon the multitude of people who surrounded us. All, without exception, who had reached the age of puberty, boys or girls, men or women, bore upon their bodies the marks of their tribe. These marks were cut into cheeks, lips, nose, chest, back; anyone seeing them knew at once the tribe to which each belonged. They bore, cut in, the marks which distinguished them.

Silently, we turned and went toward the church. The thing about which I should speak as we dedicated the church was changing and forming in my mind. On one side of the tree was in operation the ceremony of cutting the marks of the tribe into the very body of a tribal member; on the other side of the tree stood the church. These people wanted to become members of the church and to have in their place of worship "the Book which has in it the mind of God."

What are the markings on this side of the tree which should always distinguish all Christians? What are the burned-in, inerasable marks of the follower of Christ?

Paul said, "I bear on my body the marks of Jesus."

Can Christ's marks always be seen? What are they? If we are, indeed, under the Lordship of Christ there should be evidences of it.

The question to Alexander Mack was, "And how shall your members be recognized?"

It is against this background that I ask an important question as we look forward from two hundred fifty years of having been Brethren. My question is: "How shall the Brethren in the next decade, the next century, the long future, be recognized?"

I shall venture to suggest some of the marks which I think should characterize the Brethren of the future who are indeed under Christ's Lordship. I shall not attempt to relate them specifically to the Brethren of the past, since this has been done and will be done in other addresses of this anniversary occasion.

Medford D. Neher, in painting the murals depicting the emerging and developing Church of the Brethren, began with one in which the eight brethren and sisters who gave birth to the church knelt earnestly, elbow to elbow, beside the open Bible. They were seeking truth from its pages; they shared the results of this quest; their various understandings of the truth as it was revealed to each of them should be shared with one another. This picture of the Church of the Brethren is one which I hope will always be central in our future.

I. The Praying, Searching, Open Mind

I would place at the very center of the Brethren of tomorrow, as a major distinguishing mark, this prayerful, open, continuous, sharing search for truth.

It is my hope that the Brethren in the next decade, and forever, will spend much time on their knees. Prayer is easily gotten away from. The speed of our generation is tremendous. We fly across our continent in less than a night. Our speed in the next several decades will multiply even more rapidly. It may very soon be beyond what we even now imagine. Likely, more and more we all will be going someplace in a great hurry; but none of us will advance far, or really very fast, unless we advance on our knees. It is only as we search for and discover the truth of God which lies inevitably at the heart of all knowledge and can be discovered by all earnest searchers that a real future can open for us.

Prayerful searching for truth, real truth, with the open Bible central among us, is then the first answer, the first mark of the Brethren of the future.

But how shall we pray? Not all prayer is equally effective.

As the Brethren pray earnestly and inquiringly, they will not be praying primarily for strength for themselves. To pray for strength is a legitimate part of all prayer. Every Christian facing an unusual task prays for strength, for he feels his own inadequacies. Every minister preaching prays for the strength of God to bless him. The speakers on this anniversary occasion spent much time in prayer, asking God for strength because all of them felt inadequate.

But the aborigine also prays for strength and to a very different god. He decorates himself with varicolored paints, dances around his campfire, rattles his weapons, places them before a holy altar, and prays for strength to defeat his enemy, to kill those who would harm him. He prays for sharpness in his weapons; he asks the god to lengthen his arm and strengthen its power in order that he might destroy. The Hebrews also did this; some Christians have done this even until now, believing that they were calling upon Jehovah, the loving God. This kind of praying places the individual and his desires at the center. God's desires are to be bent to man's ideas and will. The Brethren of the future will not pray like that.

They will not even focus this major prayer upon asking for strength to do God's will. That certainly is a prayer admonition we hear over and over in the Christian church today, "Give us strength to do Thy will."

But even such a prayer is not enough. The Brethren of the

future will go beyond that as he prays with the open Bible before him. Saul, out of the Scripture, depicts the inadequacy of this type of prayer. He was a committed man. He knew the Scriptures well. He was a trained Biblical follower, a member of a dedicated religious order. His daily prayer was "Father, give me strength to do Thy will." But he believed that to do God's will meant to destroy all who were opposed to God's will — opposed to God's will as Saul himself understood it. Consequently, Saul's hands were bloody, his sword dripped with the blood of Christians whom he had put to its keen edge. And all the time he earnestly prayed for strength to do God's will; but it was God's will limited by Saul's understanding of it.

Then one day light from heaven struck him down; and, on the Damascus road, with his sword already drawn to slay other Christians, Saul changed his prayer and dropped his sword. His prayer became "Lord, what would you have me to do?"

This is a much better prayer. Such a prayer no longer asks, "Give me strength for myself"; it does not even ask, "Give me strength to do your will." It humbly petitions, "Give me an open mind to learn your will."

This concept, it seems to me, is one of the major contributions of the Brethren to total Christendom. This doctrine of the open mind and heart, I believe, lies at the very heart of the Brethren faith. Our assurance is not that we know His will; rather, it is that we are seekers after it, pursuers of it. We would not want to seem possessive at this point. Other Christians have held this point of view, also. But we as Brethren have made it central in our church. This is why we would never write a creed: we did not want to halt or slow down the quest for truth. I believe that Alexander Mack wanted a major distinguishing mark of the Brethren to be an open, yearning, searching mind, a mind forever searching for the will of Christ.

Jesus wanted it that way, too. "Knock," said He, "and it shall be opened unto you."

This, then, is one of the marks by which the Brethren of the future shall be recognized: they shall be prayerfully searching for truth, focusing upon the open Bible. I would not be true to my own mind, however, if I hoped to confine them to the Bible. God has ever been seeking to manifest Himself. He has left Himself nowhere without a witness. The earnest, seeking Brethren or Christian of tomorrow will be able to discover the truth of God everywhere. It is written in the stones, in the trees, in the minds and hearts of other people, in their unfolding lives and cultures.

I would even go further than this and say that some of God's truth is written in the holy scriptures of other religious groups. It is certainly to be found in the Hebrew scriptures of the Old Testament. It is also to be found in the Talmud, in the Koran, in the holy writings of every religion in the world. Not all that is written there is truth, but certainly in the writings of those whose attention was on religion and devotion God has been able to center some of His truth. In fact, Christ quoted almost word for word from some of the texts which were written before He walked upon the earth. All truth comes from God, and no ultimate truth, whether it be found in Asia or Africa, among the Hebrews or the Gentiles, cancels out any other ultimate truth. All truth belongs to the Christian. The Brethren with his open mind searches for all truth everywhere revealed in order that he might know God better. Jesus says of His disciples, "No longer do I call you servants, . . . but . . . friends, for all that I have heard from my Father, I have made known to you" (John 15:15).

I would not want to leave this point without saying that this does not make of the Christian searcher a neutral person. To be a continuous searcher for truth does not mean that one has not already discovered truth and that his life is not now being guided by the truth he already knows. God will have shown the Brethren of the future much truth; every day He will show them more. The searching Christian does have convictions. He will suffer for the truth he knows, for it is the truth of God; but always he is searching for other truth in order that the truth of God, the very life of God, may live within him.

It is in this quest for truth that the ordinances of the Christian church become helpful. They dramatize truth; they are teaching and learning devices. How better dramatize the Christian family-hood of all men than in a real love feast, the washing of each other's feet, the eating of a family meal together, and partaking together of the body and blood, the sacrificial spirit, of our Lord?

Christ knew that these dramatic ordinances were a means of growth and grace and established them for us. The Brethren of the future will so use them.

II. The Loving Heart

A second mark of the Christians, or of the Brethren of the future, is that they will be baptized — indeed, completely immersed — in love. Instead of praying for themselves or centering at all upon self, their prayer will be that they might be like Christ, that Christ might dwell within them. As the Christian prays for that and works for that, the "I" focus shifts from the center of his life and the "Thou" focus becomes central.

When we reach this point we discover that the entire philosophy of our great and highly respected Grecian and pre-Christian teachers becomes inadequate. A central word in the Grecian philosophy is *justice*. By justice they meant giving to each person the right to educate and develop his abilities until he became a well-rounded person, ready to live with other similarly developed people in a well-rounded community or democracy. Grecian education focused on producing a trained individual who would live in a good or democratic community, or state. The Grecian prayer was "Give us wisdom that we may develop our abilities and find our places in a well-ordered community or state." Christians pray for this, too. We have built our educational systems upon it. This is not enough for the individual or for his education. The focus of the Christian is not upon himself or his state. It is upon love.

His desire is that he might love God with his whole heart and his neighbor as himself. His prayer is that he might have the very spirit and life of God within him. And the best definition ever given of God was given by His Son: "God is love."

It is at this point in the educational process that the Christian college must distinguish itself. It must seek for all truth. And truth leads toward God. And God is love. If what we call Christian education does not lead in this direction it is not Christian. If the Brethren college does not teach this, is it really Brethren?

The second mark of the Brethren of the future is that he is characterized in everything, always, inescapably, by love. This is a burnt-in mark.

Love seeks not its own. Love will go a second mile. Love knows no stranger or enemy. Love will lay down its life for another. This is the distinguishing mark of the simple life; it is always love centered. "For God so loved the world that He gave His only Son," and His only Son died because He loved.

Again, the ordinances of the church are needful to dramatize for us this great love. The symbols both teach us and help to sanctify us as we seek this love.

III. Serving Hands

When the searching minds and hearts of the Brethren of the future have discovered and become a part of the love of God, the thrusts of their lives will be outward. The praying, loving Christian cannot do other than be a helpful part of his community, of the world in which he lives. The forces which dominate him are no longer centripital, that is, inward centered; they become centrifugal. He is thrust outward into society. He becomes a part of actual, redemptive love. He cannot be other than this if he prays and searches long enough before the open Bible to discover and become a part of the love of God.

The question is sometimes debated by Brethren as to whether we as Christians have responsibility for only those who are baptized Christians or whether we have so-called humanitarian responsibility for others in the world. This is a question which can no longer be debated by the Brethren of the future. Rather, being filled with the love of God and being like God, they will be impelled to serve all others. They must spend themselves for others. They must lose their lives to find life. Their love, like God's, must be for all the world. There can be no barrier, none ever, for love.

This, then, is the third mark of the Brethren.

Belonging to God, the Brethren of the future will be more than just good people in a good community. They will be sacrificing, self-forgetting people who seek always to learn new truth, to share the truth they know with all others, and to bring all others into a growing fellowship with God. They will seek to bind up every wound which God gives them power to touch. They will seek to help open every mind with whom God will let them come in contact. They will seek, under the Lordship of Christ, to help cast out all fear with love, the love of God.

This third distinguishing mark of the Brethren of the future has particular relevance to this day. Such Brethren will always be clearly recognized as peacemakers in this age of conflict. Peace will be their perpetual business.

When President Eisenhower spoke recently to the total Congress, he set forth our philosophy as a government. "We must speak from a position of strength," he said. Other governments also work from this premise. And so each government must stand ready to mete out massive retaliation when its position of strength is challenged or impinged upon.

But this very position of strength, when strength is centered on bombs and death, is a position of extreme and utter weakness. This position of strength is the "I" focus, the "I" strength. The prayer of modern states, very often, is no improvement upon the prayer of the aborigine, "Lord, give us strength, and give strength to our arms." Our governments, in essence, are still dancing around the tribal fires, painting themselves with frightening war paints, and asking God's strength upon their weapons. We are modifying the weapons, but we are not changing either the dance or the prayer. Each nation dances frantically against another. The God of love must, indeed, be far from all of this.

The end of such a dance is death. The wage of sin is death, and this is sin, demonic sin.

The Brethren of the future who are under the Lordship of Christ will not be a part of this dance of death. They must be distinguished, instead, by the earnestness of their prayer to be like God, who loved the world enough to die for it.

We, too, must love enough to suffer.

Many of us have stood by the stone marker which designates the spot where a rifle bullet brought John Kline down from his horse as he sought to minister to both sides in the Civil War. He was the kind of Brethren who must live into the future.

Dan West thought of a way to give milk to hungry babies regardless of the beliefs of their parents; water to the thirsty, food to the hungry, clothes to those who are cold.

From John Kline to Dan West to the future, a mark which the Brethren bear must be the mark of peacemakers. This cannot be something added on; it must be a burnt-in mark. It will be inerasable because the Brethren of the future will be seeking to have Christ dwell within them.

A young man from Greece came some time ago to a Brethren college. As he came to our door and we greeted each other, we asked him before we sat down, "Son, why did you come all the way from Greece to our college? Why did you pass up the colleges of other nations, and pass by the large, well-known universities and colleges of the East, to come to a little town in the Midwest to a little college like ours?"

His answer was clear and concise. He said: "I met, in Greece, some young men and young women who were digging a tunnel through a Grecian mountain to drain a valley. They were doing this in order that the valley might become fertile and food might be grown to feed my people. They were digging, not because they were paid, but because they loved people. They loved us whom they had not known and whose language they could not speak. I joined these people in digging this tunnel, and, after they were gone, I followed them to find whence they came; I wished to find for myself what it was that made them love people that much."

Those Brethren volunteers had some of the marks of the Brethren of the future.

When Alexander Mack was asked the question, "And how shall the Brethren be recognized?" his answer was clear. He said, "They shall be recognized by the manner of their living."

An oboriginal girl knelt on one side of a council tree, while the marks of her tribe were being cut in. As long as she lived the marks would remain. We knelt in the church on the other side a few minutes later and prayed that the marks of Christians, the marks of Brethren, might similarly be cut into our very lives so that they would forever remain a part of us:

> An open mind which is engaged in a continuous searching for the will and the mind of God;
>
> A loving heart; a prayerful yearning to be immersed in love, to grow to be like God;
>
> Serving hands which engage in a compelling outward thrust that makes us share all that we know and have with others, in order that the peace of God might come to us all, and so that we might help the world to sing Christ's birthday song, "Glory to God on high and on earth, peace."

These should be at least some of the inerasable marks of the Brethren in the next two hundred fifty years.

16. THE BRETHREN AND THE ADVENTUROUS FUTURE

Harry K. Zeller, Jr.

Pastor, Church of the Brethren, McPherson, Kansas; member, General Brotherhood Board; writer; lecturer; Formerly: pastor, Richmond, Virginia; pastor, Indianapolis, Indiana; pastor, Elgin, Illinois.

Anniversaries are weighted with danger. They predispose us to look backward rather than ahead. Not even the parable of Lot's wife is sufficient to shake us out of the nostalgia by which we are drawn to the past and hesitant about embracing the future.

I. Our Concept of Change

The first problem posed by the adventurous future at a two-hundred-fiftieth anniversary is our concept of change. Our eyes will turn to the past as we observe our history; they may even be glued to the past! Our research, our pageantry, our messages will all be a glorification of what has been. Spiritual values especially venerate the past. "The new is never holy," as Edith Hamilton reminds us. Faith, we are taught, is something which was once and for all delivered unto the saints — saints who lived centuries ago! "What has been must be" is the mood of faith. Especially at anniversaries we tend to speak as though faith were an antique, a period piece, if you please, which is changeless amid the swirl of change. As we reconstruct the great days in the history of the church we must guard against freezing the life of the church in the past rather than propelling it toward the adventurous future.

This anniversary ought to be the time when we remind ourselves that Alexander Mack was quite an innovator. The Reformation which brought our church into being represented a radical, dramatic break with the established past. Mack opened the Bible in the conviction that new truth would come from it. These truths were discovered, not singly lest one go off on a tangent, but in the guided communion of the whole fellowship. Having found such truth, Mack and his associates were not afraid to follow it, regarding it as the will of God.

I submit that if we went at the whole matter of religious conviction today as vigorously as Mack did, if we dug into the irrelevance of faith to the total life of the twentieth century, and if we observed the brittleness of our fixed dogmas and the failure of our faith to require any great sacrifice, we would have a new reformation on our hands. Established traditions in the life of the church may require marked change in the light of the truth which we now see in the open Bible. Exclusive practices, especially as they relate to church membership and communion, need scrutiny. Social goals, labeled socialism and communism, which may more accurately render the truth of Jesus than our capitalistic society permits us to believe, will need careful examination.

We dare not believe that Mack and his associates learned everything God had to reveal to mankind. We do not worship Alexander Mack. We are Brethren because we like the methods by which he arrived at the truth which comes from God. He expected changes still to come. We honor the insights of Alexander Mack when we make the changes which our experience with the mind of Christ reveals as essential for our time.

This was the "touch and go" issue in the formation of the church. Both Mack and Hochmann wanted open access to God and free inquiry into the spirit of truth. Hochmann feared this freedom would be bottled up in organization. He was concerned lest a new church tend to be as hard as the old church, coercing the faith and practice of the people rather than opening the windows of light and truth. Mack carried this same apprehension also, but he felt keenly the need of some structure which could press forward the faith that was in him. This was the watershed decision in the wake of which the eight were baptized in the River Eder and the Church of the Brethren was born.

Mack did not forget Hochmann's concern. To guarantee that this most fundamental truth be not lost in the organization thus formed, one of the first principles built into the Church of the Brethren was that there must be no force in religion. This represents the initial genius of the church. The Reformation broke from the old church. The Pietists continued the Reformation. If we are true to our faith, a continuing reformation will bring purifying changes into the church in the adventurous future. These changes we will not fear to make, because we are Brethren under the Lordship of Christ.

II. We Do Not Yet Know Fully What It Means to Be Christian

Let us push wider the door to the adventurous future by suggesting that this anniversary be regarded as the midpoint in our existence. We are now halfway between what the church has been and what it can be. Such a reach of faith is paralyzing. It seems too much like science-fiction crossbred with theology. Changes are coming so swiftly that they make antiquarians out of us. To contemplate more rapid and radical changes numbs our senses.

The slightest flexing of "the antennae of the future" reveals that we are destined to live in an epoch of material power and spacelessness beyond our ability to comprehend. Since this Conference last met, a whole new dimension has been added to our ken. We are now being told, "Make no mistake about it; the first man who will walk on the moon has already been born." A leading theologian in England has begun a discussion of the validity of the atonement at Calvary for any people who might be discovered to be dwelling on other planets. He wonders whether, if there are people on these other worlds, there will also be places of the skull like unto our own Golgotha. One is reminded here of the soliloquy in Ibsen's *The Emperor and the Galilean.*

Julian, the apostate emperor has brutally eliminated every shred of the influence of Christ from the known world. In his sleep he dreams that he is transported to another clime where the curve is vaster and the light more golden. Across the sweeping horizon he sees a procession led by soldiers with weeping women following and in the middle the Galilean alive and bearing his cross. When Jesus admits that he is on the way to another crucifixion, the apostate emperor cries out in agony as the procession passes by, "Where is he now? What if that at Golgotha by Jerusalem were but a wayside matter, a thing done as it were in passing? What if he goes on and on and suffers and dies and conquers again and again, from world to world?"[1]

Let us make a beginning toward this adventurous future by confessing that we do not yet know fully what it means to be Christian. We allow that God has more truth in store for us than we now know. We believe that the future may show us as much more about God as the past has revealed. The scientist is willing to say, "We do not know the one-millionth part of one percent of anything." If such humility is valid for the scientist, is it not much more essential for theologians, who proclaim the unfathomableness of God's omniscience, to be modest in their claims to know all? Such reserve would take all of the strain of authoritarianism out of our doctrine. Such humility would bring into our pilgrimage the searching mood of yearning desire to know what Christ would have us to do. All our fixed positions, our final doctrines, our firm practices would be tempered with a reticence to assume that these are the final words from God. We would come to all matters of faith and practice in the awareness that we may not be doing or believing all that Christ would have us to do and believe. Thus a new climate would surround our proclamation of truth. We would not believe our faith less helpfully, nor proclaim it with less vigor. We would embrace truth

---

[1] Hendrik Ibsen, *The Emperor and the Galilean* (New York: Charles Scribner's Sons). Reprinted by permission of the publishers.

with our whole hearts and give our soul and strength to it; but, knowing that His ways are not our ways and His thoughts are higher than our thoughts, we acknowledge that there can be more than we yet know or do which is the will of our Father in heaven.

In like manner we recognize that any attempt to limit Christ to our ideas and our practices is to betray Him anew. The New Testament stresses our oneness in Christ. In the High Priestly prayer, Jesus pleads with God to hasten the time when all people will find the unity of spirit which exists between Himself and God. It is the most moving intercessory prayer known to the human race. Our efforts to make that prayer come true have been limited and recent. Until the last two decades, denominational structures have been denominational strictures.

The way we have practiced our Christian faith has become our Christian faith. It is my duty, quite often, to secure the letters of people who desire membership in our church. A curious assortment of communications comes from the denominations. Some do not grant any letters at all. Their members are in their box! Other churches are more subtle. They do not have a procedure whereby they may transfer members. They simply report that they will drop the person from the roll. One communion conveys a "letter of dismission." Fortunately, most denominations more graciously transfer.

One day there came a young man from another country and another culture, with letter in hand. I opened his "ecumenical passport" to find inscribed within these words: "Our consistory recommends him cordially to all the consistories of all the Protestant denominations in the world, hoping that you will take him into your pastoral care and allow him to share in the celebration of our Lord's holy supper." It was as a fresh wind blowing the message of the oneness of the church of Jesus Christ our Lord around the wide world. It was as clear water gushing out of that subterranean stream of life from which all our private pools of truth are fed. It was the spirit of Christ made manifest in the mechanics of denominational procedure.

III. More Light and Truth Still Needed

Such a unity of spirit as we have in our oneness in Christ in no way lessens the need for our individual interpretations of truth as we understand them in Christ. We are required to give our particular tint or color to the whole canvass which is Christian revelation. No two men see Christ in precisely the same manner. No one man (or group of men) dares suppose that he sees all there is to Christ. Our responsibility is to express in our faith and works those facets of truth whose light Christ turns toward our hearts. As a church we are a fellowship of those whose religious traditions and insight have provided us with unique aptitudes which we are morally bound to share with other Christian people.

1. We shall continue our emphasis upon the genuine life. The spiritual sentiment tends to become routine. It gets "sot in its ways." The practices of our faith soon set an established pattern. The spiritual life early becomes a thing set apart. God's special need for the Brethren in such an hour as this may be to reiterate the truth that religion is life, not something we do while we are living. In this we can follow the tradition of Alexander Mack and the teaching of Christ. In so doing we shall meet one of the most pressing needs of Christian interpretation today.

This is an all-consuming doctrine, one not easy to preach or to practice. It plays havoc with our customary concepts of prayer, brushing aside the words we say if they are not verily the dominant desire of our hearts. This would change the character of our faith, for the way we practice our faith becomes our faith. It would require us to examine our checkbooks rather than the Conference decisions to determine what things we really believe in. It would recognize that tithing could easily become a sham if we do not also get and spend all our money in accord with the principles of the Kingdom of God. All our religious exercises would be subject to the scrutiny which requires them to be in harmony with everything else we do and integrated with all the activities of life.

Tolstoy's spiritual pilgrimage led him to a careful study of the Gospels. He discovered that the church had often distorted the essential teaching of Christ. It weighted theology on the fall of Adam, the relationship of the Trinity, and the scheme of redemption while Christ centered His teaching in the necessity for love and pity and man's duty to man. Tolstoy observed that those passages in the Gospels on which Christian dogma was based were the most obscure, whereas the practical teachings of Christ were the most definite. Yet the church consistently defined the dogmas in the most precise manner while the practical fulfillment of the teachings became an intangible requirement of faith. He came to the conviction that the real substance of Jesus' teaching was summed up in the principle of love. The problem was how to make love an effective principle rather than a sentiment. When Tolstoy accepted the literal meaning of nonresistance to evil with all its implications, much that had been obscure in the Gospels became plain, the allegorical was sheared away, and the Sermon on the Mount stood out as the heart of what Christ taught. Love became the breath and blood, the soul and sinew of being. What he believed was no longer an adjunct or even an addition; it was thoroughgoing, genuine, and all consuming; religion was life.

2. As devoutly as we may wish it to be true, the present arrangement of human affairs does not permit us to regard war as finished. The nations are absorbed in military expansion and expenditure. Economic life and diplomatic life are organized around the principle of force. Only a miracle will avert some future war. What form human conflict will take is unpredictable. Traditionally, wars have had a geographic and religious thrust. The economic aspect of war has come to the fore in the twentieth century. Quite possibly the wars of the future, if they come, may be racial or spatial in character.

Humanity is sick to the death of the travail, torture, and tragedy of war. War is the number-one public enemy of mankind.

War is a great offense to the character and purposes of God. The Oxford Conference defines it thus:

> War involves compulsory enmity, diabolical outrage against personality, and the wanton distortion of the truth. War is a particular demonstration of the power of sin in this world, and a defiance of the righteousness of God as revealed in Christ and him crucified. No justification of war must be allowed to conceal or minimize this fact.

Our unique thrust in Christendom, our peculiar witness in the world, and the special genius of our message in the adventurous future must continue to be the making of peace. In three areas we shall continue this interpretation of the gospel of Christ, as our special portion of the larger Christian witness.

(1) We shall continue to protest against the iniquity of war with the witness of our lives. As God gives us strength we shall be nonparticipants, withdrawing ourselves as far as possible from the mechanics of militarism. Because our economy is so dependent upon military expansion and such a large proportion of the tax dollar is under fee to the business of death, we shall need to increase our conviction if the witness of conscientious objection is to be decisive and effective. In a complex society, neutrality and nonviolent resistance are regarded as treason. It will be increasingly difficult to stake out a positive position.

We have a clear mandate for this faith in Jesus' insistent word that we must serve rather than be served, that we must love rather than hate, that we must give life rather than take life. The great weight of Jesus' teaching and life commits us to an even more intensive effort to rid humanity of the scourge of war. What we say and do must now breathe the conviction that made martyrs of those who refused to worship the Roman emperor.

(2) We must back up this protest with an enlarged ministry to human need. Here again we are motivated by the teaching and example of Jesus, whose stamp-sized biography was spoken by Peter, "He went about doing good." We shall need to supply mountains of material aid to meet the monstrous human needs which still crawl across our world. We shall preserve the personal

witness of our faith by continuing to send volunteers with our gifts. We shall follow the focus of mankind's distress and disaster from Europe to Asia and Africa or anywhere else in the world. We shall explore every area in which remain little strands of hope and tiny cords of faith which need only the love of others to weave them together into the bridge of existence, the way of understanding, the avenue of brotherhood.

(3) It is not enough to drive an ambulance or answer an emergency. We must cover the pit from which the wounded man was lifted, erect a stoplight to warn others of the bloody crossroads, build a barricade at the precipice over which humanity plunged. Our labor of love must envelop the total work of peace to end the total woe of war. This work will lead us to deal with the standard of living, the consideration of universal human rights, the educational needs and the nutritional lacks of all people, the spread of disease and the rise of populations, the technical assistance and the cultural heritage of the dispossessed peoples of the world, the social, ethical, moral, and religious concerns of every person dwelling on the face of the whole earth. If we thus proclaim the gospel of Jesus we deal with every concern confronting every human being on the earth. This is the ministry of reconciliation.

3. In the adventurous future we shall find anew that the answer is Christ. The Church of the Brethren will come to its own in the family of God by "following Jesus." This represents no new trend, no change from the past, but an intensification of what has been the insistence of the church from the beginning. Alexander Mack's simple words on following Christ have a classic quality: "Look wholly and alone to the express words of the Lord Jesus, and to his own perfect example, and to follow him in obedience with faith and simplicity . . . bringing every thought into subjection to the Lord Jesus." If we have had any rule of life, any code like unto a creed, it has been the teaching and the example of Christ. In the next two hundred fifty years we will still be probing the fathomless teaching and the matchless life

of Christ for fresh insights into Christian living. In Him we shall have life. Whether we walk, ride, fly, or even orbit into the adventurous future, we shall still discover that Christ is the way, the truth, and the life.

Paul exhorts us to grow up in every way into Christ, who is the head. His instruction to the church at Ephesus outlines this maturing process. It begins with the knowledge of the Son of God. It requires, interestingly enough, the unity of the faith. Its aspiration, its "stretch," its tension is toward "the measure of the stature of the fullness of Christ." In this reach toward Him we are no longer children, pushed around by every fickleness and fancy. We become solid enough in faith that we speak the truth in love. While this is taking place in us and in our church, all other parts of the body of Christ — the big churches and the little connecting cells, the orthodox sinews of faith and the sharp new truths tingling like exposed nerve ends, the fabric of society like the skin of the body, and the vital parts of its structure like the heart beating within — all begin to work properly, grow, and find the health and the usefulness that come with love. It is one of the most revealing pictures of the progression of faith, the miracle of love and the endlessness which the growth process has when we move toward Christ.

In such an hour as this, as at the hour of beginning two hundred fifty years ago, the church is drawn again to Christ. In the providence of God it is not permitted us to know what of marvel or surprise lies in the unknown tomorrow for our church fellowship. I have the faith that, whatever the adventurous future may bring, my church will be praying, in the words of George Matheson: "O Jesus, Thou never growest old to me. Yesterday is past, last year is a thing gone forever, but Thou art ever beyond. Men will never outgrow Thee nor go beyond Thee. Times shall change, customs shall change, the order of life shall change, but this faith shall abide. A new science of the stars shall dawn. The earth shall move round the sun instead of the sun moving round the earth, but there shall be no new Christ in the firmament. Thine eyes shall not grow dim nor Thy strength abated. A thousand systems shall fall at Thy side, but their crash shall not touch Thee. Thou shalt have the dew of Thy youth when the world is old. Thy feet shall touch the final ridge of the mountains and the beauty of Thy tidings shall be a joy forever. Amen."[2]

---

[2] George Matheson, in *Moments on the Mount* (New York: A. C. Armstrong and Son, 1884), pages 254, 255.

17. THE BRETHREN AND THE BOOK OF BOOKS

CHALMER E. FAW

Professor of New Testament, Bethany Biblical Seminary; secretary of Annual Conference; minister, writer; lecturer. Formerly: pastor, Raisin City, California; missionary to Nigeria.

The Brethren, both early and recent, are not to be explained on one basis alone; but a great deal can be said about them, and perhaps some of the most important things said about them will be in terms of their approach to and their use of the Bible, particularly the New Testament.

Though in a real sense true, it is not enough to say that the Brethren are primarily a people of the Book. So are all Christians, to some extent, and particularly is this true of most Protestant groups. Nor is it enough to say that the Brethren are a New Testament people. Again, it can be said with fairness that all Christian bodies in one way or another trace their thinking to the New Testament and consider it quite evident that they are New Testament Christians. It is not even enough to say that the Brethren are a noncreedal New Testament church, for a surprising number of Protestant groups share in that position as well. What is relevant and important in this anniversary year is to discover just how and in what peculiar way the Brethren are a New Testament church and then look at our present situation in the light of that discovery.

It is sometimes implied that the Brethren are people who simply take the plain teachings of the New Testament without embellishment or interpretation. While there is much truth in this, it must also be stated with emphasis that no one just picks up the Bible, or any passage within it, and simply reads it and takes its plain meaning. Quite unconsciously, perhaps, but nonetheless surely, he reads it in the light of certain presuppositions which he has made his own. Similarly, his emphasis upon certain passages, and the way in which he relates one passage to another and then from these passages derives some guide for his living, may all be unconscious on his part but may make radical differences in the results obtained. We do well, then, to examine just what are the presuppositions, spoken as well as unspoken, conscious and unconscious, with which the Brethren have, from the beginning, approached the Scriptures.

First let us acknowledge the debt of the Brethren to their predecessors and note the peculiar blend of attitudes which helped to mold their approach to the Bible. From mainstream Protestantism of the Lutheran and Reformed traditions the Brethren inherited a belief in the supreme place of the Word of God as found in and, in many respects, indentified with, the Bible. In this common Protestant view, each individual is capable of reading and understanding enough of God's Word to enable him to exercise faith and lay hold on salvation. The Brethren carried this Protestant emphasis even further, however, by insisting on more complete reliance upon the careful reading of the Scripture rather than upon man-made creedal statements or summaries derived from Scripture.

From the Anabaptist left wing of the Reformation, the Brethren inherited an intensity and seriousness of commitment to New Testament discipleship, with a radical break with the world as an act of adult choice, sealed by baptism and exemplified in lifelong devotion.

Along with the Inspirationists and the mystics, the Brethren believed that the Holy Spirit is still very much alive in the world and continues to inspire believers in the understanding of the Scriptures. From this heritage also came the sense of the "inner word" within the heart of the Christian which matches and helps interpret the "external word" of the written Scripture. Thus was born among the early Brethren the vivid concept of the possession of the "mind of Christ" by every believer.

From the Pietists, both of the churchly type and of the more radical or separatist type, came the early Brethren emphasis upon warmth and zeal in religion, as evidenced, for example, in the composing and singing of hymns and the fervent preaching of the Word. From this influence also came the emphasis upon being good and doing good in true faith-obedience to Christ, who is both Savior and Example. Of special influence upon the Brethren were the writings of a learnéd Pietist historian, Gottfried Arnold, who uncovered the practices of the first two centuries of the early church and deeply instilled in his readers the ideal of restoring as nearly as possible the primitive Christian church and its practices.

Such were the major historical streams of thought which combined to make up the particular phenomenon which we may call the Brethren approach to the Scriptures. Let us now look at this more closely, and seek to discover just how these varied aspects were interrelated for the Brethren, underlying and coloring their use of the Book of Books.

At the very center of the Brethren approach to the Bible, as, indeed, of their whole Christian faith, are Jesus Christ and the believer's wholehearted love for Him, faith in Him, and lifelong joyous devotion to Him. Nothing in the early Brethren writings about the Scriptures makes sense if this fact is omitted or overlooked. The believer is one bound to Christ by ties of love and gratitude and by a fervent desire to obey Him in every particular.

Alexander Mack, Jr., son of the leading founding spirit of the church, spoke of the first eight members as

persons [who] agreed together to establish a covenant of a good conscience with God, to accept all ordinances of Jesus Christ as an easy yoke, and thus to follow after their Lord Jesus — their good and loyal shepherd — as true sheep in joy or sorrow until the blessed end.[1]

And Mack, Sr., summarized his doctrine with these words:

> Therefore, I will advise you this, in conclusion, that you should look alone to Jesus your Redeemer and Savior (Hebrews 12:2). If you have learned from Him the teaching as it is outwardly commanded in the Testament, so that you will remain steadfast in it, and resolve yourself to sacrifice your life, your property, family, yes, all that you have in the whole world — rather than waver from His teaching. . . .[2]

Warm, fervent, steadfast, obedient attachment to Christ is the very heart of their approach to the New Testament. Special attention was given to the commands of the Lord, but these were commands to be accepted with a heart of love and zealous eagerness. In his "Answers to Gruber's Basic Questions," Mack, Sr., asks, "Why should a believer *not* wish to do the will of Him in whom he believes?"[3] Obedience then, is not a teeth-gritting discipline but the joyous desire of the free but committed lover of Christ to do anything and everything the Lord commands. Interpreted in modern terms, the true Brethren spirit was not "Do I have to do this, or that?" or "What is the least I can get by with?" Rather, it was "What all can I do to show my love for my Master?" And so the Brethren combed the New Testament for the commands of Jesus and His apostles, looking upon each imperative as a new opportunity to express love and loyalty to Him who meant more to them than all the world. It is in this spirit that Mack is to be understood when he deals with the strictness of the commandments, saying, "However, none of the teachings and ordinances of our Lord Jesus may be considered insignificant. . . ."[4]

What the Brethren sought was not more commands to obey, but a greater spirit of obedience; and, more than obedience

---

[1] Preface to the American edition of his father's writings. Translated by Donald F. Durnbaugh in *European Origins of the Brethren* (Elgin: The Brethren Press, 1958), page 121.

[2] "Rights and Ordinances," in Durnbaugh, *op. cit.*, page 404. All quotations from Mack, Sr.'s, writings are from the Durnbaugh edition.

[3] *Ibid.*, page 331.

[4] *Ibid.*, page 347.

itself, the desire to obey. It is this emphasis which makes it possible for Mack also to speak of "all the commandments of Jesus as an easy yoke" — as quoted before. The early Brethren seriousness about obedience is reflected in the reasons Mack goes on to cite for regarding even the smallest commandment as great: namely, the greatness of the Sovereign and King who has commanded them and the greatness of the consequences in terms of life everlasting "with all the gracious gifts of the Holy Spirit which believers possess" and in terms of the terrible punishments awaiting the disobedient.

Given, then, this central and all-consuming devotion to their Lord and this deep desire to follow His every command, the Brethren find three avenues open for coming to know the mind of Christ: (1) the simple word of the Scripture, particularly the New Testament, and especially the direct commands contained therein; (2) a commentary on this written word as found in the life of Jesus, His immediate followers, and the Christians of the first two centuries; and (3) the inner word of the Spirit or *mind of Christ* within the believer, which verifies and validates the other two.

As to the first of these, the simple word of the Scripture, the distinctive features were the accent on the commands of Christ and His apostles and the spirit and thoroughness with which the will of the Lord was sought out. The word of Scripture is to be taken in simplicity, humility, and all seriousness. The plain, literal sense would seem to be followed unless the literary form or context would dictate otherwise or unless the literal word in one passage should run counter to that in other passages.

Brethren read the whole New Testament and compared scripture with scripture, with a fine admixture of zeal and common sense, attempting, with a conscientiousness and an intensity that defy duplication today, to discover the precise will of their Lord for their lives. Mack, Sr., speaks disparagingly of those who take a passage out of the New Testament here or another there without considering the whole mind of Christ. Mack, Jr., in commenting on the fact that the synoptic Gospels say nothing of the feet-washing while the Gospel of John says nothing of the bread and the cup, remarks: "Therefore scripture must be understood and looked upon with a spiritual eye of love and calmness."[5] It is of interest to note in passing that while the heart of the Christian faith is to be found in the New Testament, Mack and the early Brethren made extensive use also of the Old Testament, accepting it as inspired and to be used in discovering the full revelation of God's will in Christ. It is also interesting that he once quotes from the Wisdom of Solomon,[6] one of the books of our Old Testament Apocrypha, without drawing a distinction between it and the remainder of the Bible.

With all their stress upon simple obedience to the written word of Scripture, the Brethren found themselves, however, seeking further light. Here it is that the second avenue of understanding comes in: that of the commentary on the Scripture afforded by the life of Jesus, of His followers, and of the total Christian community for the first two centuries. Said Alexander Mack, Jr., in his 1774 preface to an edition of his father's writings:

> [They] felt themselves drawn powerfully to seek the footsteps of the primitive Christians and desired earnestly to receive in faith the ordained testimonies of Jesus Christ according to their true value . . . and when they found in authentic histories that the primitive Christians in the first and second centuries uniformly, according to the command of Christ, were planted into the death of Jesus Christ by a threefold immersion into the water of holy baptism, they examined diligently the New Testament and finding all perfectly harmonizing therewith, they were anxious to use the means appointed and practiced by Christ himself and thus according to his own salutary counsel, go forward to the fullfillment of all righteousness.[7]

This is an especially revealing passage, for it helps explain not only the process by which the Brethren arrived at the doctrine of trine immersion but throws considerable light on their whole interpretive approach to the Bible. All Christian groups

---

[5] *The Writings of Alexander Mack,* Henry Kurtz, editor and translator (Columbiana, Ohio, 1860), page 143f.

[6] Durnbaugh, *op. cit.,* page 379.

[7] Henry Kurtz edition, pages 22-24.

have read Matthew 28:19; but not all of them, in Mack's day or our own, have found a threefold mode of baptism in it — a threefold formula, yes, but not a threefold form. The threefold mode the Brethren derived, as Mack, Jr., says, first from the historians; they then examined the New Testament and found the two in harmony. The second aid in finding the will of Christ for the sincere believer, then, is the life and practice of the primitive church, which became a commentary on the simple word of the Scripture.

The third avenue is the internal word of the Spirit, or the "mind of Christ" within the believer. Mack, Sr., put it this way in his "Rights and Ordinances":

> Now, the Scriptures are only an outward testimony of those things which were once taught and commanded by the Holy Spirit. The prophecies and warnings were also spoken through it. . . . True, the Holy Spirit was in the apostles in greater measure for the expansion of the gospel, yet it is the same Holy Spirit in all believers.[8]

Then a bit later he says that people cannot understand the Bible in their own wisdom or carnal minds, but each must read with his "inward ears" open. The believer "reads externally the scripture in faith and hears the internal word of life which gives him power and strength to follow Jesus."

Putting these three approaches together, then, the way to understand the will of our Lord is the written word of the Scripture, as demonstrated and illustrated in the life of Jesus and the primitive Christians and as attested and validated in the heart of the believer through the internal word of the Holy Spirit. And essentially these three agree, for, to quote Mack, Sr., further: "That which the Holy Spirit ordained for the faithful was written outwardly. All believers are united in it, for the Holy Spirit teaches them inwardly just as the Scriptures teach them outwardly.[9] And again: "This law which is inwardly written by the Spirit of God is completely identical with that which is outwardly

---
[8] Durnbaugh, *op. cit.,* page 384.
[9] *Ibid.,* page 384.

written in the New Testament. All of the latter had flowed from the inward, and is an express image of the inward living Word of God."[10]

The final stage in ascertaining the Word of the Lord comes through the active indwelling and work of that Word within the believing, obeying Christian. In a hitherto-unknown tract published by the Sauer press in 1747 this is forcefully stated in these words:

> It is of extreme importance to Christians that all the words of Christ and his Spirit be read, considered and believed with sighs and tearful prayers to God, being received with true broken-hearted contrition to the point that they transform the life of the reader gradually until the whole New Testament is written in his heart by the finger of God and his whole life becomes a living letter of God in which one can read all the commandments of Jesus Christ (2 Corinthians 3:3).[11]

Here then is the Brethren approach to the Book of Books: a warm, zealous, world-renouncing attachment to Jesus Christ and Him only in sincere eagerness to obey His every command, the latter to be ascertained by steeping oneself in the written word of the New Testament, testing it by the life and practices of the earliest Christians, understanding and accepting it into one's life by the work of the indwelling Spirit, and letting it so permeate his whole existence that he himself becomes an epistle of the living God in whom every commandment of the Lord Jesus can be read.

There are certain spiritual accompaniments which make this approach to the Bible a living reality and help steer a clear course between a shackling legalism on the one hand and a formless inspirationism on the other. Some of these have been stressed already. All of them must now be gathered together and properly related to the Brethren interpretation of the Scriptures.

First is the twofold action of a radical break with the world

---

[10] *Ibid.*, page 386.
[11] *Ein Geringer Schein des Verachteten Lichtleins der Wahrheit die in Cristo ist* (Germantown, 1747). Excerpts translated by the writer from microfilm of the book found by D. F. Durnbaugh in the Rare Books section of the Philadelphia Historical Society, entry number Ac. 221. The above quotation is from pages 1 and 2 of this tract.

and the joyful, loyal adherence to Jesus Christ and the intense desire to obey Him in everything. Without this, the true reading and understanding of God's Word cannot follow. Just how this tremendous desire to believe and obey comes about, none of the early writings explicitly tells us, but the tenor of those writings which have come down to us reflects the Pietist experience of profound contrition and repentance and a consequent inner heart-warming and enlightenment by the Spirit of God. In the Sauer tract of 1747, previously referred to, this emphasis upon true repentance as the basis for understanding the New Testament is explicitly made:

> The person who has repented has truly experienced that all the words of Jesus Christ are Spirit and life. . . . Such a person loses all desire to pervert and interpret scripture according to his own understanding . . . he will be made willing to hear everything that God has commanded him.[12]

Then along with the penitent spirit and warmed heart with its intense desire to obey comes a humble simplicity in obedience. It is the proud and rebellious man, Mack would say, who argues and evades and so complicates the plain commands of our Lord. For the true believer the commands of Christ are simple and forthright and the man humble and devoted enough to perform them will be blessed, whereas he who attempts to mix in his own desires and avoid or change the ordinances is the one who makes obedience difficult. True believers and lovers of the Lord Jesus

> have always looked steadfastly and single-mindedly to their Lord and Master in all things. They follow Him gladly in all of His commands, just as He has told them to do, and as He has shown them by His own example. They thus learn in their simplicity to understand well the intention of their Master, even in the simplest matters.[13]

With this zeal for Christ and this humble simplicity goes a third spiritual characteristic: a sense of the unity of the Word of God, or what we today would perhaps call spiritual integration. In one way this is a part of Christian simplicity in contrast to

---
[12] *Ibid.*, pages 2 and 3.
[13] Durnbaugh, *op. cit.*, page 364.

the rebellious mind which would complicate matters. This unity is threefold: (1) the inner word of the Spirit agrees with the outer word of the Scripture; (2) in spite of seeming variations, the mind of the Spirit in one scripture is in unity with the mind of the Spirit in every other scripture; and (3) believers should seek among themselves unity and the bond of peace.

Still a fourth spiritual overtone is completeness or wholeness. While Christ is the center, the whole Bible (Apocrypha included, apparently) witnesses to one divine event and possesses a wholeness and completeness of meaning for the believer that removes the necessity for a fragmentary quoting of this favorite passage or that. The whole Bible is to be read and used to find Christ's will for His followers. It is interesting to hear Mack, Sr., sum up his rites and ordinances in the father's parting advice to his son to love God and neighbor, contemplate and keep the commandments, and beware of false prophets. Here is a breadth of Biblical thought to balance the cutting edge of the radical Pietism and the sectarian Anabaptism from which the Brethren sprang.

A fifth aspect of the true Brethren spirit is its emphasis upon doing, as against creed or lip-service. As Mack well observed, actually Christ's commandments are a simple and an easy yoke, if one is just humble and devoted enough to do them and not quibble about them. Doing them brings its own reward of blessedness. It is interesting to note how much space is devoted in the early writings to the proper performance of the rites and ordinances. Especially is this true of the rite of baptism. In the 1747 Sauer tract of the three headings, "The Holy Scriptures," "True Repentance," and "Christian Baptism," over four times as much space is devoted to baptism as to the other two topics together, as important as they are. At first glance this would look like legalism or a salvation by works. To jump to such a conclusion, however, would be to misunderstand the Brethren. So great was their zeal and their devotion for their Lord and so careful were they to find the truth, and, so sharply did they differ with current practices, that they felt called to spend a great amount of time and energy explaining rites and ordinances, for here obedience was made concrete and their intense desire to obey found expression.

A sixth element of the spirit that marks the Brethren approach at its best is a certain openness to new light. This manifested itself in several ways. One was the aversion to man-made creeds which, though they expressed much truth, might, at the same time, limit or set a boundary to the revelation of new truth by the ever-living Spirit of God. Another evidence of this openness was the willingness of the Brethren to use the best scholarship of their day in their search for the mind of Christ as expressed in the primitive church.

Reference has already been made to the Brethren use of the research of men like Gottfried Arnold. A classic expression of this aspect of Brethren openness and humility is the one found in the 1774 statement of Alexander Mack, Jr. The entire passage is too lengthy to quote here, but every member of the church should peruse in detail his statement, which tells how two changes had already been made in the order of the feet-washing in the love feast and communion ceremony. At first the feet-washing service was observed after both the supper and the bread and the cup. Then further reading and comparing of Scripture led to a change of the feet-washing ceremony to a time after the supper but before the bread and the cup. Then, finally, with a new publication of the New Testament by a man named Reitz and the aid of a brother who knew Greek, it was seen that the feet-washing ceremony occurred after supper had been prepared but before it was actually eaten. Thus the order which we observe to this day was established: namely, feet-washing, the supper, and then the bread and the cup. The spirit of true humility and inquiry illustrated by these changes is thus eloquently expressed in the opening paragraph:

> We felt moved in our mind in sincere love to give the reasons why we wash feet before supper. At the same time we would say that this is our

belief and view; if a brother or any other person can in love and moderation instruct us according to the word of the Lord more fully and otherwise than is here pointed out, we should be ready to accept it not only in this point of feetwashing but also in other matters and not at all rest upon long usage but let the word of the Lord be our only rule and guide.[14]

Note the remarkable breadth of this: they are open to instruction, says Mack, not only by any "brother" (member of the church), but "any other"; and not only in regard to the feetwashing, but "also in other matters." This is a safeguard against both legalism and traditionalism, for they were eager that they (to quote his words) "not at all rest upon long usage but let the word of the Lord be our only rule and guide." It is worth noting that this was written in 1774, just before the outbreak of the Revolutionary War, the bitter experience of which served to turn the Brethren inward, to dull their adventurous, inquiring spirit, and to make them susceptible to the very legalism and traditionalism which the founding fathers were able to avoid.

Although our emphasis thus far has been upon the early Brethren method and spirit of Biblical interpretation, we are deeply concerned about the present situation in our church. Living as we do in a day when the Bible, though still a best seller, is not a dominant factor in the life of even Christian people, and in a day when much of the early zeal and fire of the Brethren for obedience has grown cold, the question must be raised and frankly faced. Are we still Brethren, the true spiritual heirs of those who gave birth to our beloved fraternity? If not, then how can we become such? What should we do? These are questions which each one must take to himself and struggle with deep within his own soul, then within his own home, within his local church, and so throughout the Brotherhood.

Let me suggest that the lessons of the past can be summed up in three directional pointers for our day. For the most part these are areas in which we today are found wanting and in which we must seek rebirth, not to return to or in any superficial

---

[14] Henry Kurtz edition, page 141.

way to imitate the founding fathers, but to rise in our day to something of the spiritual stature with which they stood in theirs. These three are: an experience, a spirit, and a method.

No one can read the authentic Brethren literature of the first seventy years of the church's existence without being struck with the fact that those Brethren had had a religious experience. So deep and so real was their experience of the living Lord that it shone forth through their daily lives, their oral testimony, and their written contributions. It is the mark of every true revival of Christianity. From it came their zeal and enthusiasm, their deep devotion, their loyalty, and their world-renouncing seriousness and abundant joy. Without it their approach to the Bible withers into barren legalism or dissipates itself in vapid emotion. With it, their use of the Scriptures is luminous and vital. We their children should not so much copy them as have our own experience of the living Christ and come fully and enthusiastically under His Lordship.

Along with the experience, and as a direct outgrowth of it, is the spirit which they exemplified. We have already enumerated some of its characteristics: (1) a radical break with the world and an intense desire to obey Christ in every particular; (2) a humble simplicity in seeking out and obeying the mind of Christ in Scripture; (3) a sense of the unity of the Spirit within the Scripture, within our own experience, and within the church; (4) a sense of the completeness and wholeness of spiritual truth; (5) an emphasis on actual doing, whether in ordinances or in everyday living; and (6) an openness to new light and a willingness to grow. These traits have marked the Brethren at their best. How often and how sadly they have at times fallen below this level only the honest historian knows, but at their best this has been their spirit. Here again, great heart-searching must take place on our part. To emulate this spirit without the profound experience of Christ which alone makes it possible would be worse than folly. But to recover, each in his own heart, and each generation anew in its own way, this same intense awareness of the living Lord, and its consequent revitalizing spiritual power, is our challenge.

The third directional pointer has to do with the method of Bible reading and study. The thorough way in which the Brethren compared scripture with scripture with "spiritual eyes of love and calmness" suggests both comprehensive and intense Bible study, a refusal to fasten upon prooftexts and clichés and to be satisfied with anything less than the clearest possible understanding of the whole mind of Christ, as revealed in Scripture and in early church history. We need to live with the Scriptures, steeping ourselves in their God-centered and Christ-glorifying approach to life. Not only that, but we should recover the proper use of the whole Bible, including those parts now avoided because of loss of interest or ignorance on our part. And, still further, church history, with its many lessons of theology, ethics, and church polity, should be studied for the light it throws on the true mind of Christ.

Might it not be right that, just as the early Brethren were informed by and found their way to an expression of the mind of Christ through the use of the best research available, so we in our day should make reverent use of ever-advancing scholarship, making sure to regard it as a servant of true Christlikeness and never a master or an idol? And is it not also the better part of godliness to keep ourselves open in our quest for the truth revealed in Christ so that if anyone, a brother or any other, can "in love and moderation instruct us according to the word of the Lord more fully" and otherwise than we have hitherto followed, we too should be ready to accept it not only on one point but on all points, so that we, like those early Brethren, shall "not at all rest upon long usage but let the word of the Lord be our only rule and guide"?

18. THE BRETHREN AND THE MODERN STATE

DAN WEST

Director of leadership training, Brotherhood staff; writer; lecturer; home, Goshen, Indiana. Formerly: Brethren relief worker in Spain; director of youth work, Brotherhood staff.

The Annual Conference of 1908, celebrating the bicentennial of the Church of the Brethren, began with thinking about the problem of government. The first address then had to do with church polity or government *within* the church. It may be more than a coincidence that the program committee set a similar problem as the beginning of our thought for this Annual Conference celebrating the two-hundred-fiftieth anniversary of the founding of the church. But this time the thought is to be government *outside* the church — the relation of the Brethren to the modern state.

Brethren always live under tension. The more we try to live our doctrines in the modern world, the more the tensions increase and the heavier they become. One of the greatest tensions for Christians everywhere comes out of the relation between church and state. And one of the heaviest for the Church of the Brethren comes in relation to the American nation-state. We Brethren always love our country, respect many of its customs, and obey its laws. But we have some doubts about the actual state. (For present thinking, the word *state* refers chiefly to government officials — persons who are authorized to act for the state.)

I. Government Is Right

We Brethren believe in government as a matter of principle. We have Scripture for it: "The powers that be are ordained of God" (Romans 13:1b, KJV). And Brethren have always accepted the governments they find — sometimes too well. We have never been political revolutionaries.

For some people on this planet, however, government is a bad thing and anarchy is their goal. In the family it may be only a temporary affair when youth try to develop independence from their elders and become persons in their own right. They seem to be anarchistic but they do accept a great deal of tyranny from their peers. Most of them, however, go on later to learn interdependence. That means some kind of government.

However, there have been sizable groups of even adults who claim not to believe in any organized government at all. During the Spanish Civil War, on many telephone poles in Barcelona posters appeared bearing Bakunin's picture and this message in Spanish: "Anarchy is the highest form of order."

Brethren would not agree to this. Anarchy is not the highest form of order.

II. The Modern State

The state is a wonderful servant, but a very hard master. And the tendency is always toward too much control and too little real responsibility. Today the state as we know it exerts more control over its people than Brethren can welcome. Now some controls are necessary, but for the best human welfare there must be a limit. We accept some controls, such as traffic laws, taxes, and wage controls, cheerfully — or soberly. Other controls, such as draft laws and some civil defense items, we accept with reservation. But when the state goes too far, the Brethren say no and mean it. For example, in a small town near the Canadian border, one civil defense official from the state headquarters was explaining that a warden had been appointed over every designated area in the town. "And that man's word is law," he said bluntly.

Quickly there came a response. Two ministers (one a Dunker) objected, saying, "That man's word is not law. This is America." Immediately the imposing-looking "house of cards" crumbled.

During most of the nineteenth century the state let us alone quite largely and we let it alone. However, in the modern world this is no longer possible either for us or for the state. Neither can let the other alone. And in the future, it seems, tensions from state controls will increase more yet.

One regional planner from Harvard University predicted that "rigid governmental and economic controls beyond all we have ever known will be required to place the community interest — and common good — before the so-called rights of individuals."

Another example: Luther Gulick of the New York City Institute of Public Administration believes that one fact is going to force us into a new type of thinking: "Most Americans will be born, grow up and live, work and die in great city areas." And he expects governmental structures to handle the problems that develop.

If these predictions are correct, every decade will bring Brethren and all other Christian groups (and everybody else) under more controls and into heavier tension with the state. But there are real dangers here. Let us look at a few of them.

1. Some people tend to glorify the state. The flag worship before important public events is one evidence of this. Flags in churches are worth studying also. Some people seem to imagine that the state has almost personal qualities and demands a supreme loyalty. In their minds, the state is no longer a servant; it is a master. One high school valedictorian this spring put the law of the land before the law of God. But this deification of the state is pure fiction. Professor Hocking would remind Brethren and everybody else that "there is no state entity, but there is a God."

Now governments are not all alike. But too many similarities seem to develop with time in modern states as well as in ancient ones. Governments tend to go beyond the restraint of evildoers in the direction of restraining the activities of persons and groups toward justice and toward common welfare. State officials are not impersonal administrators of law, but often very faulty persons like the rest of us. Sometimes they don't even average up. Then, if they are power hungry, they will tend to reach farther and farther toward increasing control of the people.

So long as the state "is not a terror to good works," Brethren feel little tension. But if governments encroach on human rights or attempt to control the church, tension increases heavily. And this is happening in America and other modern states. More than ten years ago Lord Boyd Orr, then director general of the Food and Agriculture Organization of the United Nations, complained rather bitterly over the typical attitude of government officials at the United Nations assembly. Soon after his report and his plea for more help for the hungry people of the world, he shared some of his sadness with me: "It seems that governments are more concerned about political advantage than they are about the welfare of their own people." Half a century ago, Acton saw this process also and he reminded us that "power always tends to corrupt. Absolute power corrupts absolutely."

Some thinkers believe that all modern states will go totalitarian. One novelist attempted to describe the breaking of the last human personality in the process of making him into a willing tool of the state.

In summary, there are risks as well as gains in the development of states. Brethren should be aware of both of them. Any state worship combined with grasping for power over people is dangerous. Obedience to the state is better than anarchy, but it is not the highest form of order. Here, too, "eternal vigilance is the price of liberty," as much as in Thomas Jefferson's day.

2. National sovereignty is overemphasized. The modern state accepts too little responsibility for the welfare of people outside. Often they are ignored and most of the time they are

treated as of less importance than people within any given state. As transportation and communication bring us closer together, this becomes a dangerous policy. The weather has never had any respect for national boundaries; nor have radio waves, influenza germs, hunger, or even ideas. More recently, earth satellites have no respect for national boundaries; neither has radioactive fallout.

We should be grateful for the heroic service to mankind by the United Nations but at the same time aware of its weaknesses. Here is one: The United Nations is still based on the idea of national sovereignty — every state doing as it pleases. This is just a more respectable name for international anarchy. The worship of the state feeds this dangerous idea. And the present obsession with war plans is both a result and a new cause of anarchy between states. There is an increasing need for a world government, instead of international anarchy. Now, we are more than ever before "in the same boat."

To summarize:

(1) Brethren accept some state controls. Anarchy is not the highest form of order.

(2) We cannot worship any state, nor obey it blindly. Obedience to the state is not the highest form of order.

(3) Our faith is worldwide and reaches beyond the confines of national sovereignty.

We oppose the idea of anarchy either among persons or between states. National sovereignty is not the highest form of order. By the way, church sovereignty is not the highest form of order either. Anarchy is as wrong between Christian groups as between states or people.

This tension which comes from accepting government and yet having doubts about it makes a difficult problem for Brethren to work out. What are the best relationships to the modern state?

III. Possible Relationships to the State

With the prospect of present tensions increasing and newer and greater ones developing in the future, it may be helpful to look at all possible ways of meeting them. There are two main types — running away or staying by.

1. We could run away. This is the "avoidance reaction" of which the biologists tell us. It can be either a physical or a spiritual running away. This sometimes does solve one part of a problem anyhow.

(1) By emigrating. Abraham did this; we do not know exactly for what reason. Moses and the Hebrew children left Egypt when tension with the state became too great. So did the Pilgrims, the Catholics, and the Quakers, from England. From Germany, the Mennonites and the Brethren. There have been many more groups. The national Hungarians are the most recent evidence of emigration as a way of meeting too much tension with the state. Not many years ago a small group of Quakers emigrated to Costa Rica apparently to get away from the problems connected with the military draft. As we look back on most of these efforts, we are inclined to commend the persons involved for taking this way out.

But in our modern world we have a tough problem. There is no longer any place to go with any assurance for any long time. Geographical migration does not seem to be a way out for us.

(2) By going into a monastery. As we learn more of the history of the church we have an increasing reason to be grateful for the monastery, which helped to conserve the Christian faith during the Dark Ages. Professor Floyd Mallott was of the opinion that the denominations under great stress might serve in our time a function similar to that of the monasteries during the Dark Ages. The Bruderhof movement may be a monastic movement, although some of its apologists do not think so. Insofar as it is a withdrawal from the problems incurred from the relationship of the state, it may be monastic. If state persecution comes, this — as a last resort — might be justifiable. But until then, hardly for the Brethren. We are living *in* the world, partly because we have to. But more than that — we want to.

(3) By going into a "holy" vocation. Here is a delicate problem. In the United States and in some other countries, clergymen have been exempt from military draft for a long time. And it is defended by some thinkers. It does give more freedom for them; but it does raise a doubt about what is God's will. Does He have one will for His special servants and a different will for the rest of us?

This holy-vocation method of running away has further implications, however. Alex Miller in his provocative book, *Christian Faith and My Job,* gives the opinion that the people who work in "uplift" jobs such as the ministry, social work, and teaching are really dodging the hard problems which the rest of us must face. If we Brethren are to find a real answer to this question, we ought to grapple with more of the problems the majority of mankind has to meet. From our former sheltered life, we may have become too naive.

2. We could stay by. We are not inclined to run away — at least not many of us — but more and more it will become impossible for us Brethren to run away if we wanted to. And so, we must look at the other alternatives.

We ought to have a better reason — that of wanting to stay by in order to give the witness to our faith and to help in the carrying out of our responsibilities in some way. There are different ways of doing this also. Here are four of them:

(1) Accepting the demands of the state as the will of God — "adjusting." A modern rationalization of this appears in a proverb: "If you can't fight 'em, join 'em." Most churches have done this as a matter of principle, but it is foreign to the Brethren belief. However, under stress some Brethren officials have made some major "adjustments." I mention one.

When World War I was declared in 1917, the Brethren were not ready for that kind of strain. In the uncertainty, a special Conference was called at Goshen, Indiana, in January 1918. There, after some discussion, a statement was drawn up for the guidance of the Brethren who might be affected by the war and the draft. It looks fairly harmless now, but when it came to the attention of the War Department it was considered seditious. Accordingly, some Brethren officials were called to meet some state officials. One of our men described it thus to me later: "We almost got down on our knees before Secretary Baker to take back the Goshen statement."

The first thing for me to remember is that I was not there, and so I have no judgment to offer against the men who were there. However, I cannot stop thinking about it or wondering what John Kline would have done — or Christopher Sauer, or John Naas, or other Brethren leaders in former times. Certainly I cannot fit that with anything I read about the early church in a situation where the tensions might have been even heavier. Yes, to be honest about it, we must admit that the Brethren have "adjusted" on some occasions.

Now to take the brown taste out of the mouth, let us look at an incident where the Brethren did not "adjust." It was during World War II. For some reason some official in Washington decided that civilian public service men (who were engaged in alternative service) were to be ordered to cut their way through the forest to a certain kind of timber thought best for airplane propellers. It was clearly for war purposes, and they were to do this under military guard if necessary. Well, another church official under that stress gave the instruction to collapse civilian public service if necessary. This was a distinct *no* to the state.

To improve the taste a little more, another incident may be worth reporting. The Japanese were uprooted from the West Coast because of a supposed military danger. One fine Japanese boy in civilian public service had been considered by church and state officials. And it was agreed that he would be left alone unless some unfavorable publicity should compel his transfer. But one state man changed his mind and ordered him to be shifted on very short notice. A church official presented this problem to the whole group of civilian public service men at suppertime, and they united against the edict. Yes, there were plans to put the whole group into jail. But plans were worked out so that that was not necessary. (Some thought this action was an "adjustment.")

Brethren can sometimes say no to the state. And there may be more such occasions in the future, under the greater tensions, because we cannot have any other master once we accept the Lordship of Christ.

(2) *Splitting the personality.* "My heart belongs to God, my body to the state." These are heavy words from an important source. But before we censure Martin Luther for them, we may well be very humble ourselves. We had better take a little time to study our own integrity — or lack of it — under stress. Maybe we, too, have separated part of our activities from our religion. Many of us working in defense plants or taking and keeping "blood money" from war sources (I mean the extra purchasing power) have allowed our own personalities to be split. But Brethren consciences are restless under all such incidents. This is not the best way to stay by.

(3) *Transforming the state.* With our new and growing sense of responsibility for what happens in our country we are trying to help to move the state in the direction of a Christian policy. And it takes "the long look of faith" (as W. W. Slabaugh put it); but it is commendable that an increasing number of Brethren are trying to help carry that burden.

However, this means more than just voting or telling Congressmen what we feel on important issues. It is as Professor John Brierly of Cambridge University gave it to a little handful in Geneva, Switzerland, thirty years ago: "It is your job to create the spiritual stuff out of which international law is made." This will mean long, hard toil — even agony. It includes minor compromises, with the steady temptation to make major compromises. But we can hold steady under that tension, too. "Something is borne because something is being born."[1] Brethren can contribute something toward sound government within the state and beyond it toward a sound world government. This is staying by and doing something constructive.

Some people do not believe that the state will ever be transformed, and they can find much evidence for their position. But there are some others who see further. Some years ago Jan Smuts, the former field marshall and empire builder from South Africa, was talking with Andrew Cordier at the United Nations center in New York City. When Shawcross, the British delegate, was mentioned, Smuts asked if he were not a Quaker. Cordier did not know. "I believe he is," the old warrior went on. "Anyhow, he has Quaker background. . . . You know, humanity is very tired of war. It has lost the way. The Quakers have that way. Sometime we shall have to come to that philosophy for the basis of our political decisions."

Kagawa is hopeful for his country. He said: "We are going to alter the definition of a great state. A truly great state is not necessarily big, nor rich, nor quarrelsome with its neighbor. The great state is wise, moral and God-fearing. We aim to make Japan a state with which God can be pleased."

Brethren must help make America a state with which God can be pleased.

(4) Personal and group discipleship. This means living in the modern state, but keeping spiritually clean. In this position Brethren will do what they can to carry the burdens of the state, but that is not their central task. They will not put all their eggs in that basket — nor most of them. Several comparisons might be helpful here, although they do not fit exactly. A lifeguard does all he can to teach others to swim and in an emergency to save someone from drowning. But he is not willing to drown also if he fails to save the victim. In a world of disease, doctors try to keep themselves healthy. In a real sense anyone taking

---

[1] Hocking, W. E., in *The Coming World Civilization*.

this position is not *of* the world while he lives *in* the world. Brotherhood under the Lordship of Christ means that whenever it comes to the choice between transforming the state and keeping the conscience unspotted from the world, "we must obey God rather than man." This is the major responsibility of Brethren in the modern state.

IV. Toward the Right Relationship

1. State and church should recognize that both are needed in a good society. Each one can do something, but not everything. Hocking makes much of the state's impotence[2] to motivate or furnish standards for its own functions, to provide the basis for education or for punishment, to stabilize the family or the economy. It cannot even control its own moral sources in the field of recreation. He thinks that the more complex life becomes the more the state needs the church to furnish motivation and standards for the chief functions of society, including those of the state.

2. The central motives of love and justice are valid for both church and state. At its best the state may be interested in love, but it insists on justice. The church, at its best, seeks justice, but it insists on love. The church cannot shift that central motivation. The state can implement what love creates. As Masaryk put it, "justice is the arithmetic of love."

Both of them are concerned about values which extend beyond any human life. The state has longer vision than any person. That of the church is infinitely longer — eternal. The state deals with the present world; the church does also, but it reaches beyond. Brethren need to prepare themselves for both worlds at the same time.

3. "Power-with" the state. Brethren cannot say that the church is self-sufficient without the state. For the best living we need the state, but we desire no blind acceptance of it. And we favor a continued separation of church and state.

---

[2] *Ibid.*, pages 7-15.

The time was when the church had power over the state. And recently the state has gained almost complete control over the church in some countries. We cannot accept either condition. Our target is a genuine interdependence. Like the fungus and the alga which co-operate in the lowly lichen that grows on rocks and produces soil, like the bacteria which lives in the rumens in cattle and other cud-chewing animals, like the fig moth and the fig which help each other, so church and state will become increasingly interdependent in an increasingly complex world. Biologists call it symbiosis. Here, however, the church is the prime mover of the pair. The church furnishes the eggs and hatches them; the state rightly furnishes the laying house. Hocking says that "the state is dependent for its vital motivation upon an independent, religious community."[3] Brethren cannot be content with any kind of anarchy.

States must come to learn the "power-with" principle also — a larger symbiosis. If churches learn it first, they can be more convincing to states.

4. The state is right in putting some tension on the church for basic motivation and for standards of the good life. And, more than either of these, for examples of good living. *Fortune* magazine made an appeal of this type to churches at the beginning of World War II. Schools, hospitals, relief agencies, and many others have been born in the church and taken over by state officials. Many ideas on technical assistance came largely from the efforts of missionaries. This is right. The state can serve society by not allowing the church to become smug or lazy. Religious liberty is a wonderful blessing. But if we ever take it for granted, it will trickle through our fingers. The state can help the Brethren appreciate religious liberty by insisting that it be re-earned locally in every generation. If we have to go a thousand miles or a hundred years away for new evidence, it is never quite convincing to us or to the state — or to our youth.

---

[3] *Ibid.*, page 46.

5. The church must also keep a tension on the state in the direction of:

(1) Honesty. "The whole art of government consists in the art of being honest," said Thomas Jefferson.

(2) Religious freedom as the complexities of life increase. This includes freedom for everybody, not just for our little group. This toleration of minorities is often awkward. It means a "war of persuasion in a world of free wills."

(3) Human welfare on a world scale. The church must also keep a tension on the state to enlarge horizons to take in more people and the larger welfare of the whole world. This has been happening, but it must increase. This includes: food for every person on a basis that builds self-respect; health for every person within the limits of knowledge; education for every person to both the privileges and the responsibilities of world citizenship; and learning to live together helpfully as people on a "shrinking planet." We are working in this direction in the heifer project. And we welcome every honest co-operator. This includes churchless and stateless people too. Toynbee is optimistic here: "Our age will not be remembered for its horrifying crimes, or its astonishing inventions, but because it is the first age since the dawn of history in which mankind dared to believe it practicable to make the benefits of civilization available to the whole human race." All of this under God. Something like this could be a real beginning of a sound world government.

A rather homely illustration might be helpful here. Some years ago, after a very strenuous summer in western camps, I had the opportunity of doing a little fishing in the ocean. It was genuine fun to be a member of a good-natured group of forty persons dropping lines and hopefully holding poles over the side of a barge anchored five miles out from the shore. It was exciting to watch somebody else a few feet away pull up a fish from one hundred feet down. It was more exciting to pull in one yourself. But the real aim was to catch a yellowtail.

All at once my line grew taut. There was tension aplenty

as my line was moved about in the water by something big on the other end. Of course, I held on and wound my reel. By an unwritten law everyone else on that side of the boat pulled his line back in to give me free room to land my fish. And advice came in from all sides. One bit of it I remember: "Hold her head up!" I was trying to do that, but my unskilled arms could not do it. As in a good many other fish stories, the big one got away, even before I got to see it. Maybe it *was* a yellowtail.

But the advice still holds. It is the church's job to hold the state's head up — on honesty, on religious liberty, and on world planning for human welfare.

As citizens, individual Brethren have something of a sliding scale of citizenship. In totalitarian states like Nazi Germany we might have slid to near zero. Some Mennonites still hold to that policy in other countries. But in some states the citizenship of Brethren might approach one hundred percent — more like that of some Friends. The more nearly the policy of the state approaches the mind of Christ, the fuller can be our citizenship. The farther it shifts away from the mind of Christ, the smaller our citizenship must become. But the tension must always be in the same direction, toward more responsibility to match our religious liberty — and to match our faith, whether we have religious liberty or not. This is part of what will help to transform the state some day.

We Brethren have a long way to go ourselves, but we have the task of doing more than our share to keep tension on the state toward Christian brotherhood as the highest form of order. In our changing world the possibilities for this are increasing along with the risks of the space age.

Let me summarize again:

(1) Anarchy is *not* the highest form of order.

(2) Obedience to the state is *not* the highest form of order.

(3) National sovereignty is *not* the highest form of order.

(4) To meet the intricate problems, Brethren will not run away in any sense; nor will we adjust to the state on any major

problem. Further, we cannot allow any major splitting of personality. Instead, we will take on the Herculean task of transforming the state. But more than that, we will maintain a personal and group discipleship to our Master as our major responsibility. Then we shall have much to share with a needy state and a needy world toward Christian brotherhood — the highest form of order.

Somebody described the early Christians as "absolutely fearless, absurdly happy, and always in trouble." That does not yet describe us Brethren. Sometimes we miss it on all three counts. But as we build a group integrity appropriate to a Christian culture we shall become increasingly self-respecting and fearless. As we live closer to our Master we shall become happier deep down. And as we venture out beyond conventional practices we shall come into increasing tension with the modern state, with always enough trouble to keep life interesting and heroic. Can the modern state be transformed? All of them? There is no light answer, but "for the Christian to give the world up as lost is to give God up."[4]

It is the duty of the Brethren and all churches to keep at this unfinished task until "the kingdom of the world has become the kingdom of our Lord and of his Christ." This idea cannot be fully expressed without music. Handel's *The Messiah* does it better. Brotherhood under the Lordship of Christ is the highest goal for the Brethren and also for the modern state.

---

[4] *Ibid.*, page 108.

19. THE BRETHREN AND BIBLICAL ETHICS

W. Harold Row

Executive secretary, Brethren Service Commission of the General Brotherhood Board; chairman, National Service Board for Religious Objectors; minister; writer; lecturer; visiting instructor in Christian social ethics, Bethany Biblical Seminary. Formerly: pastor, Richmond, Virginia; national director of civilian public service, Brotherhood staff.

The focus of Brethren interest has been on Christian living rather than on creed, or ritual, or even on the Bible itself for the Bible's sake. We have insisted that Biblical faith requires practical, ethical living. Alexander Mack, Jr., listed "training in righteousness" as one of the primary purposes of Bible study. Brethren have a theology, but it is nonsystematical, nontechnical, and noncreedal. Some have referred to it as a theology of "religion as life." D. L. Miller wrote a half-century ago: "In the subtleties of speculative theology the church takes but little interest. She is chiefly concerned in giving willing and cheerful obedience to the plain simple commands of Christ Jesus." Our theology has been simple in structure, Biblical in reference, and life centered in concern. It is a way of life more than a way of thought; a way of doing more than a way of talking.

Brethren for the most part accept Christian ethics as generally understood in the larger Christian community. The norms of Christian conduct for most areas of daily living are rather well understood and accepted in theory, though less honored in practice. The term, *the Christian Way,* therefore has meaning, at least in the Christian community itself. The purpose of our inquiry today, however, is to pose, and then attempt to answer, the question as to whether there is *a Brethren Way of Life* which has discernible and desirable emphases within the larger body of accepted Christian ethics. And my answer, in a sentence, is that there is a Brethren Way, within the Christian Way, which is definable, defendable, and desirable.

For the early Brethren the essence of Christian living consisted in the imitation of Jesus. John S. Flory said that they "were exemplars of an everyday type of Christianity," and that they carried "their religion into the affairs of daily living." Alexander Mack wrote that Christians should "look wholly and alone to the express words of the Lord Jesus and to his own perfect example." My favorite description is that of Floyd Mallott: "The Brethren are truly characterized as a company of people who seek to exemplify the type of life expounded in the Sermon on the Mount. . . . We thus think of the Brethren as Biblical, Pietistic Mystics. . . . They are imitators of primitive Christianity."

Brethren are heirs both of the Pietists and of the Anabaptists. From Pietism we inherited our zeal for a primitive, Biblical faith and the emphasis on practical goodness. From Anabaptism we inherited our attitude of nonconformity in relation to culture and our emphasis upon the "gathered church of the truly converted who lived up to the New Testament ethic" (Durnbaugh). Mack wrote that the true Christian "must be separated from the body of Satan, the world, . . . all unrighteousness, and . . . all false sects and religions."

I. Seven Propositions

1. Brethren ethics are essentially Biblical ethics. Brethren have been a people of the Book, but they have in the main taken an instrumental attitude toward the Bible — truth in order to goodness. According to D. W. Kurtz, the Bible enables man "to live the life of goodness, and love, through the power of the Holy Spirit." From Pietism, we accepted the corollary truths that (1) every Christian should read the Bible, and (2) Bible

reading should lead to the good (godly) life. Brethren always have believed that the answer to the question of what it means to be a Christian is to be found in the Bible, especially in the New Testament, and more particularly in the teachings of Jesus. They understood the New Testament to be the norm for all doctrine, the "rule of faith," and the "guide for conduct."

The Brethren canon in theory has been the entire Bible. But in practice our Brethren canon is considerably more limited. We have put major emphasis upon the New Testament and within the New Testament upon the Gospels and a few other scattered passages containing exhortations to and examples of Christian living. New Testament teachings most respected by us include: Matthew 5, 6, 7, 18, 25, 28; Luke 4, 10, 14; John 3, 13; Romans 12; 1 Corinthians 11, 13; Galatians 5, 6; Ephesians 5, 6; Philippians 2; Colossians 3; Hebrews 12, 13; James; 1 Peter; 1 John. A Brethren canon of Scripture is Scripture widely and regularly used by the Brethren. In the main, we have preached the elements of Christianity as given in the Sermon on the Mount, and we have found these treasured emphases repeated in other New Testament passages.

Brethren interpretation of Scripture has emphasized the obvious and the practical. C. C. Ellis wrote: "God gave us the scriptures, not only that we might learn the truth, but that we might live the truth. We need it for guidance in the right way." Rufus D. Bowman most clearly defined our method of resolving apparent contradictions in the ethical teachings in the Bible. He insisted that the Old Testament be interpreted in the light of the New Testament and the New Testament be interpreted in terms of the mind of Christ. Further he said: "God through Christ is the central source for New Testament authority, and the light from which the Old Testament should be studied."

2. Brethren ethics are ethics derived from faith. Christian ethics are preceded by Christian theology. The *didache* (the teaching) depends upon the *kerygma* (the proclamation). This makes conduct, though secondary, an essential deduction from

faith. Ethics "expresses in the imperative mood what theology states in the indicative," according to Sidney Cave. The New Testament is first concerned with what God has done, and only then with what men ought to do. The Christian ethic rests on the truths of historical fact. It shows what men must do in relation to what God has done. Christian ethics are theocentric; moral problems are to be seen from the perspective of God's will. We begin from the revelation of the nature and the will of God as this has come to us in Jesus Christ. Brethren, even in the most churchly act of their faith, approach the Lord's supper (*agapé*) not as a purely religious act in the usual sense of a sacrament, but as the central place of meeting with God in remembrance of the obedient act of His Son, from which they go out into the world with new strength and humility to do His will. "We love because he first loved us" (1 John 4:19). Even "to regard the Sermon on the Mount as ethics pure and simple is completely to misunderstand it, for the ethics of the discourse is through and through religious ethics, and the ethical life to which it points is impossible of attainment without the help of the religion which inspired it" (L. H. Marshall).

3. Brethren ethics are primarily the ethics of obedience. Christian ethics are both an "ethics of duty" and an "ethics of ends," "duty" being represented by the will of God, and "ends" as the realization of the Kingdom of God. The first stresses aspiration, achievement, the good act. Duty ethics are illustrated by Kant, Calvin, Brunner; end ethics by Aristotle, Aquinas, Rauschenbusch. Brethren ethics are a mixture of both, especially in this century, but are fundamentally an ethics of obedience. "This do" is a recurrent command. We are more concerned with the question, "What is right?" than with the question, "What is man's chief good?" Ideals are secondary to duty. Supreme loyalty is to God, not to self or to society. For Jesus the central maxim was "Thy will be done."

Prominent in the writing of the early Brethren was the concept of following Jesus (*Nachfolge* — following after). This *imitatio Christi* motif is deeply rooted in our history, as it was in the New Testament. Perhaps we have at times stressed this too much, too mechanically. Christ calls us to obedience, not merely to outward imitation. Ours is a discipleship ethic. Christian ethics are epitomized in the words, "Have this mind among yourselves, which you have in Christ Jesus . . ." (Philippians 2:5). We are not called simply to be a group of little Jesuses, but rather "to the measure of the stature of the fullness of Christ" (Ephesians 4:13). The gloomy Dean of St. Paul's, W. R. Inge, reminded us that "one of the reasons why there are so few Christians is that Christianity is a very stern creed, a creed for heroes, while we are good-natured little people, who wish to have a good time, and to give others a good time." We have responded sympathetically to Romans 12:2: "Do not be conformed to this world but be transformed by the renewal of your mind, that you may prove what is the will of God, what is good and acceptable and perfect."

4. Brethren ethics are the ethics of love. The heart of the Christian ethic is love as *agapé*. Paul Ramsey speaks for a growing number of ethics teachers when he declares, "There is no obedience, no response to God, there are no religious duties beyond this: 'Thou shalt love'; and love fulfills every legitimate obedience." Or Waldo Beach and Richard Niebuhr writing thus: "The early Christian church stated in one sentence what it has learned about man's duty from its Lord and from the prophets and law-givers who preceded him. That sentence read either 'love your neighbor as yourself,' or 'walk in love as Christ loved us.' Over and over again this is presented as right conduct." Jesus presented "obedient love" as the operative principle of man's moral duty: "You shall love. . . . Love one another. . . . Love your enemies."

New Testament ethics are not primarily an affair between man and man but between God and man-and-man. We are to love our neighbor after the manner of God's love toward us. Brethren have regarded the two love commandments as equally binding, and thus have escaped both the error of medieval mysticism, which gave too exclusive an emphasis to the vertical dimension of the commandment to love God, and the error of the modern social gospel movement, which has overemphasized the horizontal relations of the commandment to love one's neighbor. Brethren have rejected the prevalent dualism between personal and social ethics (cf. Brunner's limitation of the scope of Christian love to person-to-person relationships and his use of justice as the norm in all other social relationships). We have maintained that love is both relevant and essential to every human situation, both as ultimate norm and as immediate goal. (Richard Niebuhr recently defined the purpose of the church as the increase among men of love to God and of man to man.) Justice is to be understood as a means for love's perfection in society. Justice is love's servant, never its master. Similarly, freedom as a goal of the good life never determines love, but love requires and issues in freedom. "Love is law's fulfillment."

5. Brethren ethics are the ethics of right relationships. Love is not so much an abstract principle as it is a cohesive, active spirit. It is not some giant lever whose fulcrum rests upon the shoulder of God and by which we can mechanically move mountains of opposition or even protect our friends from their enemies. *Agapé* love is non-utilitarian, noncalculative, and nonprudential. We do not love in order to win friends or influence people; we love in order to "fulfill the law of Christ." We understand love as *agapé* (loving others because God has first loved us) rather than love as *caritas* (loving others to please God). Love is relational; more specifically, love expresses itself in the familistic pattern rather than in the pattern of social contract or coercion. Nothing is more characteristic of the Brethren than their family pattern of doing things. Both our theology and our practices of brotherhood have been expressed largely in family idioms — characteristic of the New Testament. Even Annual Conference continues to be more like a big family reunion than a convention.

6. Brethren ethics are the ethics of redemption. "God was

in Christ reconciling the world to himself, not counting their trespasses against them, and entrusting to us the message of reconciliation" (2 Corinthians 5:19). This text in its setting gives us the assurance of our own hope in Christ and sets up before us our task in the world as ambassadors for Christ. In a sense our ethics are the ethics of failure, in respect to both ourselves and those to whom we minister. Perfectionist ethics relate to our call and obligation in Christ, not to our achievement nor to our appraisal of others. Our ministry in Christ is to all men everywhere, especially to the weak and the hurt, the despised and the neglected. These we serve not because (like Eugene Debs) we are one of them or they are one of us, but because "while we [all] were yet sinners, Christ died for us."

7. Brethren ethics are the ethics of the good life in the good community. The early Brethren fully accepted the axiom of Pietism that "to be religious is to be good." We have resisted stubbornly every attempt to make religion a substitute for goodness (thus our enthusiasm for the Epistle of James). For us righteousness is goodness, and goodness is the expression of the character of God, who alone is perfectly good. We would accept Luther's observation that "the good man is not good because he does good things, but the good man does good things because he is good." The order is important. Righteousness expresses itself in doing good, but the reverse is not necessarily true. "Good consists in always doing what God wills at any particular moment" (Brunner).

Our Brethren emphasis is on "life lived in community" — *Gemeinschaft*. This is sound, even if at times, and in some particulars through most of our history, we gave too narrow definitions to community. We have, with a few notable exceptions, resisted the temptation to absolute perfection which is always individualistic and not social. Brethren generally have rejected the perfectionist and individual tendencies toward celibacy, monasticism, and social unconcern. The Brethren conception of the church was not so much in terms of institutionalism as in terms of community. The church as a "holy community," the

Gemeinschaft der Brüder, emphasized brotherhood, democratic organization, the love feast as the central act of worship, human relations based on Matthew 18, mutual aid and material assistance to the needy, especially to those of the fellowship, and the church as a redemptive community modeled on the primitive, apostolic church. Brethren social ethics have been based more upon the idea of brotherhood than on the idea of the regenerated Christian individual. However, we have stressed such personal Christian traits as integrity of speech, purity in morals, simplicity in dress, and neighborly helpfulness.

II. Religion as Life

"Religion as life" — a central thrust in our heritage — logically implies the good life in the good community, and is based upon the initial and perpetual "good news" that "God was in Christ reconciling the world to himself." There is a holy matrimony of good deeds and "good news." What God has joined together, let no man put asunder!

This whole analysis of our Brethren social ethics needs the correction of some of its obvious weaknesses and omissions. Space permits only a listing here. We need to remember that the Brethren Way is not the whole way or the only way, but one body's interpretation of the Christian Way. We have often succumbed to a literalistic, legalistic morality. We have tended to make the teachings of Jesus too simple and to use them too mechanically. We have too much limited our ethics to person-to-person relationships, too much to the ethics of a single community, and have failed to see their relevance to social structures. We have been more concerned about "what is right" than about "what is relevant." We have relied on moral influence rather than on political power in reference to social decision. We have been slow to include the orders of society as under the Lordship of Christ. We have not sufficiently understood the nature of power, justice, freedom, and corporate evil. We have tended to emphasize love at the expense of justice, when justice is the social requirement of love. We have thought of sin too much in personal terms, thus neglecting the complex social dimensions of evil. We need to understand more fully that at every point of preventable evil in our world, our Lord calls us, both as a body of Christ and as individual citizens, to heroic action, both ameliorative and remedial. We need to be aware increasingly that the ethic which is peculiar with us needs to be universalized, even as it needs the corrective of other ethics. But we dare not hide the light of our ethics under the bushel of current ethical confusion. Brethren social ethics may be *over*simple, but in this kind of a troubled world they are also long *over*due.

In conclusion, we need to be both grateful and repentant for our past Brethren social witness — both joyfully "fulfilling our heritage" and redeeming our past by "re-writing pages of our history" through ever-new deeds of love and kindness. We need to recommit ourselves heroically to these fuller dimensions of our faith — action to match our faith and faith to match our action. We need to realize more fully what we must do together in the world as a Brotherhood because of what God has done for us through Christ. We must listen together to the Word of God. We must keep our minds open to the constructive testimony of the newer voices of Christian social concern, even though they may seem strange to us at first. We must ever experiment with new truths and new techniques in social education and action. We must engage in "doing the truth" in order to learn new truth. We must always keep our deeds of love a respectable distance ahead of our words of love.

Brethren always have regarded the "cup of cold water" as an authentic and necessary note in Christianity. This has kept our faith practical and relevant to the problems of everyday living. For us, Christian ethics are always social ethics. But we have also understood that the "cup of cold water" is to be given "in the name of Christ." Thus the deed of mercy is no isolated act of human kindness born alone out of the human heart, but rather the issue of obedient love wedded to Biblical faith. For us Christian ethics are always Biblical ethics, both as to origin and as to validation. The "cup of cold water" defines the nature and the field of our social obligation. The concept of "in the name of Christ" validates our service and provides us with grace sufficient for every need.

Last night the moderator again raised the question of Alexander Mack, namely, "And how shall the Brethren be recognized?" He responded by a thrilling and relevant commentary on Mack's own answer, namely, "They shall be recognized by the manner of their living." In other words, by their ethics. I leave with you the same question rephrased as "And how are the Brethren to be known today in our troubled world?" If not by their dress or speech, meetinghouses or mode of baptism, resolutions or books, then certainly by their way of life. "You will know them by their fruits" (Matthew 7:20). And Paul delineates the fruit of the Spirit as "love, joy, peace, patience, kindness, goodness, faithfulness, gentleness, self-control," adding, "Against such there is no law." He then admonishes us: "If we live by the Spirit, let us also walk by the Spirit. . . . Bear one another's burdens, and so fulfil the law of Christ." And then, "Let us not grow weary in well-doing, for in due season we shall reap, if we do not lose heart. So then, as we have opportunity, let us do good to all men, and especially to those who are of the household of faith" (Galatians 5: 22, 23; 6: 2, 9, 10).

20. THE BRETHREN AND THEIR CULTURE

Kermit Eby

Professor of social sciences, the University of Chicago; minister; writer; lecturer. Formerly: executive secretary, Chicago Teachers Union; member, United States Commission for Reorganization of Education in Japan; assistant director of education and research for the C.I.O.; member, Federal Advisory Committee for the United States Office of Education.

As I have written on other occasions, one of the most exhilarating intellectual experiences of my life occurred when I received the insight that the founders of our church were as much the product of their time and environment as of divine inspiration. Furthermore, I was fascinated to discover that the problems our ancestors faced were not dissimilar to our own.

Included in our forefathers' experiences were war, tyranny, and persecution. Time after time during the seventeenth century, the Palatinate was overrun by warring armies. The destruction of the Thirty Years War is a familiar story. In the last quarter of the seventeenth century, the French invasion made a virtual desert of the Palatinate, in order to prevent its rich fields from supplying sustenance to these enemies of France.

Religious persecution did not die out with the end of the religious wars, however. The established churches at that time — Lutheran, Calvinist, and Catholic — brought various persecutions to bear upon the nonestablished ones, despite the guarantee against this in the Treaty of Westphalia. The smaller Anabaptist and Pietistic sects had not even this guarantee; their doctrines, particularly pacifism, made them odious to the rulers. Finally, constant political and economic oppression practiced by the rulers of the German state added to the people's burdens. Despite soil fertility, mild climate, and skillful agriculture, the peasantry of the Palatinate eked out a meagre existence because of the encumbering taxation in money and produce levied by exploitative landlords. Our ancestors, then, were the victims of distressed times, the products of historical crises. Like other people in other times under similar conditions, they set out to discover whether there was any meaning behind the travail of their lives. The external ferment was internalized, and they came to the conclusion that Christianity had not failed — it was simply untried.

Pietism, beginning with that of Phillip Jacob Spener in the late seventeenth century, was characterized by a conviction that the Reformation had not gone far enough, that "the purification of doctrine" needed to be followed by a "purification of living." Pietism stressed a resignation of spirit, obtainable only through contact with Christ. For the Pietistic Christian, Christianity is a religion of practice rather than one of theory, of ethics rather than theology. Our ancestors were more concerned with Christian character and conduct than with the relation of man to divinity. The essence of character was love, and that of Christian conduct was sincerity. Pietists were humanitarian. Today our relief program is an expression of our earliest tradition. To me, the most significant fact in Brethren history is the response of our forebears to the historical and human conditions of their lives. They were the heirs of a long period of religious ferment, religious wars, and a superimposed peace in the name of religion. Tragic as the time was, however, it was not an era of spiritual sleep; men sacrificed, suffered, and died for what they believed.

The Brethren, then, came into historical being because events brought about their existence. When the state persecuted them, they rejected it! Being victims of force and violence, they made reconciliation their goal. Confused by the state's interpretation of religious truth, they stressed a fellowship of believers. All of this, of course, is common knowledge. It is Brethren history and as such has been repeated many times.

In short, our ancestors believed that the essence of the Christian way of life was the anticipation of Christ's way and the enactment thereof. Unlike the Mennonites, who maintained historical and cultural roots in Europe, the Brethren came to Pennsylvania as an isolated body (which, incidentally, is a fact that played a significant role in the attitude of the two groups toward history and research). Both the Brethren and the Mennonites came to a Quaker Pennsylvania. The pacifism which in Germany made them aliens, in Pennsylvania made them allies. The agricultural proficiency developed in the Palatinate flowered in the rich soil of Lancaster and neighboring counties — so much so, in fact, that it became a truism that a Pennsylvania Dutchman had an instinctive ability to locate good farm land. Finally, the new world was not large enough to permit diverse cultural and linguistic islands to coexist. (For instance, I can talk "Dutch" whenever there is need or opportunity.)

It seems to me that the most significant factor in the persistence of these islands was that they were permitted at all. Differences in language meant both a departure from common cultural roots and alienation from the prevailing culture. For example, the Lutherans spoke German. Because Lutheranism had its roots in Europe, European pastors brought their books and ideas when they came to the American missions. But, the Brethren had no such roots in Europe. The impetus which Christopher Sauer and his son gave to a responsible witness was not maintained. (Interestingly enough, it was a converted Lutheran in these Brethren islands, Henry Kurtz, who gave the Brethren the push which revived their interest in education and culture.)

Christopher Sauer has always intrigued me. His was the dilemma of wishing to avoid Caesar but realizing that it was an impossibility. (His wife, on the other hand, spent fourteen years with Conrad Beissel in the Ephrata cloisters. She carried separateness to its logical conclusion. There, I suppose, Caesar let her alone, but her husband had no such escape.) In the new world, Sauer's ethic came into conflict with new problems. New social groups such as Indians and non-German Europeans, and new institutions such as slavery and indentured servants, simply shifted the focus. Often, like those of his descendants, Sauer's criticisms were inclined more to be merely negative and not suggestive of remedial action or reform. Like many of those who followed him, whose interest in peace involved them in economics and politics, Sauer's pacifism involved him in the politics of the French and Indian War. Space does not permit the development of a critique as to just what Sauer's contribution to the history of Pennsylvania and the Brethren was. But, the point I wish to make is worth repeating. A man with a Brethren heritage cannot escape involvement with the larger world if he takes his heritage seriously. All *good* Brethren live in tension. Consequently, they are, or should be, aware of the conflict between Christian values and secular ones.

Thus, the thesis of this paper is not new. Those who espouse Christ cannot be wedded to the world. One cannot, as the Bible states, serve both God and mammon. (If I may be personal at this point, I would point out that this is my life witness. The most profound sadness I know lies in the fact that I realize that Baugo, my home church, exists now for me only in memory. Thus, since I cannot return there, I devote my energies to building a world true to Baugo's image. This, no doubt, is as old as the desire of man to build a city of God. But, enough of this!)

The Brethren contribution to the world, then, can be measured in direct proportion to the conflict with its culture. From my experience, I have concluded that social progress is precipitated when the dedicated man (the spark) strikes the social situation (the tinder) and ignites it.

Our ancestors' greatness lay in their uniqueness — in belief, character, and witness. The uniqueness of a Dunker, at its best, involved more than his mode of dress. As much, it included the "queerness" of the man who lived in the world by otherworldly standards. Such men are always unique!

Now, let us examine certain of the attributes of a sect and see how the Brethren qualified as sectarian witnesses in terms of their world. A sect, as we have seen, usually arises in a period of disorganization in a given society, a phase wherein reintegration of the community is effected. This is true of the Brethren genesis. The Brethren were the products of disorganization in Germany. As settlers in a new world, they were the beneficiaries of a half-century of comparative peace. With the coming of the Revolutionary War, their pacifism led to a diaspora as they were literally forced into the wilderness. They lived in their isolated communities and biologically and culturally inbred. With inbreeding, tolerance gave way to disputation. Externals became increasingly important as reasons for holding on to them became more obscure. Our ancestors settled down into the way of life which characterized them for almost a hundred years, and still does in the several areas where the Brethren are isolated. Fundamentally, they believed themselves to be a sect in tension with the world. Caesar (the state) and the mores of the prevailing society were to be avoided as much as possible.

During this period of withdrawal, the chief intellectual demand on ministers and elders was the searching of the Scriptures, to prove the validity of the Dunker way; total immersion, the simple life, the Lord's supper — all had to be defended. Consequently, Brethren heroes were those who could defend the Brethren uniqueness in debate. As time passed, however, sectarian groups tended to institutionalize their convictions, and individuals motivated by them were both unique and convinced. For example, in my youth I was impressed by how much Mennonites and Brethren had in common, and yet how different they were. This was true to the extent that often they would rather convert one another than sinners!

Briefly, then, a sect in its collective life produces sectarians. For example, I too would share the belief that

there is a typical Mormon and his personality, furthermore, can be described. He is usually in favor of a highly centralized institutional organization; he is ruled by a characteristic system of theology; he believes in private property controlled to a certain extent by a theocracy. Likewise, there is a typical Shaker. This one holds private property to be undesirable and even against the will of God. Moreover, to the Shaker, all sexual intercourse is immoral and there is a long list of sentiments that define this individual. *There is also a typical Dunker, neither conservative like the Shaker, nor ruled by a central hierarchy like the Mormon* [italics mine]. He belongs, as most sectarians do, to the one true church. But, each sectarian belongs to a different "true church" than the other. The Dunker regards it as obligatory to be immersed in water, facing forward each time. He must ceremoniously wash his brother's feet and give him a holy kiss of love, keeping himself unspotted from the world.[1]

Today, this observation of Dunker uniqueness is hardly true. Conformity to the world's values, and not tension or conflict with them, is true of us today; we have come full cycle. We began by being convinced that the world was evil and ought to be avoided; but now we have evolved to the point where we feel that it is good (and with our help can be made better). In other words, we began with the Mennonites and ended with the Quakers!

The question to which we need to give our attention, therefore, is what brought about this transition. The answer, of course, is that we have evolved from a group in conflict with its culture to one respected and relatively at peace with it. We are now well on our way to acculturation. Yet, since to state a fact is not to establish one, let us proceed to the task of proof.

But, before continuing, perhaps I should define culture. In Webster's language, "culture has a Latin derivative, from the Latin *to cultivate,* or the act of developing by education, discipline, learning." The following is quoted for those who want a more comprehensive definition:

The term culture is used to signify the sum total of human creation, the organized result of group experience up to the present time. Culture includes all that man has made in the form of tools, weapons, shelter, and other material goods and processes; all that he has elaborated in the way of

---

[1] Ellsworth Faris, "The Sect and the Sectarian," in the *American Journal of Sociology* (supplement to the May 1955 issue), page 8f. Reprinted by permission of the University of Chicago Press.

attitudes and beliefs, ideas and judgments, codes and institutions, arts and sciences, philosophy and social organization. Culture also includes the interrelations among these and other aspects of human, as distinct from animal life. Everything material and immaterial created by man in the process of living comes within the concept of culture.[2]

For example, most sociologists and economists agree that social institutions have two purposes: (1) to insure to men the supply of material means of good living, and (2) to give men the fullest possible scope for creative activity. This, however, is a secular approach to social institutions. The sectarian, if he is true to his vision, is both a creator and a creature of a "Kingdom of God." His is a vision of the nature of the life in which God's will is accomplished.

To put my thesis bluntly, there is not a choice for the Brethren, if they wish to survive, other than to reverse the secular trend. We must emphasize the Kingdom of God — not that of the world — and internalize the uniqueness which was so obviously externalized in my youth. Pietism, in the words of James H. Nichols in his *History of Christianity,* means an individualism and internalization which seeks to build within it the significant religious fellowship — the concern was not so much for institutional expression as for personal approbation of religious truth, subjective religious experience and personal devotion — ascetic discipline."[3] I can plead in defense of this easily, for I am convinced that the internal is significantly influenced by the external, by the way we live and earn our living. We are the products of our roots, heritage, and memories.

We Brethren were once "queer" people. To affirm this fact we had only to look into a mirror. My grandfather, Monroe Schwalm, was a Dunker and proud of it. Unfortunately, some of his descendants are Dunkers and ashamed of it.

But it is not my feeling, or my point, that we ought to return

---

[2] Edward Reuter, "Race and Culture," in *Principles of Sociology* (ed. Alfred M. Lee) (New York: Barnes & Noble, Inc., 1946), page 140. Reprinted by permission of the publishers.
[3] James H. Nichols, *History of Christianity* (New York: Ronald Press, 1956).

to an isolated plain-clothed position. Nonetheless, I must insist that Brethrenism died when the secular world took over the responsibilities which once were met by the fellowship. Brethrenism is an expression, at best, of a face-to-face ethic. Therefore, when we took care of our widows and orphans and the aged, provided insurance through mutual aid, and operated as a fraternity, we gave meaning to our love feasts and feet-washing and salutation with a holy kiss. When we no longer gave relevance to these ceremonies by tangible deeds, they tended to become symbolic. Or, to put it another way, when insurance, social security, and old-age pensions came in the front door, the apostolic church went out the back. Brethrenism, I am convinced, cannot survive except that it go beyond charity by taxation.

Paradoxically, it is in our heifer program, in our voluntary service, that we are yet Brethren. This, too, is perhaps a manifestation of acculturation. Unable to maintain our face-to-face kingdom in our communities, we would ease our consciences by exporting it. But maybe we are destined to be yeast. When we came into being, and through prayer, suffering, and exile evolved the faith which is ours, we were victims of history. Today, when our prosperity is tied to war and preparation for war, we are the beneficiaries thereof. Even a secular government knows that our relief programs have other positive consequences than those which result from charity. There are also political consequences of great significance. Hitler and Stalin were not beyond sparing great artists (if they added to their countries' kudos abroad)!

It is the closed community, the one which has built into its very fibre an ethic, which nurtures followers. It is no accident that family churches, closed communities (often patriarchal ones), continue to survive and produce witnesses.

The Amish and the Hutterites know this without the benefit of sociological research. They are also living witnesses to the fact that the way men make their livings is a paramount determinant of the course their lives will take. Without being an economic determinist, I would argue that Brethren and Mennonites are doomed by urbanization and secularization. For, the way men and women earn their livings determines to a large extent the kind of lives they live. The Brethren farmer lived close to the basic rhythms of life. He saw the seasons come and go, saw the sunrise and the sunset; birth and death were intimate realities. The ultimately decisive factors in his life were in God's hands. He realized this, but his city sons and daughters are more deterministic, less intimately interdependent. The urban man believes his environment is controllable. Every day he sees what machines can do. The modern Brethren farm is machine operated and is relatively an isolated economic unit. Today, the hard-surfaced road, the automobile, the radio, the television, and other modern devices orient the farmer to his urban environment. Atomization, in sociological language, is the result.

For years I have been writing about Baugo, the church of my boyhood. I have intimated that it no longer exists except in memory. Today, those who worship at Baugo go to church on Sunday morning, and then follow their separate ways. When I was a boy, the service ritual had meaning, for the brotherhood of the love feast was expressed in the necessities of life. In order to get certain tasks done, we had to exchange labor. But not so today. Now, the market is more significant in its impact on life than is the neighborhood. The market is impersonal; the neighborhood was intimate.

Again, this point need not be elaborated. It is enough to repeat that (1) the Brethren came into historical prominence because of their uniqueness; (2) they maintained their identity by institutionalizing a way of life; and (3) their survival was uniquely contributed to by the way they lived and earned their living. Today, all these factors have changed. We are "respectable," assimilated, and urbanized, and we are becoming more so daily.

From my viewpoint, it appears too that it is the tolerance of which we, as a New Testament church, boast that has contributed to our assimilation. As our externalized uniqueness disappears, our internalized differences go with them. We are at home with Baptists, Methodists — in fact, with almost every group in Protestantism. I might add that we are welcome. The residual traces of conscience and diligence do not make us good church workers.

What I am suggesting here is not that we develop a theology giving New Testament emphasis. It is a little late for that. I am simply saying that the Lutherans, conscious of a history, affirmers of a theology, and more liturgical than we, are less easily assimilated. They have a creed; we merely an affirmation.

But, lest we become overly despondent, let me say that we have one advantage. We are historically pacifists (if not statistically so), and I hope that we are so convictionally. That, at least for a minority, creates a tension. It is our built-in dialectic. Frankly, it is the only real hope for survival.

Permit me to elaborate by using a non-Brethren example. Several years ago, lecturing at Goshen College, I asked, "What are the ways in which we are unique?" The only positive answer I got was "We believe in peace; we are a peace church." Several of the students wanted to hold on to *this!* Similarly, it has long been my thesis that social motivation in most Brethren springs from a common core. This gives me a clue for possible survival. We can begin with our peace witness and make it the point of departure for understanding our history, our heritage, and our dedication. Recently, Donald Royer of Manchester College wrote a Ph.D. thesis on the Brethren peace witness. It was from his study that I received my insight. Pacifists, he found, largely were produced in two places: elder-dominated family churches, and institutionalized churches related to our colleges and headquarters. In the one experience the conviction grew out of the religious heritage; in the other out of study and rational experience. Of course, there should be a blend of both. But, so long as there is a minority of Brethren holding on to this part of their heritage, they will inevitably be in conflict with their culture. I may add that they will also produce the tensions which will stimulate the church. For example, there are two Quaker bodies: the Friends Church, prosperous and respectable; and the Friends Service Committee, radical and adventurous. Thank goodness the latter stimulates the former! We too have had, I believe, a few debates between the Brethren Service Commission and those representatives of the more traditional means of salvation. There are other examples of possible tension, but the above serves ably as an illustration.

Since I am no longer a young radical (but I hope not consequently a tired one), permit me to recall the birth of the "Hundred Dunkers" at Winona Lake. Dan West, John and Ben Stoner, and I were convinced that the church which nurtured us has much to give the world which it was not giving. We decided that it was ours to see that it did — without the benefit of hierarchical blessing. If I may be a bit immodest (now that the passage of time has served to permit greater tolerance), let me say that I feel our mission has been, in some degree, accomplished. I am grateful for this fact — grateful that it was the Brethren sense of fellowship which made it possible. I do not think it a weakness to love men with whom one differs.

So, if we would survive — and I think we have much to give and so *should* survive — it is necessary for us to understand that the church must be reborn with each generation. Pentecost can hardly be institutionalized. To accomplish this, I would deliberately set out to make every Brethren child conscious of his roots and his heritage. I would begin with that which is uniquely Brethren — peace, reconciliation, and stewardship of life and property. (But here I am repeating myself, for this comes out in every chapter of *For Brethren Only*.[4]) Nevertheless, I will repeat my thesis: "Brethren values, if understood properly, are forever in tension with the secular. There is and must be an everlasting tension between the Kingdom of God and the kingdom of man. Brethren, if they *cannot* be unique, *can* be nothing."

---

[4] Published by the Brethren Press, 1958.

In conclusion there is little more to say than this: Brethren were born in crisis, and they witnessed their faith in protest against that crisis. This was their European phase. In America, Christopher Sauer, because he loved his fellow men and believed in peace, inevitably became involved when he witnessed to a better way. Heifers to Europe grew out of similar sensitiveness.

The study of history, if it has any purpose at all, should make us conscious of our heritage. Everything I believe has grown out of my discovery of the significance of my inborn beliefs. Perhaps this is because I lived outside of it for so many years. Suffice it, however, to say that my intellectual problems have boiled themselves down to one. It is this: "How can we give meaning to the Judeo-Christian ethic, a face-to-face ethic, and one which nurtured us in face-to-face relationships, meaning in a society increasingly complex, with decisions ever further removed?"

Today, it seems to me that the exigencies of history, technology, and the bomb have brought us face to face with the realization that survival of our civilization and ideals is dependent on the universalization of this ethic. There are no islands. Communication and travel make the world a neighborhood. But, living side by side does not necessarily insure that we will come to love each other. In fact, the French and the Germans have been neighbors for generations. Paradoxically, the Brethren are becoming known for their world brotherhood as the intimacy which once defined it is disappearing.

No, there is not an alternative. Each man must experience for himself the occurrence of conversion and decide for himself just what his commitment will be. Once we know personal experience, a new dimension enters into our lives — a dimension which demands that we live by the law of love, as expressed in human communion.

It is by this means that our survival is possible — by this means only.

21. THE BRETHREN AND BIBLICAL RECONCILIATION

T. WAYNE RIEMAN

Director of religious activities, and associate professor of religion at Manchester College; writer; minister; lecturer. Formerly: pastor, Lombard (York Center), Illinois; pastor, Waynesboro, Pennsylvania.

I. NEEDED — ABOVE ALL ELSE

More than anything else, the world needs reconciliation!

Our world is a tragically broken world. It is torn asunder — split into alienated groups with chasms of ill will separating people from people, faction from faction, nation from nation. The brokenness affects nearly every area of the life of man.

Two of the most powerful nations in human history are at each other's throats. They co-exist in a tedious balance of power that fills the world with a sense of dread and terrifying anxiety. Both brandish weapons of ultimate destructiveness and they keep piling them higher and higher in a sort of frantic trust in the might of violent weapons. Meanwhile, military leaders finger the buttons which may trigger us into the annihilation of the human race. Gigantic multidimensional propaganda machines keep grinding out misinformation to keep the fearful morale in both nations high. Statements by national leaders on both sides bristle with belligerence.

Each side knows that an all-out atomic war will be the last war for our civilization. Massive retaliation is the announced policy of both nations — one a so-called "Christian nation." Each is poised, ready to strike. Great ocean-spanning and space-soaring ballistic missiles, able to deliver hydrogen explosives from New York to Moscow in twenty minutes, are in aimed readiness. A circle of Strategic Air Command bases rings the Soviet Union. B-47's are in the air around the clock on patrol "missions" from these bases. Each crew carries a lethal load, with the explosive capability of all of the bombs and all of the ammunition expended by all of the planes of all of the nations of World War II.[1] Distant Early Warning radar screens are supposed to alert us so that any enemy atomic attack will bring instant and terrible reprisal. Massive retaliation is the announced policy. Should either nation misjudge the other, or someone become trigger happy — the atomic war would be on.

The brokenness of our world has many other dimensions.

We are beset by racial tensions. Little Rock is a symbol of the mood and the explosive possibilities in many communities in our nation. Rigid, artificial barriers exist. We dare not point an accusative finger at the South. Northern cities are as unprepared as the South. Indeed, many of our Midwestern towns are unprepared for the inevitable changes. Feelings of estrangement and hatred emerge from the nearly insurmountable barriers which some of God's children have erected to keep others of God's children "in their places." Ours is a broken world. The world needs reconciliation more than it needs anything else!

The church of Jesus Christ, meant to be one universal worldwide body, is a broken church. Two major groups within it claim to be *the* church and disclaim the validity of all other forms and expressions. One of the larger groups, Protestantism, has splintered two hundred fifty times and despite significant mergers the process never seems to end. This brokenness infects the whole body of Christ. In thousands of towns of our nation we have crippled little churches of different denominations with meager programs competing with each other rather than joyously co-operating. There is very little joy in the success of another

---

[1] George Barrett, "On Patrol With 'The Weapon,'" in the *New York Times Magazine,* April 1958, page 16.

denomination — especially if it is near our home. The Lord's table, to which all are invited by Jesus Christ himself, cannot be shared because some groups self-righteously insist that their form is *the* way and they disclaim the validity of all others. The church itself is a broken vessel and in need of reconciliation.

Our century has been called the Century of the Homeless.[2] It will be remembered for its tired, dispossessed millions who cannot go home. Other men or nations have erected barriers or boundaries which shut them off from home and country. Hatreds fume and smolder. Justice does not come. Bitterness, estrangement, and a sense of alienation beset them. These people live in captivity. They are the broken people. It was to such — the blind, the brokenhearted, the bruised, and those in bondage — that Jesus gave His reconciling ministry.

The world needs reconciliation more than anything else. It is a broken world. Nations are at each other's throats, or are engaged in subtle intrigue to dominate all others. One race and then another shows recalcitrance. Christ's church sings much too glibly, "All one body we," for it is a church divided and deluded with its own self-righteousness. Edwin Dahlberg, president of the National Council of Churches, says: "There seems to be a fundamental hardness of heart — a stubborn unyielding spirit — throughout the life of humanity today." He points out how it clutters up the life of the family, makes us unwilling to see another's point of view, blocks negotiations between labor and management, causes walkouts in the United Nations, stalemates disarmament conferences, and embitters the life of religion.[3]

Man is in a tragic predicament. This is not new, but the dimensions of it are different. Collective suicide and the reduction of God's good earth to a radioactive ash heap were never previously possible. Now we teeter on the brink of a hell of our

---

[2] Dan Raffensperger, "Century of the Homeless," in the *Gospel Messenger*, January 4, 1958, page 3.
[3] Acceptance address upon election to the presidency of the National Council of the Churches of Christ in America, reprinted in the *Gospel Messenger*, January 18, 1958, page 3.

own making. There seems to be some fundamental declination in man which elevates his own ego to the place of sovereignty. This shuts man off from his neighbors and drives him to selfish domination over them. Unbridgable chasms emerge. Men are estranged and alienated from each other. Worst of all, men are estranged from God. His sovereign claims are rejected in our rebellious egocentricity. Alienation is the clue to man's predicament. *Estrangement, bitterness, brokenness,* and *meaninglessness* — these are the words describing man's situation.

More than anything else, the world needs reconciliation!

Perhaps the Church of the Brethren was born for such a day as this. Isn't this our destiny, our reason for being? Reconciliation has been a central doctrine of our faith and practice. To bring reconciliation to men who live in disharmony with God, to reconcile men with men and with their own highest destiny is the greatest work in the world. Somehow reconciliation must be effected, though even to suggest it implies, in the minds of some, moral turpitude. We will be called naive, impractical dreamers. But the Brethren, and all who take Jesus seriously, know that the gospel of Jesus knows nothing of retaliation and armed violence and the inevitable alienation. Instead, we are confronted inescapably with the startling injunctions: "Love your enemies, do good, bless them that curse you." This is the ministry of reconciliation which has been given unto us.

What is reconciliation?

II. The Gospel of Reconciliation

Reconciliation is the activity of God to restore man to right relationships with Himself and with others.

The Bible assumes that man needs help, that he is sick, lost, and alienated from God and man. Adam's sin of rebellious self-sufficiency is the sin of mankind. After his sin Adam felt estranged, sought to cover his nakedness before God, who knows all things, and tried to hide. Somehow the sin of the father is transmitted unto the third, fourth, tenth, and hundredth generations. The Cain-Abel estrangement symbolizes man's tragic predicament throughout the ages. Men are alienated from men. Murder, violence, hatred, and Lamech's retaliatory threat of vengeance seventy times seven are the marks of nearly every age of man.[4]

Man's estrangement is of three kinds: 1. He is out of harmony with God — is rebellious and self-sufficient, runs his own life, and refuses to accept God's sovereign claims on his life. 2. He is out of harmony with his fellow men; his self-centeredness makes him forget who his neighbor is and his utter dependence upon him. 3. He is out of harmony with himself; there is warfare among his many selves, and every man is far from the destiny which God has ordained for him.

There are many who deny the truth of such an analysis. Some are like Henry David Thoreau. When he was near the point of death his Calvinist aunt asked him a timely question: "Henry, have you made your peace with God?" To this Thoreau answered very pleasantly and confidently: "I didn't know we had quarreled."

The Bible assumes that there is a gulf between God and man that can be crossed only by God's initiative. This gulf is often described as sin. It separates man from God, man from man, and man from his own highest personal destiny. The Bible assumes also that man is incapable of effecting this reconciliation.

St. Augustine confesses the predicament of his early life apart from God. He recalls his "past foulness," the "carnal corruptions of his soul," the "fog of lustfulness." He stank in the eyes of God, he says. He played the prodigal and committed thefts. "I was foul and I loved it," says he. In the midst of this he cried out: "Who can disentangle that complex twisted knottedness of our little lives?" Through all of this he felt the mercy

---

[4] Genesis 4:24.

of God pressing upon him. While he was running away, God was close on his steps, trying to turn him back. This is the "good news" of God. He will not let go of us. Augustine discovered that God was frustrating him, making him restless in his sin, and that there is no rest until a man rests in God.[5]

The core of the Bible is good news — the good news of what God does for us in our lostness, loneliness, and self-willed separation from Him, other men, and ourselves. It is God's will that the world should be reconciled.

God is love. He loves us in our lostness (Luke 15). He seeks for us until He finds. There is no escaping God, whose mercy endures forever. God was in Christ reconciling the world unto Himself. In Christ we see the cosmic peacemaking effort of God. God so loved the world that He gave His Son that all who believe in Him and trust their lives to Him might have eternal life — the life God intended for them. God is greatly pained at the alienation of man. God sent His Son not to condemn the world but that the world might be saved. God's judgment is inevitable. There could be no good world without it, but His chief business is redemption (John 3:16, 17).

The gospel is a gospel of reconciliation. God was in Christ reconciling (2 Corinthians 5:19)! Paul testifies that "we also rejoice in God through our Lord Jesus Christ, through whom we have now received our reconciliation" (Romans 5:11). It is a gift to be received. We do not reconcile ourselves to God. Indeed, we cannot. But there is good news — while we are yet sinners, engulfed in our own self-willed life, which shuts us off from God and alienates us from our fellows, God reaches down to us, forgives us, and cuts the knot of our entanglement. He takes the initiative. He comes to us where we are and calls us to respond. Most of the New Testament is testimony of lives reconciled to God through Christ.

Spurgeon used to tell the story of a very poor widow whose

---

[5] *The Confessions of St. Augustine,* translated by Edward B. Pusey (New York: The Modern Library, 1949), pages 3, 29, 35.

source of income was so small that she could hardly pay the rent and keep food on the table. Her minister, knowing the measure of her poverty, gathered a substantial gift to help pay the rent. Taking the gift to her door, he knocked for admittance but was unable to gain entrance. Later he met the widow on the street and told of his call. She admitted that she had been there all the time, explaining that she thought it had been the landlord who came for the rent. In that manner we often shut God out!

God knocks on the door of every life. He comes with a gift of love, forgiveness, and inestimable mercy. Many of us have mistaken the nature of God. He is not a taskmaster who comes to collect the rent and to lay burdens upon us. He comes with a gift — the gift of eternal life — His life for us. He comes to set us free from all that locks the door between ourselves and God — all that alienates us from our Father and our fellow men. When God's love is met by man's repentance and self-surrender, estrangement is transformed into the mutual personal relation of Father and child.

When reconciliation has been offered and accepted, the gospel of reconciling love becomes an ethical imperative. After Paul proclaims that "God was in Christ reconciling the world unto himself," he adds, ". . . and entrusting to us the message of reconciliation" (2 Corinthians 5:19). Proclaiming this message is our ministry — a ministry to bring men to union with God through Christ. Evangelism is at the heart of our faith.

There is another dimension to our ministry of reconciliation. When men are not right with God they are wrong with other men.

We all sin against our neighbors far and near, and are sinned against. We offend and are offended. Estrangement results; wide chasms separate us; enmity abounds. We wait for the offender to make restitution and it does not happen. Jesus lays the ministry of reconciliation upon the one who is offended (Matthew 18:15-18). It is his responsibility to initiate the first step in reconciliation. He is to go to the offender. The fault is to be pointed out privately and with humility. There must be no disparagement or belittlement, no holier-than-thou attitude. The purpose is to win the offender. If the offender stubbornly resists, reconciliatory overtures continue in the presence of a friend. If this is unsuccessful, the matter is brought before the church so that the whole force of the reconciling community may play upon the estrangement.

How far shall these efforts for reconciliation go? How often shall a brother sin and we forgive him? Surely there's a limit to this! Peter raised this question and suggested what he thought was magnanimity, though it limited forgiveness to seven times. Jesus' answer is unequivocal. He raised the number to infinity. There shall be no limits to forgiveness! The backslider, the alcoholic, the deviant, the sinner must be forgiven as often as necessary. This far must efforts to reconcile go. It is not reconciliation unless it is costly. Seventy times seven does not mean being a doormat, but to go on forgiving until hatred is gone from one's own soul and as long as recalcitrance continues.

This is the faith of the Brethren.

III. Reconciliation — the Faith of Our Fathers

Reconciliation was a central tenet of the faith of our founding fathers. D. W. Kurtz claims that the doctrine of peace was the first principle which they laid down.[6] M. R. Zigler insists that from the beginning to the present day "our main objective around which all else revolves is peacemaking."[7] The records give ample evidences of this central concern.

Donald Durnbaugh tells us that the founders came to the conclusion that it was necessary to form a church organization if Matthew 18:15-18, regarding the settling of disputes by the

---

[6] D. W. Kurtz, *Ideals of the Church of the Brethren*, reprint from the *Gospel Messenger*, November 18, 1933, pages 8 and 11.
[7] M. R. Zigler, *News Briefs from Europe*, page 3.

church, was to be followed. Ever since 1732 this passage of Scripture has been read at baptism.[8]

The tremendous concern regarding baptism was indicative of their zeal for right and harmonious relations with God. Baptism was a covenant of good conscience with God, a sign of obedience to His command.

Brethren commitments to the Lordship of Jesus Christ had far-reaching social implications: second-mile religion, turning the other cheek, returning good for evil, and clear-cut disapproval of force, violence, and bloodshed. These were, in a real sense, tests of the faith. If commitment did not result in a new way of life, it was not real. John Naas refused to accept induction into the military guard of the king of Prussia because he had Jesus Christ as Lord and Captain. Andrew and Martin Boni refused to carry weapons or appear for military drill because these things set men against men and ended in bloodshed and violence. They were incompatible with Jesus' gospel of reconciliation and unlimited forgiveness.

There are many rites, practices, and beliefs which indicate the centrality of the gospel of reconciliation in Brethren life and thought. Anointing symbolizes the recognition of the necessity of the right God-man relationships and provides the opportunity for one to respond to God's gracious overtures during an excruciating crisis in life. The deacons' visit, prior to the love feast, sought to face every member with the acid test in relationships to discern whether men were right with God and their neighbors. Matthew 18 has been employed innumerable times to relieve tensions and ill will.

The Brethren emphasis on reconciliation was unique. From the Reformed faith Mack and his followers received the stalwart doctrine of salvation by faith with its central concern for proper God-man reconciliation. The writings of our founders seem to assume this and address themselves primarily to a neglected

---

[8] Donald Durnbaugh, in the *Brethren Adult Quarterly,* April to June, 1958, page 37.

part of the doctrine of reconciliation — man's relation with man.

The reconciliation of man with man was focused for the early Brethren. When one recalls the times in which the founding fathers lived, the reasons for this emphasis become apparent. The aftermath of the Thirty Years War, the pillaging and bloodshed, and the coercive belligerence of the established churches made reconciliation and unlimited forgiveness the sharp cutting edge of the gospel. Discipleship involved loving God and man, unlimited forgiveness, and outgoing efforts to effect reconciliation between God and man and man and man, and religion that turned the other cheek when offense was given. This was the faith of the Brethren.

Unless one probes deeply one might conclude that the early Brethren were exclusively concerned with the reconciliation of man with man. This, however, was not the case. The Brethren founders were nurtured in the Reformed faith. They assumed and accepted God's reconciling activity in Jesus Christ, salvation by grace, and justification by faith. Mack's nearly overwhelming emphasis on baptism symbolized his great concern for obedient response to God's reconciling activity.

D. W. Kurtz asserts that peace was the first principle laid down by the Brethren in 1708. What is meant by this? Biblically, peace means three things: (a) peace with God, involving faith, repentance, and reconciliation; (b) peace in the human heart, the fruit of peace with God; (c) peace with all men, brotherhood through reconciling love, second-mile religion, all fruits of peace with God.

All of this was very meaningful to the Brethren. The doctrine of reconciliation or peace, as applied to their situation, meant a few other things: (a) no force in religion; religion must be a free response to God in faith; (b) no litigation in pagan courts (except when granted permission by the church); willingness to suffer wrong; and (c) willingness to suffer in the ministry of reconciliation.

The Brethren have been persistent, but not always consistent, in their concern for and practice of the doctrine of reconciliation. Their insight into the meaning of the love of God and the love of man was correct: humility, repentance, unlimited forgiveness, second-mile religion, suffering rebuff and abuse for a turned cheek. Their lives, however, were not always in accord with these professions. Even Alexander Mack acted in an unreconciliatory manner toward Hochmann (to whom the Brethren owe a great deal) on one occasion — calling him a false prophet and a hypocrite.[9] Someone married outside the church at Krefeld. One group would have excommunicated him. Despite John Naas's efforts to reconcile, the group suffered a tragic severance.[10] Such sins of the fathers were transmitted through ensuing generations. A number of splits occurred through the years: the Ephrata experiment, and the tragic divisions of the 1880 period. Presently the spiritual children of Alexander Mack are divided into five groups. They, like children who have quarreled, have little conversation with each other; and our efforts toward reconciliation have not been salutary. We must humbly confess our sins of haughtiness, our unloving and unreconciliatory spirit which led to these tragic divisions. This is the dark side of our heritage. It is shameful, but we must face it.

There is, however, a brighter side of the picture! We are heartened by the persistence of the concern for reconciliation. It runs like a golden thread back and forth through the fabric of our history. Hundreds of references can be made to the persistent centrality of the doctrine of reconciliation.

From the beginning, reconciliation has been the central principle of the Brethren. The church was organized so that Matthew 18:15-18 might be effectively obeyed. The feast of love, baptism, and the anointing service symbolized different responses to the reconciliatory work of God in Christ. Naas and Mack were unending in their efforts to keep the spirit of reconciliation alive.

---

[9] Stated by Donald Durnbaugh in the *Brethren Adult Quarterly*, April to June 1958, page 53.

[10] *Ibid.*, page 63.

Becker was responsible for reuniting the somewhat spiritually and geographically distant Brethren in America. After 1732, Matthew 18 came to be read and was nearly raised to the level of a membership vow. The Sauer motto on the printing press, "For the glory of God and my neighbor's good," and the strong pacifist principles of both father and son are salient and practical expressions of the reconciliation doctrine. Nonresistance was emphasized continually by our forefathers. In the eighteenth century the Brethren were known as defenseless people. They would sooner suffer pain and death than inflict wounds and death on others. The 1875 Conference describes the church as a "peace association."

The most thrilling expressions of our ministry of reconciliation have come since 1850 with our entrance into higher education at that date in an effort to claim the minds of men for Jesus Christ, the initiation of a worldwide mission program in 1875, and the birth and flowering of a service program after 1941.

The times in which we live have laid tremendous claims upon us. The world needs, more than anything else, reconciliation. What shall we Brethren do?

IV. Brethren — Born for Such a Day as This

God's will for us is reconciliation. The gospel speaks of a God who comes to us to help us and to reconcile us to Him, our neighbors, and ourselves.

God has given us the ministry of reconciliation. Literally, He "put in us" the word of reconciliation (2 Corinthians 5:19, 20). In a special sense we have been called to this ministry. For two hundred fifty years, peace and reconciliation have been our central concerns. Now the world, more than ever before, needs reconciliation. The Call program is not of man, but of God. It is our chance to do the most significant thing our church has ever done. Now is the hour! When gigantic nations, armed with earth-shaking and civilization-destroying weapons, hurl invectives and threats of massive retaliation — this is the day for which we were born. This is the day for a program of massive reconciliation for the total life of mankind.

Our central message is peace and reconciliation. Surely we were born for such a day as this! This is our day of destiny. We have been in training for two hundred fifty years. Now is the hour! We cannot change our past, but we can help shape the future.[11]

We need a bold new program of reconciliation. What will it be? The dimensions of such a program must be reckoned by the needs of the hour. Edwin Dahlberg, speaking at a White House Conference on Mutual Aid, called for a program involving giant steps, imaginative daring, and dramatic character:

> We beg you to apply the same bold, creative imagination to the non-military approach to peace that you have already applied to military defense.
> The world is weary and disheartened by the continuing plans for massive retaliation. We yearn for someone to lead in plans for massive reconciliation, on a global scale, and look for the day which we believe to be at hand now, when all of America's great wealth, resources, and power shall be dedicated to that end.[12]

What will be the characteristics of a program of massive reconciliation and how shall the Brethren participate in it?

1. It will begin with repentance. There is no hope for our ministry of reconciliation until we see our own self-righteousness. Brethren have tended to give absolute devotion to "our" causes, values, ordinances, and Biblical interpretations. We have elevated certain ideas, rites, and forms of worship to the stultifying creedal level. This is a violation of one of our basic tenets — no creed, but openness for new light. Our fellowship has been a bit exclusive, whereas the gospel is for all. We have been unconcerned about racial and social injustices. Our mission and service programs are continuously crippled by lack of financial resources; meanwhile we lust after longer, lower, and wider cars, after

---

[11] Ira Frantz, in the *Brethren Adult Quarterly,* April to June, 1958, page 124.
[12] *Why Christians Support Mutual Aid and Reciprocal Trade* (New York: Department of International Affairs of the National Council of Churches, April 21, 1958), page 2.

kitchen gadgetry, after more luxurious homes, after the things that our misused money will buy. God, have mercy upon us!

2. It will be evangelistic. Evangelism seeks to bring all men under the Lordship of Christ. This will be "Operation No. 1" in the life of the church. It is inevitable if Brethren take seriously the Great Commission and believe that the gospel is for all men.

We Brethren have been very timid. For two hundred fifty years, reconciliation and peacemaking have been the core of our faith. The world needs reconciliation more than it needs anything else. Now is the hour for us to proclaim it daringly and lovingly. Rise up, Brethren! Have done with lesser things.

3. It will be a costly program. Of course, it will involve a vastly increased financial program. Next year our budget ought to surpass the goal, and we must look forward to even greater increases in subsequent years if we are to give as God has prospered us. The greater costs, however, are in nonfinancial matters. The reconciling love of God is costly — to Him. Reconciliation is always costly. Many of our reconciliatory efforts fall short because they do not go far enough and do not cost enough in terms of sacrifice and suffering. Mack and others "counted the cost," and then proceeded. It was not too costly for Mack to give away his material possessions to help the needy, or to run the risk of death to perform baptism in accordance with Bible instructions. Christian Liebe suffered imprisonment and servitude in the galley ships. John Naas hung by his thumb and toe. Christopher Sauer's printshop was confiscated.

Massive reconciliation will be a most costly enterprise. It may involve suffering, humiliation, and lost prestige and property. It may mean foregoing many of the privileges we now enjoy. It will surely mean sharing, first until it hurts, and then until it becomes a joyous experience.

Our service program has made a significant beginning, but . . . the fact remains that we still live in luxurious homes, eating until we are overweight, driving shiny, highpowered automobiles, and worshiping in finer and finer churches with carpeted floors and cushioned pews while people in India and China die of hunger and Koreans have been reduced by war's ravages to such depths of poverty, filth, and disease as are beyond our imagination.[13]

Massive reconciliation calls for something vastly more costly than what we have done to the present time.

4. The church must become a reconciling community. By the providence of God the Church of the Brethren has had an opportunity to help heal the breach between a nationally known criminal and society. This is precisely what we ought to do — a thousand times a year. Every church ought to be engaged in such reconciliatory work.

There are few communities which do not have alcoholics, the mentally ill, moral deviants, parolees, or prisoners who desperately need the supporting power of a loving fellowship which will accept them as people and offer them unlimited forgiveness when they fail or flounder. Alcoholics Anonymous is working well and joyously at this task. Some churches are making significant strides in this ministry. May their tribe increase! Every church ought to be a "bureau of reclamation."

Nearly every community or church has within it some people or groups who are at odds. Positive ill will and hatred exist. This is the hour for massive reconciliation — first in our own churches; then we will become fit vessels for the larger work of reconciliation in our world.

The world needs bridges. We ought to be bridge builders. The church must cross racial, social, national, and economic barriers or it is not the church. When will the Church of the Brethren stay in a community and provide the reconciling leaven as people of other races and strata move in? When will the Brethren be truly Brethren?

5. The church must be one church. There is only one church — the church of Jesus Christ. To speak of "churches" or of "our church" is to speak in error. A divided church is a contradiction; it cannot be a reconciling church.

---

[13] Ira Frantz, *op. cit.*, page 125.

Let the Church of the Brethren become a reconciling church, bridging the breaches which separate Christian from Christian. This may mean the end of denominations; it may lead to organic union. Surely it means the end of competitive denominationalism and divisive sectarianism. Our ministry lays this ecumenical task upon us — to reconcile all children of God into one universal fellowship of Christ. Whether it succeeds is never the issue; whether it is right is! We are to seek to reconcile, regardless! Reconciliation on an ecumenical level will be costly. Some of our love for peripheral matters, for form and ceremony, must be done away with. It will cost this for us and other groups. But let it be said unequivocally: *no one will have to give up anything that is part of the gospel of Jesus Christ,* though any peripheral concern must suffer castigation and be reduced to proper size. Overemphasis of one doctrine, rite, or form distorts the gospel and gives rise to divisive denominationalism.

6. It will be a service program. John Oxenham's insight is right: "His service is the golden cord, close binding all mankind." Service in Christ's spirit is a work of reconciliation.

Cups of cold water, relief goods, heifers — these must be given in increasing measure to meet the physical needs of the dispossessed. Food continues to be the primary problem of our planet. The cries of hungry children will haunt us who claim to be our brother's keeper. We will share, not only our surpluses, but also economic aid, capital funds, and technical skills so that these people can be both self-supporting and self-respecting. Such aid ought to be prompted, not by our desire to win political friends and advantages over our enemies, but by love of people, freedom, peace, and justice. Economic aid ought to be separated from military considerations and enormously expanded. Tariff walls must be lowered and reciprocal trade agreements encouraged. Our student exchange program might be expanded to include teachers, farmers, craftsmen, and technicians in many fields. Brethren Service is a revolutionary innovation with tremendous reconciliatory potentialities. Can it be expanded?

A bold new program of reconciliation must include our active participation in a persistent campaign for justice for the teeming, exploited masses of mankind. Reconciliation has social implications. It involves those issues that breed fear and tension. The inequities suffered by our own Negro citizens symbolize in kind the injustices of people everywhere. We must all work at this where we are: in the South, in sleepy Midwestern towns, and in the great Northern cities. Is your church ready to open its doors and membership to those of all races? Will your church invite Negro families to come and live in your communities — assuming responsibility for housing, living wages, acceptance in the community, and membership in the church?

We ought to awaken public opinion to the folly of our preoccupation with military affairs. Trusting in an obsolete defense network of Distant Early Warning radar stations and the Strategic Air Command is futile. The utter bankruptcy of a foreign policy predicated on military terms, and bristling with threats of "massive retaliation" and statements about the "brink of war," must be exposed. These are *absolutely incompatible* with Jesus' ethics for enemy dealings: love, bless, do good, and pray for those who despitefully use us. One of the surest ways to lose a struggle with a fanatical force is to become fanatic. To be sure, great power blocs do not take God into account; this dare not mean that we must leave Him out and adopt the tactics of the opposition. We can do business with Russia. Fifty thousand people gathered in one spot in England on Easter Day to protest the insanity of the continued testing of nuclear weapons. Now is the time to channel the great discoveries of our age away from the realm of terror into the service of mankind. To be silent when we ought to speak is one of the gravest sins.

V. Conclusion

God raises up men and groups to meet needs which arise. Moses, Abraham, David, Amos, and Paul were called and responded to God's call. Two hundred fifty years ago our church was called into being. It could well be that we were born with this unique emphasis on peacemaking and reconciliation for such a day as this. For two hundred fifty years He has groomed and trained us for this hour when the world needs — more than anything else — the gospel of reconciliation.

The Call which follows our anniversary celebration is not simply a program. It is God's call to help lead the world out of its warring madness, its bondage to bitterness, its brokenness, and its alienation from God and man.

22. THE BRETHREN AND THE ECUMENICAL CHURCH

KURTIS F. NAYLOR

Pastor, Prince of Peace Church of the Brethren, Denver, Colorado; under appointment as Church of the Brethren representative to the World Council of Churches and director of Brethren Service in Europe. Formerly: member, National Youth Cabinet; Brethren Service worker in Ecuador; administrative assistant for Brethren Service in Europe.

"The human symbol of our time is the Outsider. While an unprecedented physical unity marks the world of our time, the human family today is rifted by chasms, unprecedented by their number, their breadth, and their depth. Today in how many ways and in how many spheres of human existence has a man become an outsider! The *refugee* without a country of his own, the *migrant* without a home in his environment, the *negro* segregated in his institutions, the *dweller* in the inner city, are symbols of contemporary man. His life lacks a sense of at-homeness, he is forced in a real sense to live outside the environment of which he may be a physical part.

"It is also true that the average man is becoming strange to himself, a literal 'Outsider' as regards his inner world! How many men do not know themselves. Their life has no real significance; they have no personal sense of vocation; there is nothing in the beyond which beckons them."[1]

---

[1] John A. Mackay, "Eternal Imperative in a World of Change," *Theology Today*, Volume Six, Number 1, page 90. Reprinted by permission of the author and the publisher.

Men today live as spectators in their world, never allowing themselves to be involved in living situations, never becoming committed to great ideas or great causes. Nevertheless, they crave fellowship; they want to be understood; they wish to belong somewhere, to someone, or to something that they have never found.

Elfan Reece of the World Council of Churches recently told of visiting the refugees in the Middle East. In talking with one of the men he asked him, "What would you most like to have?" The man paused a bit and then said, "I would most like to have a key." "A key?" said Dr. Reece in surprise. "Yes," said the man, "a key to a house, that I might have a home."

Tonight the question facing us is: "Do we have a key to give to the men of the world that they might have a home?"

It is just in this situation that we must face the fact that God calls His church, His people, that they might be His ministers to the men of the world. God always calls man in his sin by calling him first in judgment. But God calls man not only in judgment, but in His grace and power in order that!

We, the Church of the Brethren, in this two-hundred-fiftieth anniversary year, are called to expect great things from God. This is the "Day of the Lord." Our time is one of God's springtimes.

We are called to expect a great summons from God rather than to protect ourselves, or to enshrine our heritage, or to harden it into an idol for our own worship. We are not even called here to report to one another how good we are or how well we have done. But we are called here to confess that God —

There is a breath of air moving through the whole body of Christ, here and throughout the world. This is the voice of the Living God, who in judgment, grace, and power is calling to His church in order that the world might believe that Jesus was sent by Him.

As we gather here in this Annual Meeting, it may be necessary that we concern ourselves with program and problems, with the planning and the progress of what we have and are to do. But we must never forget that this concern with our inner life and the outward work of our labor in the "vineyard of God" is to be always in the light of the call of God in order that the world might believe that Jesus is the Christ.

It is in the light of this that I would call our attention to the two passages of Scripture read for us this evening (Genesis 12:1-3, and John 17).

I. God's Call to Abram

God called Abram, and you remember that this summons to leave homeland and kindred and to go out to a land shown him by the Lord follows hard upon the debris of the fallen tower of Babel.

Men had sought in their own strength to build a tower. A tower so high that it would not only reach God, but would in fact be high enough to overshadow God. A tower of such grandeur that it would enable man to replace God and in his own strength and power be the ruler of his own destiny.

Man's pretensions collapsed in ruins before the judgment of God. But it is interesting that as the idolatry of man lay in ruins, then, precisely, came the call of God to Abram. The call of Abram was a call to be a blessing to all the families of the earth. This was a call to oneness not in pretension and human might but to the oneness of blessing and being blessed.

This call to Abram, which we call a covenant, is the golden thread of the Old Testament. The epic of Israel is the account of the winding, halting pilgrimage of the people of God toward their destiny with Him — a destiny of servanthood and obedience. This journey of service and obedience was and is to be the vehicle for God's benediction and guidance, not only for His people, but for all the nations of the world.

The bondage in Egypt, the Exodus, the wandering in the wilderness, the entering of the promised land, the glory of David, the wisdom of Solomon, the magnificence of the Temple, the fall of Jerusalem, the Exile, and the Return are but epics in the hesitant response of Israel to the call to be the servant of God and His instrument of blessing to all the families of the earth.

Over this trek was the constant and steadfast call of God, who, now in judgment against the false righteousness and pretensions of an exclusive nation and now in grace and mercy to go out in power through obedience to His will, continued to speak and labor with His people in the events of history.

II. God's Call to the Church

This covenanting call of God hung over His people. That they sometimes in faith and obedience responded, and sometimes in idolatry and sin rebelled, comes to a focus in an Upper Room. This is the new covenant of God through Christ.

Jesus ate a meal with His disciples. He washed their feet. He gave them the embodiment of Himself in the bread and the wine as the perpetual rations for the journey of faith, to be the mystery of His living presence among them.

It is almost as if it were happening tonight. We can see them leave that Upper Room to wend their way through the silent streets of Jerusalem. Jesus walks with a heavy heart, but with confident steps of trust. The disciples are now animated with expectation and now paralyzed with uncertainty and fear.

They come to the Temple square and cut across its courtyard. They stand in the shadows talking, and there the Lord pours out His heart. "I am the true vine, and my Father is the vinedresser. . . . A new commandment I give to you, that you love one another . . . as I have loved you. . . . When the Spirit of truth comes, He will guide you into all the truth."

The disciples are now silent as they stand in the Temple courtyard in the intimate presence of the Lord and He says, "Let us pray."

This is the neglected prayer of our Lord. Here, as the Lord lifted up His eyes to heaven, we feel the very throb and compassion of His heart pouring forth. We sense here the miracle which is the life of His church. In the "disorder of men we glimpse the order of God." Amidst the threat of impending doom and the despair of men, the prayer of God comes clear and sharp: "That we may be one, even as God the Father and Christ are one, that the world may believe that He is the Christ." This is no prayer for grandeur and greatness in the church, but a prayer for the greatness of God's mission to the whole world.

William Temple has called the ecumenical movement the great new fact of our time. Our text for this evening guards us from seeing this as but an ideal or a dream of men. What we are dealing with here is the prayer of God, the divine reality of the living God. The churches in the community of God are not called to oneness in answer to a wishful dream of men. God's judgment has shattered these empty illusions with the tumbling down of the towers of Babel all across the landscape of the world. God has not abandoned us to those brief rapturous moments and lofty moods that come over us like a dream. God hates visionary dreaming; it makes the dreamer proud and pretentious. If we fashion a visionary dream of our own ideal of the united church, we sooner or later demand that it be realized by God, by others, and by ourselves. We enter the presence of God and the fellowship with our demands, with our jaws set, and judge the Brethren and God himself accordingly.

The Lord prayed that we might be filled with joy. Since God has already laid the only foundation for our fellowship, we have joy because He has bound us together in one body with other Christians in Jesus Christ, long before we ever enter into common life with them. We enter into that common life not as demanders, but as thankful recipients. This is our joy in that we thank God for what He has done for us in giving us our brethren in the other churches who also live by His call. Here is our gratitude for what God has given to us in the others as a sign to us of His richness and grace.

We ought never to enter a service of worship either in Annual Conference or at home in our own congregations but that we breathe a prayer of joy for the richness of God's worship in the ritual of silence which is a Friends' Meeting or for the glory of prayer, vestment, and liturgy which is the Episcopal or Orthodox service. The first order for us as we seek to make halting steps in obedience to God in oneness that the world might believe is joyful thanksgiving for our brethren in the other churches.

Second, Christ did not pray that we might be taken out of the world. We must see our divisions and consider the problems created by them against the background of the paganism of the unconverted whether overseas or in our own country. At every turn our divisions hinder our service. They blunt our appeal to the general public at home and abroad.

The fundamental anomaly of our day is that any two disciples of our Lord should not be in communion with one another. We are so used to this state of things that we seldom pause to appreciate its gravity. We fail to see that it makes a mockery of the very prayer of our Lord.

We are one not because it is "nice to be together," but because we are intimately related to Christ. The basis of all spiritual reality is the clear, manifest Word of God in Jesus Christ. The community of the Spirit is the fellowship of those who are called by Christ; and the brightness of our light is the shining rays of God's love in that while we were yet sinners He loved us.

The world yearns and groans for genuine community. But, with all our yearning, our towers of Babel lie in ruin and the tumbling minarets of our dreams have crashed around us in chaos and confusion.

In this very situation, as the call came to Abram so the call comes to the church to answer the prayer of her Lord that we might be one as He is one with the Father, that the world might believe that He is the Christ.

The unity of the church is essential to the complete discharge of her commission. She is called to give witness to the one God and to provide universal fellowship for all mankind. Plainly we cannot do either of these things effectively if we are divided and therefore fail to be ourselves in the fellowship into which we call the various nations and the many sections of the nations.

I recall my first trip into Germany with M. R. Zigler. I shall never forget coming into Ulm. It was one of the first war-scarred cities that I had seen. The desolation of rubble was all around us. We slowly picked our way to the center of the city; there stood the great church spire reaching in majesty to the sky! Brother Zigler turned to me and said, "Kurtis, whenever you see the rubble and the ruin, don't turn away too quickly. You must walk among it, see it, and feel it until you sense the anguish of the people who suffered here and our sin that caused it." Then, characteristically, he added, "But do not despair. Always look up for the message of God."

Christ not only stood in the Temple courtyard of Jerusalem lifting His eyes to Heaven in prayer, but He stands in the courtyards of this Conference and in the courtyards of all our congregations in prayer. The message from God to His church is in the prayer of His Son our Lord that we might be one as they are one. We are not to pray to be taken out of the world, but that as the Father is in Christ and Christ is in the Father we may be in Him that the world might believe that He is the Christ.

We are called to be consecrated in truth. This truth is in the Living Word of God, who walked among us and who dwells with us in glory. We are the heralds of God's good news. This fact has no primary place for the preaching of judgment save it be seasoned and flavored with grace. What we have to say about the seriousness of the human situation is but the prelude to our speaking the saving word to our fellow men. What we preach is the gospel of salvation wrought out in the Christ-Event. This has introduced a new situation between God, the world, and the adversary, and has placed the destiny of man on a new footing. Every reality in the world and in history is in some way related to this central event and relative to this absolute point of reference.

Dr. Visser 't Hooft, the secretary of the World Council of

Churches, has brought into focus the well-known vision of Ezekiel concerning the dry bones. Ezekiel sees the bones coming together. They are again covered with sinews and flesh and skin. But that is not sufficient, for there is not breath in them. Unity by itself is nothing; it may even mean death. It is only when the breath of God comes upon the bones that "the whole house of Israel is truly gathered and united. Unity in the Biblical sense is God given, which means new life.

On the night before His crucifixion our Lord prayed that the plan of God may be brought to its consummation in the glory of the new creation. Now it has often been suggested that this profound unity is to be understood only as a spiritual and invisible unity. But this is to deny the very evidence of the text. This unity is to be visible that the world might be convinced.

It has become fashionable to criticize proposals for union as merely something called pragmatic. This kind of thinking must be sharply challenged. Certainly a desire for unity which subordinates truth to administrative convenience, or a unity to build a bulwark against Roman Catholicism or to rival the pomp and power of the nation states, or a unity that ignores the convictions, treasures, and traditions of our various families of God is something other than that which the Holy Spirit produces. But to call pragmatic consideration as something other than the divine prayer is to miss the real point. We are called to unity for a very practical reason — that the world might believe that Jesus is the Christ. This is not the manipulation of men, but it is the very call of God. Our Lord's prayer binds us in the church and the churches unmistakably to God and His relation to the world.

The unity of the church is the sign and instrument of the salvation which Christ has wrought. In so far as a church exists in separation from the other members of the body of Christ, this is a contradiction of the gospel; and we stand before the world convicted of living in sin and of having submitted ourselves to some partial emphasis of the faith rather than to the whole counsel of God.

There is one Lord, one faith, one atoning act, and one baptism by which we are made participators in the glory of God. In so far as we, who profess to share that faith and that glory, that atonement and that baptism, fail to agree and come together in one body, we publicly proclaim our disbelief in the sufficiency of that atonement.

Therefore the world does not believe because even in the church it does not see the power of the atonement so real and so meaningful that all mankind in all its infinite variety and contradiction can find there its lost unity.

To say that the church must be one is to return to the prayer of our Lord in answering obedience. We are drawn together by the work of the living Holy Spirit so that we cannot but recognize Christ in one another.

To face one another in Christ is to face the ultimate secret of the church's life, which is life-through-death in Christ. "For whoever would save his life will lose it; and whoever loses his life for my sake, he will save it" (Luke 9:24).

We believe in the power of God to bring forth new life. It is in Christ that we will find our fractured ideas and broken life reknit into His body and quickened by His living blood in the resurrection which is from God.

We cannot confront the world with the call to be reconciled except that we, in the church, first of all become one in our reconciliation in Him.

It is in the hard stubbornness of the world that the church is turned again to the source of her power and the fountain of her life, which is God in Christ.

III. God's Call to the Brethren Today

Happily this Biblical doctrine is also close to the very origin of the Church of the Brethren. It is part of the thinking of Alexander Mack. Mack differed with Hochmann on this very point. In the little village of Schwarzenau, with all the discussion and the eddying currents of spirit that flowed in and out of the windy streets, Mack after careful study of the Scriptures came to feel that there must be some visible embodiment of the body of Christ in a living church. The unity of the persons in Schwarzenau was to be in Christ made real in Bible study, in the ordinances, and in the mission of the church to the world in brotherly obedience.

I am confident that a sincere and honest acceptance on the part of the churches of the obligation to bring the gospel to every creature will lead us to reassess our unhappy divisions and cause us to take seriously the very great danger we are in by them.

God is again meeting His people in the hard facts of our situation in the world. This is just as He met Abram in the rubble and ruin of the tower of Babel. We are not here dealing with only a matter of theological discussion but with the very mission of the church. We are called to come in answering obedience to the prayer of our Lord.

Our task in this anniversary year of the Church of the Brethren is threefold. First, we must call the church to a new acceptance of her missionary task to the whole world. Secondly, in obedient answer to the prayer of our Lord we must do everything in our power to extend the areas of co-operation between all Christians in the fulfillment of that task by seeking to draw all into fellowship with Him and through Him, being united each to the other. And, third, we must see that it is time for the Church of the Brethren to press with all vigor the necessary steps, the encounter, and the discussion leading to full organic and visible union with some other church in the family of God, so that the day may be hastened when all the family of God shall be united in Him, that the glory which was given in the Son may be given to us, that we may be one even as the Father and the Son are one in order that the world might believe that Jesus Christ was sent from God. Is the time not ripe for us to take this bold and adventuresome step in obedience to the call of God and the very prayer of our Lord?

We ought to go forth in the full confidence that this is the call of God — to get out of the arid confines and the "Egyptian bondage" of our own smallness to wander in the wilderness preparatory to entering the promised land of God's covenant. Short of such a leap of faith in obedience, we can in no wise expect that a needy and hesitant world will believe.

This is the key to the house that mankind might indeed have a home, which, please God, will be but the preparation for the mansion of life eternal.

23. THE BRETHREN AND THEIR INTERPRETATION OF HISTORY

WARREN F. GROFF

Associate professor of Christian theology, Bethany Biblical Seminary; minister; lecturer; writer. Formerly: pastor, Beech Run church, Pennsylvania; assistant in instruction, Yale Divinity School; associate professor of religion, Bridgewater College.

In this anniversary year, when we are being reminded of the happenings and the inner meanings that are vital in our community's experience, it is especially fitting that we should raise the question: "Where did the early Brethren stand and where are we today in the understanding of history's ultimate origin, meaning, and direction?"

For the most part, our Brethren forefathers did not deal directly with this matter. One looks in vain for a systematic discussion of the interpretation of history in the writings of Alexander Mack. He does approach the question of the "end" of history directly at a few places, notably in *Rites and Ordinances (Rights and Ordinances)* in connection with a discussion of the reward of believers and the judgment of unbelievers. This topic comes up again in his work entitled *Ground-Searching Questions (Basic Questions)*.

However, the scarcity of direct references does not mean that the Brethren lacked an interpretation of history. Mack's treatment of other themes in the works mentioned presupposes a reading of history. His well-known comments regarding "universal salvation"—to which we shall return later in this presentation — are part of a larger scheme of interpretation which is at least implicit throughout. History includes those happenings that are remembered because of their creative effect upon persons in community. A pattern of interpretation is implied in the way people respond to meaningful events in concrete life if not in systematic statement. It is apparent that the Brethren saw themselves as sharing in the dramatic and decisive "Event of Christ," to which the New Testament principally bears witness. Therefore, in their testimonies to what this Event has done and meant for their life in community they give expression to an interpretation of history which, as we shall see, stands firmly within the Biblical perspective.

Our task here is to set forth and evaluate some of the major themes in that pattern of interpretation which is implied and presupposed throughout their life and thought if not directly stated by the early Brethren. We shall then raise the question as to where we stand today in the reading of history.

I. The Chief Clue

Jesus Christ is the chief clue to the meaning and direction of history. The early Brethren stand with the New Testament witnesses in testifying that the cluster of events connected with Jesus of Nazareth, the "anointed" of God, has had a unique impact upon life. This segment of history illuminates the rest. Jesus Christ has changed the way we look at life. Because of His coming we understand more fully what we ought to be and what, by God's grace, we may become. His exemplary life, His authoritative teachings, His sacrificial death, and His victorious resurrection constitute the "center" of history in the light of which "beginning" and "end" become evident. His coming, as Alexander Mack would put it, has brought into history a dramatic and decisive call for a life of loving obedience to God, symbolized in the deepest instance by water-baptism.[1] It is to Jesus Christ that

---

[1] See Alexander Mack, *Rites and Ordinances,* especially the section entitled "Water-baptism" (quotes from the edition of 1888, by the Brethren Publishing House).

we turn for primary insight into history's dynamic, pattern, and goal.

II. Personal, Purposeful, and Providential

When Jesus Christ serves as our primary clue, history is seen as personal, purposeful, and providential.

History is personal. The Brethren would agree with the over-all Biblical view that historical events are not simply the result of blind fate. They are bounded by the intention, ordering, and continuing activity of God, the sovereign Lord. It is He who gives history its deeply personal nature. It is He who is the Creator of all. It is He whose power and glory are mirrored in nature, the setting for life in community under God's sovereign rule. It is He whose reality and work declare that man is not simply a "cosmic orphan" but a creature with a noble destiny. It is He who has made man "in his image" and has given him dominion over the works of His hands. It is He who has created man with a persistent restlessness until he finds his rest in the One in whom he lives and moves and has his being. It is He who has taken the initiative in calling into being a "covenant people" and in sending His Son into the world to fulfill that "covenant." History, thus, is not the more or less mechanical outworking of an impersonal process, but fundamentally a drama in which the God of Abraham, Isaac, and Jacob, the God and Father of our Lord Jesus Christ, is the chief agent. History is personal, for in the beginning is God!

History is purposeful. In and through Jesus Christ, the inaugurator of the "new covenant," as in His preparatory work in calling out the nation of Israel to be His "covenant people," God has declared His interest in and pattern for history. As understood by the Biblical witnesses and the early Brethren, history is purposeful as the arena of divine-human encounter. That which basically gives meaning to historical events is the coming of God to man. The concrete involvement of God in history reaches its climax in the Incarnation, whereby God personally enters life.

In the specific and perfect manhood of Jesus of Nazareth, He reveals the quality of life that history is to manifest: life in loving obedience to the sovereign Lord. History is purposeful, for in the center is Jesus Christ, who, in His life of radical obedience, reveals the pattern for all of life!

History is providential. Purpose is revealed dramatically in the "Event of Christ" at the center of history. But even as purpose implies the One who is the initiator of purpose, the God who is in the beginning, so it points to the fulfillment of purpose, the end of history. For this reason, a view of history that stresses purpose is inevitably eschatological, i.e., concerned with end, or fulfillment.

Quite clearly, the Brethren would share the conviction of the New Testament community that history is not simply a wearisome cycle without beginning and end. The mood of the writer of Ecclesiastes basically would be foreign to them when he argues:
"What has been is what will be,
    and what has been done is what will be done;
    and there is nothing new under the sun."[2]
On the contrary, history not only has dynamic and meaning but also direction. History has a destination and does not simply repeat itself or come to the end of the line. This is so because the God who is the Creator, who has acted in the coming of Christ, is acting still and will act in bringing history to its fulfillment. God has acted in sending His Son into the world to live, minister, and even die so as to deepen and purify His "covenant" with man.

But this is not the whole of the Biblical proclamation, which so clearly informs the early Brethren. The Christ who lived, taught, healed, died, and rose from the grave comes again in glory, judgment, and renewal. The note of eager expectancy regarding the near return of Christ is found again and again in the New Testament. *Maranatha* — or, "Lord Jesus, come! Thy

---
[2] Ecclesiastes 1:9.

kingdom come!" was the earnest prayer and life orientation of the New Testament participants. The time of God's action, or of Christ's coming, may catch one unprepared, as is illustrated by the man going on a journey without telling the exact hour of his return. The time of God's action in Christ is near, as is typified by the parable of the fig tree and its ripening branches. What is the significance of this claim that Christ comes again? This is saying essentially: "In the beginning God" and "In the end Jesus Christ." History, in other words, has not only its pattern but its end in Jesus Christ. The first coming of Christ is our present clue to what life is all about. The "second coming" points to the fulfillment of God's purpose for history. History is providential, for in the end is the consummation of God's action in Jesus Christ!

In the life orientation and writings of the early Brethren one finds clear evidence of a view of history as personal, purposeful, and providential, even if it is not stated in this particular way. This could be illustrated by reference to the thought of Ernest Christopher Hochmann, a German Pietist who was vitally connected with the early Brethren. It is likewise clear in the thought of Alexander Mack. As he sees it, history has its beginning in the eternal and almighty God, whose sovereign will must be taken into account whatever the topic under consideration: water-baptism, the Lord's supper, excommunication, church divisions, oath-taking, personal examination, love and faith, the external and internal Word, matrimony, worship, the reward of believers, and the judgment upon unbelievers.

Further, Mack finds history's purpose centrally revealed in Jesus Christ. He never tires of emphasizing the need for loving obedience patterned after Jesus Christ, the loving and obedient Son. An oft-quoted sentence from *Rites and Ordinances* illustrates this reading of history's purpose. "It is therefore very good to look wholly and alone to the express words of the Lord Jesus, and to his own perfect example, and to follow that only in obedience with faith and simplicity, and bring every thought into subjection to the Lord Jesus."[3] Here is life as ordered by the sovereign will of God. Here is history's pattern and purpose.

Mack's writings imply that history has providential direction as well as dynamic and purpose. God has not ceased acting. He is even now working toward our sanctification, which is rooted in His eternal intention and is oriented toward the future for its consummation. "Since there is but one God and but one Spirit, this same one Holy Spirit can will nothing less but what his will was many hundred years ago, namely, our sanctification."[4] God the Spirit works as the "internal teacher" who parallels and illuminates the Scripture, which teaches us "externally."[5] Further, God's providence is leading history toward judgment upon unbelievers and the eternal reward of believers. For Mack, then, God's action is not only past, but also present and future. We are living in the transition period between Christ's "first" and "second" comings. But this does not mean that elaborate schemes regarding the "end of the age" are possible or necessary. The early Brethren took the caution of the New Testament: "But of that day or that hour no one knows, not even the angels in heaven, nor the Son, but only the Father. Take heed, watch."[6]

III. Divine Judgment and Renewal

We have already touched upon a third basic theme in the interpretation of history which, we are urging, is at least implied in the life and thought of the early Brethren, informed as they were by the Biblical proclamation: History as the drama of man's encounter with God reveals the ever-present realities of judgment and renewal. God's coming action in Jesus Christ involves a *no* in relation to all false values, demonic powers, and wrong decisions. And yet the sovereignty of God's love offers an even more fundamental *yes* relative to all creatures. God judges, but His

---
[3] Mack, *op. cit.*, page 61.
[4] *Ibid.*, page 50.
[5] *Ibid.*, especially the section entitled "Of the Internal and External Word."
[6] Mark 13:32-33a.

judgment is redemptive. He "plucks up and breaks down, destroys and overthrows," but He also "builds and plants."

In Hochmann's *Confession,* which was widely known and endorsed by the eighteenth-century Brethren, we find a recognition of this two-sidedness of God's work. On the one hand, Hochmann writes:

> I have been infallibly convinced from God's Word that the glorious Christ sitting at the Father's right hand will soon break in and will thrust all the heathen powers from their seat. . . . And now because the Kingdom of Christ is so near at hand, I confess that . . . I have learned from God's Word to reflect more upon the rising sun of justice than upon the high powers of the world soon to depart; for that will last into the eternity of eternities, but these will soon have reached the limit, by the great impending judgments of God.

Convinced as he is of the sovereignty of God's love, on the other hand, Hochmann confesses: "As in Adam all men have fallen, so also must all men be born again, through the other Adam, Jesus Christ; if this were not so, it would necessarily follow that Christ were not powerful enough to restore the human race. . . ."[7]

Renkewitz, the learnéd biographer of Hochmann, describes this twofold theme of judgment and renewal in Hochmann's preaching even further. Christ's coming action, already breaking in upon history, is viewed as the approaching "day of wrath." Still, the deepest reality is God's love, which Hochmann describes with such words as *ocean* and *abyss*. In fact, God's sovereign love is fully itself only as all wayward creatures finally are brought back to the One who created and nurtured them.[8]

Alexander Mack shared basically this view of Hochmann. He speaks, on the one hand, of the imminent judgment upon unbelievers. Their state is tragic. "When they consider all things, how they did not love God as the chief good, and thereby have forfeited all that great salvation, then such a torrent of pain and misery will overwhelm them, which no tongue can express.

---

[7] Quoted in M. G. Brumbaugh, *History of the German Baptist Brethren in Europe and America* (Elgin: Brethren Publishing House, 1899), page 83ff.

[8] Heinz Renkewitz, *Hochmann von Hochenau,* especially pages 375-382.

For they are banished from the presence of the Lord, and from all the saints."[9] On the other hand, Mack's stress upon the reality of blessedness is equally vivid and moving. "Yes, it will make their joy still greater when they shall behold the Lord Jesus in his great glory and majesty, with his many myriads of angels and saints surrounding his throne and singing with great fervor and joy, Hallelujah, so much so that heaven and earth shall be filled with the sound. . . ."[10] Mack manifestly shares the conviction of Hochmann regarding the sovereignty of God's love, for he is unwilling to assert, from his study of the Bible, that the torment of unbelievers is altogether without end. He is cautious, however, in proclaiming a view of the ultimate restoration of all creatures. The reward of the restored unbelievers will never match the reward of those who are obedient to Christ in the time of grace. Further, people are not to put their trust in eventual restitution to the neglect of the call to decision here and now.

As typified in the thought of Hochmann and Mack, the early Brethren reflect a firm hold on two truths that are both deeply rooted in the Biblical witness and in Christian experience: the radical character of human decision in relation to God in Christ and the sovereignty of divine love which yearns for and persistently pursues each wayward child, or the coming of Christ in judgment *and* renewal. They wisely seek to preserve both insights, in spite of the difficulty in getting them together in a coherent system. Their reluctance to proclaim an abstract doctrine of universalism is commendable, for this denies too quickly the radical significance of human decision. But they also validly witness to the sovereignty of God's love, which nurtures and sustains but does not force human response. Are we not all finally dependent upon God's love and gracious action on our behalf? The Apostle Paul writes: "Therefore, since we are justified by faith, we have peace with God through our Lord Jesus Christ. Through him we have obtained

---

[9] Mack, *op. cit.*, page 65.
[10] *Ibid.*, page 64.

access to this grace in which we stand, and we rejoice in our hope of sharing the glory of God."[11] Acknowledging the eternal seriousness of human decision and the mystery of God's sovereign love in relation to man, can our prayerful hope for all mankind be anything less than to share in the glory of God in Christ Jesus?

IV. Where Do We Stand Today?

Where do we stand today as Brethren? In what, fundamentally, is our faith? In the God of Christ's coming, the God whose purpose for history has been made plain in Jesus Christ, the God who even now is at work to bring history to its fulfillment? Do we live so as to acknowledge the sovereign activity of God as the primary power in the world, today and tomorrow? Are we oriented toward life as obedient disciples under the Lordship of Christ? Or have we exchanged the faith of our fathers in God's coming action in Jesus Christ as the goal or "end" of history for a contemporary substitute?

In the Western world the alternatives confronting us have not been either the Biblical view of history's "end" or the total negation of meaning and direction in history. Even if the New Testament eschatology is neglected or repudiated, we have not often been tempted to follow some of the major Oriental religions and philosophies which look upon history as a wearisome repetition of sameness, and which therefore conclude that escape from the tiresome "wheel of existence" is the highest goal of life. Rather, the temptation for us has been to adopt some alternative reading of history's purpose and direction, some alternative view particularly of history's end.

By default, if not by intent, have we perhaps adopted what Halford E. Luccock, in commenting on Mark 13 in the *Interpreter's Bible*, calls the modern American's secular apocalypse?

He looks for a world of wonders which science and industry will provide. He has exchanged his august faith in God's coming action for a faith in the kind of plastic heaven that comes out of a factory. We are

---
[11] Romans 5:1-2.

kept in a state of nervous excitement with prophecies of the world of tomorrow, a paradise of chromium and ceramics, of helicopters and television, of egg-shaped automobiles and layer cake houses, of skyscrapers of glass and clothing made of soy beans! What a trade! Heaven for earth, the coming of Christ in the life of the world for the coming of a salesman's paradise.[12]

Are we really oriented toward God's coming action in Jesus Christ or, to mention a related idolatrous substitute, is our faith most deeply in the might and power of our own hand? The Book of Deuteronomy records the recurrent temptation that goes along with technological progress. The Israelites have come out of the desert into the relatively rich land of Palestine. They have begun to amass wealth and land. Now they face the peril of self-deifying pride. Since their stomachs are full and they are surrounded with bountiful possessions, hitherto-undreamed-of comforts and gadgets, they face the temptation to assert baldly: "We have gained this by our own industry and good sense." They are warned by a sensitive writer in the seventh century B.C.: "Beware lest you say in your heart, 'My power and the might of my hand have gotten me this wealth.'"[13] As Brethren in the midst of a culture marked by the greatest prosperity and technical advance to be found anywhere in human experience, where ultimately is our faith? In the God of Christ's coming? Or in the power and might of our own hand?

Have we as Brethren adopted the idolatrous substitute of our own righteousness and program of good works? The Israelites in coming into the rich heritage of Palestine also are warned by the Deuteronomist against saying: "It is because of my righteousness that the Lord has brought me in to possess this land." In this anniversary year, as we rejoice in the rich heritage that has come to us, is our faith fundamentally in the God of Christ's coming, who ever judges even as He renews? Or is it even more in our own righteousness and goodness?

---

[12] Halford E. Luccock, in the *Interpreter's Bible* (Nashville: Abingdon Press), Volume VII, page 863f.
[13] Deuteronomy 8:17.

Let us penitently, obediently, and expectantly dedicate ourselves to the God of Christ's coming. Let us open ourselves to the coming of that day when we shall behold the Lord Jesus in His glorified humanity. Contrary to what might be expected, such an orientation toward the future does not make us indifferent regarding the present. Given this penitent, obedient, and expectant openness to God's action in Jesus Christ, action that is not only past but present and future, we shall find ourselves less timid and half-hearted in our evangelism, less fearful and defensive in our ecumenical conversations, less preoccupied and anxious about our own survival, less complacent and accommodating in the midst of a pagan culture, less susceptible to the twin perils of legalism and sentimental Pharisaism in our program of good works. Alexander Mack explains the present impact of this future hope in these words: We may be aware even now that in the day of Christ's coming "believers will wonder why they themselves, while in this world were not more willing to give body, life and all they had, out of love to this heavenly King and his holy doctrine."[14]

---

[14] Mack, *op. cit.,* page 64.

24. THE BRETHREN AND BIBLICAL PROCLAMATION

JOHN B. GRIMLEY

Missionary to Nigeria; minister; educator; writer; artist. Formerly: pastor, Pitsburg, Ohio; director of missionary education and recruitment, Brotherhood staff.

Up on the side of Wamdi Mountain in northeastern Nigeria there are several grottoes formed by the way in which gigantic boulders were rolled together in ages long gone by. In these grottoes I viewed the Margi "engagement paintings." They had been done in red ocher on the grey rocks, daubed from the painted bodies of the young men who made the paintings during their engagement ceremonies. In the main they were stick-figure drawings of men and horses and spears — spears of the old iron-shafted and iron-spangled type. According to my guide, a Margi man, these paintings had been made on these rocks from "as far back as men first took wives."

But something new had been added. On the ancient and crumbling rock, also painted with red ocher, some Margi lad had printed J-O-H-N followed by the number *1957!*

Yes, on the crumbling rock of pagan animistic religion and culture a new message had been written — the message of Jesus Christ and His church. My guide reached up and pointed to one of the paintings and said, "That one is mine, the one I painted thirty years ago." That was just about the time that Brother H. Stover Kulp first arrived in Margiland, traveling close by that very mountain.

This Margi man and I sat down in the shade of the great rocks and their paintings. We were held in the spell of the traditions of the years gone by. We fellowshiped together, talking of the virtues of the old and the new; we talked of the vices, too.

On the way down from the mountain we passed several old "god pots." They had been thrown out at the time of their owners' deaths. And I said to my guide, "Do you have one of these in your house?" (Every Margi man must have such a shrine.) Quickly he looked up and answered, "Oh, no! I threw mine out some time ago. I'm a Christian now."

Something new had come into his life. Figuratively speaking, he had already died, died to the pagan way of life. He had thrown out his little "god pot" and had taken in the New Man, the living Lord, Christ Jesus.

Throughout the world something new has been added — the church of Jesus Christ.

When God called Abraham out from the polytheism of his ancient day into the worship of the one God, something new had been added — faith.

When God called Moses out from the degradation of slavery and the pleasures of sin in Egypt into the light of the freedom of man under law, something new had been added — hope.

When God cried out through the prophet Isaiah in the fortieth chapter of that book and mentioned "good news" in just so many words, and for the first time, "O Zion, herald [proclaimer] of good tidings," something new had been added — expectation.

When faith and hope and expectation were united and fulfilled in Jesus of Nazareth, something new had been added — experience! The message of redemption and freedom in Christ had not only come as a new fact in history, but it was also destined to take root quickly in the experience of men.

This message of Christ — the historic fact alive in experience — is the very essence of our Brethren Biblical proclamation.

On the first page of Brother J. E. Miller's book, *The Story of*

Our Church, before "our story" had really begun, we find Alexander Mack and another "on a preaching tour proclaiming the gospel as best they have been able to understand it from long study . . . and full obedience to all New Testament teaching."

Biblical proclamation has been at the very heart of our Brethren life. But not always has that proclamation gone far beyond our own meetinghouses and our own hearthsides. A spirit of openhearted search for the truth which the Brethren had does not lend itself readily to bold proclamation to others. But while the church as a whole was slow to grasp the responsibility of proclaiming the Bible message to outside groups, there were, nevertheless, individuals even during the very early days of our church history in America who had a deep concern at this point.

I am not a historian. I am a proclaimer of the message of Christ to West Africa. But I understand from talking with Brother Austin Cooper, one of our church historians, that even as David Livingston once stood on a high prominence in the heart of Africa and felt his soul stirred by the smoke of a thousand cooking fires, so also Brother George Adam Martin in the early eighteenth century stood on Allegheny Mountain, and, looking down into what is now Brothers Valley, beheld the vast area of the Shawnee Indian nation and saw a vision of proclaiming the message of Christ to the Indians — a vision which apparently was never fulfilled. Likely it was never fulfilled because of the trials of the Revolution and the inexorable rolling west of the wagon wheels. But the spark of "proclamation" was there and the right wind was sure to blow it into flame. Brother Christian Hope and Brother Wilbur Stover and our other early missionaries were that wind, a spirit from the heart of God.

I. Motivation

Today churchmen are trying to define just what the right motive and just what the right strategy for proclaiming the gospel to the world might be.

From the time Wilbur Stover and other young people of

his day persuaded the church of its responsibility to proclaim the gospel to the whole world, the Great Commission has in itself been a great motivating force in our Brethren outreach to the world. It, we believe, expresses the whole intention of the New Testament. "Go into all the world and preach [proclaim] the gospel to the whole creation. He who believes and is baptized will be saved; but he who does not believe will be condemned."

Jesus said, "Go!" What more is needed? It is not possible to disobey, for Jesus said, "If you keep my commandments, you will abide in my love." Paul said, "I was not disobedient to the heavenly vision." He was compelled in obedience to go forth. "Go, and I will be with you!" is a command which cannot easily be ignored. Obedience is strong motivation! And with the present breakdown of disciplines this is to be emphasized.

However, there are other motives to consider. I remember reading, when I was in school, a missionary article which stated that one of the strongest motivating forces of the great nineteenth-century missionary awakening was the belief that those without Christ were lost and bound for hell. The article was suggesting that a new motivation be found since hell had cooled down considerably!

I have chosen to quote the Great Commission as recorded in Mark, not because it is shorter than the Matthew record of it, but because it contains an element which the Matthew record does not contain. "He who believes and is baptized will be saved; but he who does not believe will be condemned."

Now I know that this part of Mark is not in the oldest manuscripts, but nevertheless the mind of Christ and also His specific statements are in total harmony with it. We must remember that it was not Paul who sharpened the sword of God's judgment, but Jesus himself. Jesus not only painted in glowing colors the joys and satisfactions of being in fellowship with God through Him; He also drew out in lurid colors the agony of separation from God.

Jesus said, "I am with you always, to the close of the age."

And He said also, "The Son of man will send his angels, and they will gather out of his kingdom all causes of sin and all evildoers, and throw them into the furnace of fire, there men [men! in the place prepared for the devil and his angels!] will weep and gnash their teeth."

And Peter, who knew from personal experience the deep, ever-forgiving mercy of Christ, nevertheless says, "The day of the Lord will come like a thief, and then the heavens will pass away with a loud noise, and the elements will be dissolved with fire, and the earth and the works that are upon it will be burned up."

It is possible in this hard world that as a retreat from reality we put too great an emphasis on the grand statement which expresses the great mercy of God, "The final judgment of God on all human history and on every human deed is the judgment of the merciful Christ," and slight the fact that Jesus himself taught that this great mercy can be effective only in the lives of those who repent, those who now in this life are delivered "from the dominion of darkness and transferred . . . to the kingdom of his [God's] beloved Son, in whom we have redemption, the forgiveness of sins."

It is not difficult in these days to imagine the heavens passing away and the elements dissolving with tremendous heat! As both Biblical and secular history well illustrate, man has often been the one who himself is the instrument of God in bringing God's judgment to bear.

It has been suggested that man is even now on the verge of sufficient power to bring the terrible prophecy of Peter to fulfillment! Did you read about the theory of one present-day astronomer? His theory is that the exploding stars which have been seen are likely evidence that men on far-distant worlds have reached this explosive era in the passage of their history just a little earlier than we are reaching it!

The judgment of God hangs over us, and not only over us who are "enlightened" and thus the more responsible, but also over all men everywhere. All men are lost without Christ. We can see that plainly enough here in America. But it is more difficult to feel so about those far away. Downstairs is a display crying out, "LOST, 500,000 pagans." From this distance from our responsibility in Nigeria it may not seem very self-evident. But when you are there, the impact is indeed clear that they are now lost in their ignorance, filth, and sin. *Now,* I say. And unless this present condition changes, it will continue, according to Jesus, in terrible consequences in the life to come. The fact that the church is now founded in most countries of the world does not lessen the force of this motivation.

Yet Jesus is filled with boundless compassion and longsuffering, not willing that any should perish!

Compassion on the level of human need is one of the great motivating forces in the proclamation of the gospel. Jesus had compassion upon the multitude and healed them all!

In our church areas abroad the compassionate services of the hospitals, the schools, and the agricultural programs are not hooks upon which to catch the unwary. They are the expression of the compassion of Christ. It is impossible for the church to exist in the presence of the four dread horsemen of ignorance, oppression, famine, and death without responding to them in active service. It is the compassion of Christ which causes missions to continue to serve in Mohammedan lands even though there are no converts and the future looks no better than the past.

As I was leaving Nigeria on furlough I scanned a book by a British author who was searching for the all-inclusive motive for the proclamation of the gospel. He spoke of the state of the lost, the near return of Christ, compassion, and obedience to Christ's command, "Go." Then he said that the deepest motive for Christian expansion today is Christ. I agree with him, for in saying *Christ* we say it all!

One of the greatest threats to the proclamation of the Christian message to the world today is the eclectic tendency to throw all religions, as our Nigerian brethren would say, "into one bag," and to bring them all together in one grand sigh of man in his evolving toward God. This is the thought William Blake expressed when he wrote, "As all men are alike, though infinitely various, so all religions, as all similars, have one source." This is very far from the New Testament teaching that "there is salvation in no one else [but Jesus], for there is no other name under heaven given among men by which we must be saved."

We must resist every attempt to equate Christianity with other religions, whether in relation to source, content, or goal.

However, within the framework of the Christian faith, we must be eclectic. It is not "this *or* that," but "both *and*." Life is complex. Human nature is complex. The Bible presents the human spirit in a great struggle with God — and a great struggle with Satan. Thus there is a great variety of emotion and of religious experience. There is a variety of drives and motivations contained in the Bible and in the Christ of Calvary.

We need the total motivation available in Christ.

We need a keener discomfort in our realizing that those without Christ are lost now and facing a terrible doom. I wish it were not so! It is a terrifying situation. We need a keener discomfort in our contemplation of it.

We need a deeper compassion for those suffering in mind and body, a compassion which will motivate us to use every means in our power — and where our power runs out to bombard the storehouse of God for the power to help all those in need the world around.

We need a greater realization of the urgency of being instruments of God's grace to bring men into the Kingdom of God *before* "the Lord descends from heaven with a cry of command" and closes the door! But I wish we had *that* long to work at it! Many doors have already closed and more are continually threatening to close.

We need a more sincere desire to obey the command of Christ to go into all the world. It is a command which He makes in love for the lost and in love for us. Unless we, the church universal, go, they cannot hear; and without service for Him our own Christian lives must shrivel and die.

II. SHARING AN EXPERIENCE

Now, with all these motives in mind and understanding that they are all bound up in One, Christ Jesus, I would suggest that the deepest motive of all in proclaiming the "good news" to the world is sharing an experience.

In using the expression, *to the world,* I have in mind not only the bush country of Nigeria, where blood still bathes the backs of brown-skinned maidens receiving their tribal markings and where infanticide is practiced and mothers still die in anguish and terror on the birth stone. I have in mind not only the lands of the East and the lands of South Africa, where power struggles too vast for us to contemplate are in progress. I have in mind not only our great neighbor to the south, that for many centuries has been held in darkness by a medieval religion. Nor do I have in mind only the many areas in Europe where great social forces are brewing and throngs of refugees are in dire need.

In using the expression, *all the world,* I have in mind also the "jungles" of America — the Skid Rows, the Little Rocks, the sophisticated suburbias!

And to reach all of these — "the whole creation" — our motivating force is that of sharing an experience, the experience of "Christ in you — Christ in you the hope of glory." Not only your hope of glory, but the hope of the world.

Jesus said, "You are my witnesses." In Acts, again and again the Christians said, "We are witnesses of these things." They in actuality were more than just observers of a historic fact. To those who saw them they must have been exhibits — living exhibits of the risen Christ in personal experience, exhibits of the fact that if "anyone is in Christ he is a new creation." This is clear not from teaching but from observation!

This experience must be shared. The Holy Spirit, who brings

Christ to us and us to Christ, is Christ in us — Christ in experience. He moves us to share this experience with others.

We do not so much have a message to proclaim as an experience to share.

III. Strategy

In sharing this experience of Christ on a worldwide scale, what shall our strategy be? Let us consider just two aspects of our strategy for today in the sharing of this experience. First, ecumenicity. In the deepest spirit of thorough co-operation with our brothers of every Christian group we must work for the winning of the world. In unity, fulfilling the prayer of Christ that we be one, there is strength.

The church abroad is enjoying a great amount of freedom and joy in this respect. But in Nigeria there are instances where the church must drag devitalizing weights! Those who by God's grace brought them into being have often been fearful of their particular identity. Our African brethren have shown absolutely no fear at this point.

Fifty to one hundred years ago the tribes of northeastern Nigeria were being attacked by foreign forces. The tribesmen greatly outnumbered the invaders, but there was no unity. Each village had its own mountain in which to hide, its own peculiar god to which to offer vain offerings. There was no single unifying force available to them. Not even fear bound them together, for they feared each other as much as they feared the enemy. The final result was total subjection.

Those invaders of the past are still present in Nigeria. They are not raiding with the sword and fire, but with political pressures and small informal Koranic classes. The small fast-growing church sees in Christ the unifying force for capturing the land by the sword of the Spirit. Only as we have full freedom in Christ — freedom to co-operate with all Christian groups — can we truly help them in Nigeria, and in every other land, to be victorious in this spiritual struggle. In the freedom of co-operative fellowship we have opportunity to share the special experience of the Brethren.

And the second important aspect of our strategy for today is mobility. Both in the field and in the offices of administration we must be willing and ready to move quickly. The great people movements of the world do not wait until we are ready. The wind blows and we hear its sound! Such movements do not always come when anticipated. But it is most urgent that we are mobile and ready to move into every opportunity as soon as it appears. Set programs, plans, and the "long view" are all swept away by the urgency of the hour.

We read that in the days of Marco Polo, China was ready for a people movement. But the church was struggling with itself — rotten at the heart. It had no experience of Christ to share. The opportunity passed. Mass conversion of China to Christ in that early day might have set a very different pattern for the history of that land.

It is a gracious coincidence which brings the Call program and the two-hundred-fiftieth anniversary of our church together. For we are in need of the Call no matter what our age might happen to be. We are called now to share our experience of Christ in a way we have never done before. The proclaiming of the Biblical message of Christ has cost something; we have our martyrs — both abroad and here at home, men and women who have shared an experience! What has it cost you? What experience do you have to share?

Is the Book of Books to you, as a Brethren, only an ancient manuscript recording historic facts? Or is it a living, soul-searching experience bound into all your life situations, showing you the living Word in the written page?

Are the ethics of Christ for you, as a Brethren, only a goal toward which to strive? Or has His code of honest and high moral conduct become your life experience — Christ ruling even your subconscious?

Is reconciliation to you, as a Brethren, just a "peace" teaching?

Or has it become an experience for you with God and your fellow man?

Is history to you, as a Brethren, just a matter of dusty volumes through which you plod as a beast of nature bound by fate as the beast is bound by instinct? Or is history for you a mysterious and fascinating experience of existence — existence in the Kingdom for such a time as this?

Is Biblical proclamation no more to you, as a Brethren, than a calculated presentation of the facts within the framework of tradition? Or is it an experience of Christ which is radiant and unrestrained, yet which, in dignified fashion, extends to all?

It is most urgent that we share this experience of our living Lord! The link between God and the lost world is you. It is all of us working together now through the Call. Our task is greater now than ever before in the history of the world.

A month ago today, we took the plane at the Kano airport, in Nigeria, to begin our trip home for furlough. As the big four-motor plane lumbered out onto the airstrip for the take-off, I had to wonder about the great ship's ability to fly. The wings, carrying those tremendously heavy motors, seemed to shake and tremble in a most alarming way. The whole plane seemed very cumbersome and unwieldy. But then, suddenly, the power was turned on, and the great airship seemed to come alive! And in a matter of moments, we were air-borne! If the Call program seems cumbersome and unwieldy — if its goals seem beyond our abilities — then the Power needs to be turned on! When the Holy Spirit in Christ Jesus enters our lives, we will come alive, air-borne by the Spirit of God. The impossible will become a reality.

That night, flying over the Sahara Desert, I aroused myself from slumber and looked down. I was amazed to see the lights of some kind of desert installation shining brightly directly below. Each light sent its message up through the Stygian darkness. But each light was in its place in the total pattern of the installation! Individually they shone, but not alone. Each found its fullest meaning in the beautiful pattern of the whole. I do not know what they represented, but I feel that they are a parable of the part which each of us must play in the total program of the Call.

About four in the morning, I again aroused myself and found that dawn was breaking. It was a beautiful sight with the light streaming brilliantly in a long horizontal line from the east through the darkness toward our plane. And suddenly, it was daylight. From seventeen thousand feet up, I looked down and saw the waters of the Mediterranean Sea! Yes, it was there that Day broke upon the world. It broke through eternal darkness almost two thousand years ago. That Light is still shining in darkness and we have the promise that the darkness will not put it out.

As Brethren, proclaiming the good news of Christ, motivated by a vital experience, ecumenical and mobile, let us continue the proclamation of the Word, going into all the world and proclaiming the gospel to the whole creation.

25. THE BRETHREN UNDER THE LORDSHIP OF CHRIST

Paul M. Robinson

President, Bethany Biblical Seminary; president, Church Federation of Greater Chicago; editorial associate, the Pulpit; minister; lecturer; writer; member of the General Brotherhood Board. Formerly: pastor, Ambler, Pennsylvania; pastor, Hagerstown, Maryland; moderator of Annual Conference, 1956.

It is most significant that in this anniversary year we have directed our thought to the Lordship of Jesus Christ. Here we come to the central affirmation of the Christian faith. In a magnificent expression of divine revelation that is both prophecy and praise, the Apostle Paul in writing to the church at Philippi declares of God's Son: "Therefore God has highly exalted him and bestowed on him the name which is above every name, that at the name of Jesus every knee should bow, in heaven and on earth and under the earth, and every tongue confess that Jesus Christ is Lord, to the glory of God the Father" (Philippians 2:9, 10). All the names given to Jesus and all His relationships with His followers seem to find their fullest expression in this one word, *Lord*.

The earliest statement of faith in the New Testament church undoubtedly was the simple clause, "Christ is Lord." Professor Oscar Cullman has stated that "the affirmation that Christ reigns over the whole universe is the historical and dogmatic nucleus of all Christian creeds." After more than nineteen hundred years of Christian experience, and in this two-hundred-fiftieth year of the Church of the Brethren, we can express Christian truth no more profoundly or make no confession more demanding than to say, "Christ is Lord." Christ is greater than all our thought about Him. He not only stands in the center of history but must also be at the heart of our lives. He is the King of kings and the Lord of lords.

The word *Lord* is almost startlingly out of place in our current secular vocabulary. Modern man has been in revolt against the kind of authority which it suggests. He wants to make his own declaration of independence from any obligation beyond his own choosing. His motto is freedom. He believes himself to be the master of his fate and the captain of his soul. Here precisely is the peril of the twentieth century. The undisciplined expression of man's genius may well become his own undoing. Freedom needs a Lord to keep it free. The rightful Lordship of Jesus Christ over the lives of men is written into the constitution of the universe. When men make Christ their Lord, life holds together. When we try to free ourselves from Him, both personal and social life fall apart. If we try to build peace on war or a social order on injustice, truth shouts from the housetop, "You can't do that. 'Except the Lord build the house, they labor in vain who build it.' "

As we read the simple Gospel accounts of the life and ministry of Jesus, we are amazed at the way His authority was accepted by the common man. Without the benefit of all that our theology has taught us about His wondrous birth as the Incarnate Word of God or about His sinless saviorhood, these early disciples were so impressed with His right to be their Master that they called Him Lord.

What was there in this strange itinerant preacher that so compellingly drew men to Himself? He walked by the Sea of Galilee, and the fishermen when they heard the call, "Follow me," dropped everything and followed. He called a tax collector, with a lucrative income, who left behind his chance to make a fortune. Jesus offered no security, only danger. He offered no material gain, but, rather, the loss of all that had always seemed important. But there was something in His personality that held men captive.

The authority of God was in every word that He spoke. For never a man taught as this man taught. The purity of eternal goodness was in His life, for He dared to say, "Which of you convicts me of sin?" and no one could answer Him. Even in His death, when the powers of wickedness had done their worst and He hung dying upon a cross — shamed, disfigured, and defeated — the executioner exclaimed, half in wonder, half in fear, "Truly this man was a son of God!" (Mark 15:39). And on that glorious morning when the disciples hurried to Joseph's lovely garden only to find empty the tomb where they had laid Him, they discovered what the whole world has rejoiced to know — that He was now the Lord of death and life. If Jesus needed any further demonstration of His right to be their Lord, His resurrected presence so strongly convinced them that they cared nothing now but to witness to His transforming power.

The church, therefore, became a resurrection society. Daily the drama of death and new life was re-enacted in those who became His followers. The first disciples were not much interested in formulating statements of belief or dogma. They simply said, "Come and see. We are witnesses." It was the living Lord, whose Word was not confined to the pages of a leatherbound book but which was let loose in the world like a two-edged sword, that became their authority. It was not a set of purposes, not a system of ethics, not even a closely knit fellowship, but a living person.

A. E. Taylor, a discerning writer of the twentieth century, in *The Faith of a Moralist* goes so far as to say, "The disciples accepted the Lordship of Christ because they were first convinced that they had in themselves the actual experience of a new kind of life with God at the center." Here was One who not only opened to them new doors of truth, but who satisfied the deepest hungers of their souls. He touched their lives and they were whole. This has much to say to the Brethren in this moment of our history: "Be a church of the resurrection." The church is an imperfect, sinning society, to be sure. But if it is anything, it is a fellowship of those who have through confession and forgiveness encountered the living Lord and have found in Him new life.

So Christians in every generation have come to accept the authority of Jesus for their lives, because they have found in Him the way, the truth, and the life. He is the Alpha and the Omega, the beginning and the end. In Him all things cohere. When He is Master, life finds its truest meaning. Paul Tillich has put it this way: "Even the greatest power and wisdom could not more fully reveal the heart of God and the heart of man than the Crucified has already done. These things have been revealed once for all. In the fact of the living Lord we discover the true reality of God."

When a person was baptized into the church in apostolic days he was asked to make the simple declaration, "Jesus Christ is Lord." This was not so much a confession of faith as a pledge of allegiance. A lord is one to whom another belongs. *Lord* is the word that is used to the master by the slave. To say then that Christ is Lord means simply that our lives are in His hands. We are no longer our own. We belong to Him.

This is the beginning of discipleship, but it is only the beginning. It is not enough simply to say, "Christ is Lord." It is possible for us to declare our loyalty to Christ with our lips but to be utterly lacking in the testimony of life which bears witness to His control. Jesus himself declares that "not every one who says . . . 'Lord, Lord,' shall enter the kingdom of heaven, but he who does the will of my Father who is in heaven [Matthew 7:21]. Why do you call me 'Lord, Lord,' and not do what I tell you? [Luke 6:46]. You call me bread and eat me not; you call me the way and walk me not; you call me the truth and believe me not; you call me master, and obey me not. If I condemn you, blame me not." True discipleship means simple but absolute obedience to Him whom we own as Master. We have faith enough to follow wherever He leads us, for, as Emil Brunner has declared, "faith is obedience." Unless all that we say we believe about Christ ends in our serving Him, it is not real faith.

It is interesting to note that the early disciples never argued this point. They simply accepted it. Becoming a Christian meant surrender to Jesus Christ. In a day when Christianity meant many other things, Alexander Mack and the small band of earnest seekers after truth in Schwarzenau restored this basic principle to the heart of their spiritual pilgrimage. For the Brethren, Christianity has always been discipleship. The primacy of this fact has influenced the life of the church beyond measure. Across these two and one-half centuries of our existence, we have not been very articulate in setting forth what we believe in any kind of systematic statement. But like the first-century disciples, we would rather say, "Come and see. We will show you what we believe by what we do."

The concern for obedience has also had a marked effect upon the rites and the ordinances of the church. We have endeavored to follow literally His commandments in symbolic acts which demonstrate important spiritual relationships. So, even though the physical act has all but lost its relevance to everyday experience, we still want to wash one another's feet because Jesus said, "You call me Teacher and Lord; and you are right, for so I am. If I then, your Lord and Teacher, have washed your feet, you also ought to wash one another's feet" (John 13:13, 14). But we know that obedience must go beyond the literal fulfillment of outward observance. We must have the spirit of Jesus in our obedience. We must recognize that when we rightly insist upon the validity of the symbolism of outward forms, whatever they may be, we also stand in the peril of losing the meaning of that which is symbolized. The literal observance of an outward rite is one of the easiest ways to get Jesus off our hands. We may try to fulfill the obligations of spiritual obedience with a ritual, which is much easier. So at the Lord's table we may break bread with our brother in obedience to Christ without feeling any love for him at all. Or we may wash his feet with proud and unyielding hearts or even with a spirit of detached disdain which makes the service a mockery. We make Jesus Lord not through any ritual or even by any confession, but through surrender and obedience.

This relationship with Jesus Christ which accepts His Lordship over life therefore becomes a highly personal concern. It is not enough for us to belong to a corporation which is called by Christ's name or to a fellowship that has acknowledged His Lordship. Every Christian in a most personal and intimate way must declare in his own life as well as in word, "Thou art my Lord." The people of God must in the very truest sense become Christ's men and women.

Our churches are filled with people who have not really faced up to the ultimate demands for surrender which Christ lays upon His followers. They know the gospel. They try to live decent Christian lives. They have a high sense of moral responsibility. But they have missed the heart of what being a Christian really means. They have never given up the direction of their own lives. They have never confessed the spiritual bankruptcy of life without Christ, or through death to self have never been raised to newness of life in Him.

I must confess that I have been greatly disturbed about the large number of inactive members on our church roles. It seems to me that we are neither honest with ourselves nor with the host of nominal but unparticipating church members who pad our statistics when we continue to regard those who obviously have no vital relationship with either Christ or His church as members of His body. There is no such thing as an inactive Christian; nor is the church a refrigerator for the stored piety of the saints. I cannot help but feel that we have spent too much time at this Annual Conference discussing the forms by which we observe our faith, and not enough in consideration of their true meaning. The real problem in the church is not so much how people are baptized, but that too often nothing seems to happen when they are baptized. If the Church of the Brethren is to meet the challenge of this hour, we must call our congregations to penitence for the perilously casual response we have given to His demands and lay upon every member of every local church in this historic year the solemn understanding of what it really means to be a Christian.

One of the thrilling and challenging aspects of the Anniversary Call is that it confronts us all not only with the need of good stewardship of money to extend Christ's Kingdom but also first with the basic commitment of self, after which our gifts come naturally. Dostoevski, in his book that has had a current revival of interest, *The Brothers Karamozov,* has one of his characters say of his religious experience, "An encounter took place. A commitment was made." This is exactly what it takes to make Christ Lord.

But lest the Lordship of Christ over the lives of His followers appears to be a burdensome or cheerless relationship, we should quickly understand that, paradoxically, through this surrender we find our greatest joy. In the parable of Jesus, the merchant who was seeking the perfect pearl did not utter a sigh of disappointment when he found it, because of its great cost; he gladly traded all he had to possess it. A young man standing before the marriage altar to be joined to the one whom love has made dearer than his own life does not come reluctantly to this new relationship because it means he is surrendering his freedom as a bachelor to go out with whom he chooses where he pleases. His devotion to his beloved brings a joy far greater than the price he pays to make her his wife. He makes a new commitment gladly because he has won her heart and he loves her. In this love and through this commitment he finds a joy and a freedom beyond anything he has ever experienced without her. Christ does not impose His Lordship upon us. He loves us and wins us by His love. We make Him Lord because we love Him; and we discover that in this surrender we find our truest freedom and our greatest joy.

As Jesus Christ is Lord of each of His followers, He is the Lord also of the fellowship of those who believe in His name — the church. He not only wants to be the Lord of the church; He *is* the Lord of the church. The church is His body and His bride. Without His Lordship, the church ceases to be the church. A son may deny his father and may live in a way that does not recognize his parent's fatherhood. This does not for a moment alter their physical relationship. So, the members of the visible church may not always live as the true sons of God and may even deny their Lord, but the fact of His Lordship remains. We need, on this significant occasion and every day, to acknowledge His Lordship in such a way that the church fulfills her destiny as Christ controls her life.

Now when I speak of the church, I am thinking of the one true church, holy, universal, and apostolic, of which we in the Church of the Brethren are a part. Christ has no unique Lordship over the Church of the Brethren. He is the Lord of the whole church. May God grant that our uniqueness may be that in the fellowship of the Brethren He shall in all things have the preeminence.

We have in these days together been evaluating our heritage. How grateful we must be for the eternal truths which have been interpreted to us through God's prophets among us in these two hundred fifty years! We are debtors to our fathers in ways beyond our ability to understand or express. Insights and truths which are timeless in their significance have been brought through the faithful witness of succeeding generations into the life of the church today. We are grateful for dramatic symbols which have been our cherished means of expressing deep spiritual truths.

I feel that sometimes we have claimed exclusive rights to these because they have been rather uniquely limited to the heritage of our own fellowship. We have even called them Brethren doctrines. If they are only Brethren doctrines, we had better soon forget them. If we value them only because of a human heritage, they become idolatrous. If, however, they are truly an expression of Christian faith and order, then they have validity not only for the Church of the Brethren but for the whole family of Christ. What insight into the meaning of Christ's Lordship for His church we have, let us share without hesitation with Christians everywhere. If we would be true to our heritage, we must constantly seek to do for our generation what Alexander Mack did for his — bring the truth of the gospel into the life of today.

The perils of conformity have been rather clearly understood by the Brethren across these two and one-half centuries. Our fathers never hesitated to be different if under the guidance of the Holy Spirit they believed themselves to be right. I pray that the Church of the Brethren will never compromise a single conviction because of the pressures which will be increasingly upon us to conform to any theological or ecclesiastical pattern which may be the mode of the day and the hour. We must bear witness to the truth even though it means that we as a church stand alone. In this true nonconformity, we follow in the tradition of the church in Jerusalem and of the Brethren in Schwarzenau. It is foolish and impossible for us to try to be a first-century church. We do not live in the first century. Neither can we return to the world of Alexander Mack. But we must be a twentieth-century church which, like the true disciples in every age, lives under the Lordship of Jesus Christ, who is the same yesterday, today, and forever.

Our witness begins with the timeless truth of the gospel. We are still under His commission to "go . . . and make disciples of all nations" (Matthew 28:19). Before Christ can be our Lord, He must be our Savior. With all of the advancements of science, the insights of psychology, and the knowledge gained by education, there is still no other name under heaven whereby men must be saved. The problem of our times has been that we have tried to build the brave new world of tomorrow on our own terms. Never before in history have we developed so many brilliant minds or unlocked so many of the secrets of the world around us. Never before have been provided such thrilling possibilities for richer, fuller living. Yet at this very moment when man seems to reach the pinnacle of his achievement, we stand in more tragic peril of the complete disintegration of the human race than at any other time in the history of mankind.

We know enough about the ethical and spiritual implications of sin to live better lives. We know enough about the cruelty and injustice of racial segregation to build bridges of brotherhood. We know enough about the causes and effects of war to abolish it forever from the face of the earth. But we haven't the moral courage to live like sons of God. In the words of Will Durant, we are spiritual pigmies in giant frames. Until we bring all we know and all that we can do under the control and Lordship of Jesus Christ, we are lost. Our education is lost. Our industry is lost. Our social institutions are lost. Our nations are lost. Until all of life is touched and redeemed by the power of the living Lord, mankind is lost. To this the church must declare its witness upon a trumpet with no uncertain sound. The startling words of Martin Luther, "Every Christian must be a Christ to every other man," come to have a profound and abiding significance for the evangelistic task of the hour.

I rejoice in our growing concern that we faithfully fulfill Christ's commission for our lives. Too long we have been satisfied to conserve and nurture our established churches without endeavoring to extend our interest into the wider areas where Christ's influence is desperately needed. Our goal to establish twenty-five new churches each year should not challenge us simply because it may satisfy our desire for recognition or produce a less embarrassing set of evangelistic statistics. We must be motivated by a genuine concern for the souls of men. Across the world, the fields are white unto the harvest. Doors are opening in lands where the younger churches unite with us in proclaiming Christ's Lordship. As ideas are struggling for possession of the souls of men in these years of crisis, which may well be one of God's awful springtimes, let the church proclaim the whole gospel for the whole world.

Not only must the Church of the Brethren declare the saving power of Jesus Christ to all the world, but we must recognize our oneness with all others who under the Lordship of Christ share this witness. I am glad that the Church of the Brethren is a part of a glorious fellowship of love throughout the whole wide earth.

We are committed to participation in the life of the ecumenical church. To me this more recent concern for a greater unity within the church of Christ is as truly a valid part of our heritage as anything that has ever come from the pen of Alexander Mack. In these relationships with other Christian bodies, our own historical principles of unity without uniformity serve us well. We are not the only church with a great tradition. Ecumenical cooperation does not require stripping down our beliefs to the least common denominator of faith and trying to live on that. Rather, it recognizes our differences but seeks to bring each to the other the fullness and the richness of our varied insights and traditions. So, as one great victorious church, we seek to find the meaning of Christ's Lordship wherever it may be found. Let the Church of the Brethren share with the universal church her commitment to one Lord, her witness to one faith, and the power of one baptism.

The Lordship of Christ further demands that we must follow His way of life. It is significant to me that the earliest designation of Christianity was *the Way*. Brethren have little difficulty in understanding this. If life is truly committed to Christ, we seek to live as He would want us to live. This does not in any sense mean that our emphasis upon the good life becomes a gospel of works. It simply recognizes the fact that we cannot call Jesus Lord and not do the things He commands. We recall rather proudly that once it could be said, "A Dunkard's word is as good as his note." Can this still be truthfully said in every Brethren community?

This emphasis upon the Christian life does not end in mere personal piety. The New Testament makes it abundantly clear that one is not right with God who is not also right with his fellow men. Therefore, the Church of the Brethren, if she is to live under the Lordship of Jesus Christ, must continue to devote herself to a ministry of reconciliation and Christian brotherhood. I am grateful for the way God has been able to use our church to prick the conscience of both the church and the world for their participation in the folly and tragic sinfulness of war. Through our witness to the message of peace and goodwill, we ourselves have come to understand better what it means to be peacemakers. I am thrilled to see young men and women dedicating a year or two or three of their lives in volunteer service or through some other experience to some ministry of love. In this they are being about the business of their Lord. I trust that it may be said of every one of them as it was to me of representatives of our church in Germany by a German pastor, "They came to live among us like Jesus Christ."

Now when all the world is an armed camp, when distrust and superstition would destroy everything that love and understanding would create, let the Brethren under the Lordship of Jesus Christ continue to be His ambassadors of goodwill — peacemakers who demonstrate in their lives and service the healing power of love. On the world's long road to Jericho, let us not turn aside from need wherever it be found but devote ourselves in the name of Christ to a ministry of both body and soul. Well may we find our own mission in the prophecy of Isaiah 61:1 so beautifully fulfilled in the ministry of Jesus:

> The Spirit of the Lord God is upon me,
> because the Lord has anointed me
>   to bring good tidings to the afflicted;
> he has sent me to bind up the brokenhearted,
>   to proclaim liberty to the captives,
> and the opening of the prison to those who are bound.

Now there have been times in our history when we have been not at all sure that the church had any business trying to redeem a world that was admittedly outside the control of Jesus Christ. But let us be reminded that this is the world God so loved that He sent His only-begotten Son to redeem it. We who call ourselves by His name ought certainly to have as much concern for it as He has. Christ is not only the Lord of the church but the Lord of all of life, of the economic, the social, and the political areas of our existence as well as of our souls. The gospel is designed for the life of man in the world and not apart from it.

Therefore, the Christian cannot withdraw from it as some good people want to do, or as the bad people want the good people to do. The Christian must learn how to be in the world but not of the world. The Lord working through His church will continue to seek to win all men unto Himself and to bring their lives under His control. "For he must reign until he has put all his enemies under his feet" (1 Corinthians 15:25). "The kingdom of the world has become the kingdom of our Lord and of his Christ . . ." (Revelation 11:15).

This reminds us that under the Lordship of Jesus Christ the Church of the Brethren must give witness to the gospel of hope. In these dark days of uncertainty, the Christian lives in the assurance that Christ is the Lord of history. He has overcome the world (John 16:33). We inhabit no alien land but live in a conquered territory. We live in the light of the victory that has been won. The Savior of the world no longer hangs upon a cross, thorn crowned, nail pierced, despised, humiliated, and rejected. Now the risen Lord, He is seated at the right hand of God, the Father, where He is the judge of men and nations. The future belongs to those who belong to Him. The church lives out her mission in the knowledge that He shall reign for ever and ever and that every knee shall bow and every tongue confess that He is Lord.

So we come to the solemn moment when we must ask ourselves, "Is Christ the Lord of my life?" He is the Lord of the church. He must become the Lord of the nations. But what about my relationship to Him? It is well enough to talk about the Brethren under the Lordship of Jesus Christ, but what about the brother? We shall make no great advances in extending the Kingdom of our Lord until we who are members of His fellowship have a deeper experience with Him. His Lordship over the church becomes meaningful only when He is the Lord of those within the church. Together, with lives surrendered, we let Him work His miracles in the world around us.

I like to go to Orchestra Hall, when I can, to hear the

Chicago Symphony Orchestra. Before the concert, every musician is free to play any tune he chooses in any key at any tempo. The result is a kind of bedlam that is tolerated only because of what is to follow. This is freedom, yes, but it is not music. Then the conductor steps to the podium and raps for silence. The symphony begins. The musicians are no longer free to play as they wish. Now they are under the direction of a great conductor. They all play the same number in perfect rhythm and in the same key. What is the difference between the bedlam of the warm-up and the beauty of the symphony? Each musician now, whether playing the violin or the cello, the clarinet or the bassoon, has a master. Each finds his true fulfillment in his surrender to him.

Let this be a parable of the Church of the Brethren as we stand in this dramatic moment in our history. Ours is a dynamic mission. To us as to all the church has been entrusted a gospel that is the power of God and the salvation of the world.

As we begin the second quarter of a millennium of our history, the Church of the Brethren will stand daily at the crossroads of our destiny. Will our heritage become for us an asset or a liability? A springboard or a millstone? We are no longer a sect, but will we become a confessional church or a confessing church? Will we be a voice, or an echo? Will we become a part of the deep problem of mankind, or a part of God's answer? Will we serve the gods of our own creation, made just our size, or will we dare to live under the Lordship of Jesus Christ?

Only we and our children, and our children's children, can answer. But answer we must! And you must answer now for your own life. Look deep within yourself just now, where only you and God can see. How much of your life is under the control of Christ? Here lies the real answer to the church of tomorrow. Let His Kingdom come in us. Let His will be done in us and through us, until the kingdoms of this world become His Kingdom, and He shall reign for ever and ever!

26. THE BRETHREN AND DESTINY

CALVERT N. ELLIS

President, Juniata College; minister; lecturer; writer; member, General Brotherhood Board. Formerly: president, Pennsylvania Association of Colleges and Universities; chairman, Commission on the Arts of the Association of American Colleges; member, Advisory Committee on Education to the United States Congress.

I feel very humble to speak about the Brethren and the future. It would be much easier to glorify the past or even to analyze critically what has gone before. However, I am thankful that the mood of the Brotherhood is not to look back but to move forward. This two-hundred-fiftieth anniversary celebration has a *Call* attached!

Reading the bicentennial addresses of fifty years ago, I found that the mood was definitely to conserve, almost to preserve. The word of Brother J. W. Lear has unfortunately come true — "the edge of their boldness had worn away and their efforts were exhausted more nearly within the bounds of their own families."

However, a new spirit has been moving among us! From our church publications and educational institutions came the drive which sent our missionaries to India and China and Africa. Any group of Christians which sent missionaries overseas could not remain the same! Our missionaries co-operated with other Christians before the church in America lost its false pride of exclusiveness. Our colleges and seminary have fostered the missionary movement and brought to focus the ideas which have thrust us out into the world.

The Second World War gave the Brotherhood a new direction. It was not a case of buying a substitute to do the fighting for the boy who conscientiously could not bear arms. Nor was it only a case of noncombatant service or in extreme cases going to jail — although these alternatives were chosen. A new technique was developed which performed necessary service and provided a testimony: Brethren Service was born! This has been the most important part of our witness in the last twenty years.

The most recent decade has seen a growing emphasis upon establishing new congregations — home missions, we used to call it — and building new church houses, or edifices. As we are reaching out, we are changing!

This brings me to the subject I have been assigned, "The Brethren and Destiny." It is an imposing subject, and I do not profess to be a prophet or to have any unusual insights. I will simply outline my thoughts on the world mission of our fraternity, our place in the church of Jesus Christ. I pray that each of you will consider this subject and ask yourself the questions I have asked as I thought of the Brethren in the years ahead.

What is the mission of the Brethren in this hour? How and where can we make the largest contribution to the church of Christ? We have learned that it is not our church in the sense that we make the rules; it is His church — the church of Jesus Christ. We are His witnesses and His servants. We have discovered the vast riches of grace, the love of God in Christ, which we share with all who are His, whatever their creed or color.

This is a tremendous change in point of view and will affect our future. The gospel is not something to protect or preserve; it is good news to share in life and word! The gospel or an office in the church is not something to be proud of, but a privilege which calls for our best efforts.

We Brethren have been thrust out into the world. We may nostalgically *look* back to the isolation of the nineteenth-century farm home — but we can't *go* back! The high school, the television, and the comics bring the world to our children. The vast majority of the laymen work in factories, schools, and offices and belong to labor unions, federations, and clubs. We establish new congregations on the basis of comity, and ministers and laymen belong to councils of churches.

The change is a great challenge and also a great hazard. Do we have any distinct contribution to make to the church of Jesus Christ? Do we have a specific call to this generation, a witness so impelling that it will challenge the best minds and the prophetic geniuses among our children and our neighbors?

If we do not have a challenging witness, our denomination will be lost; our more intelligent children will join other fellowships and our epitaph will be "His grandparents were Brethren." But I took the responsibility of leading our thoughts in this closing hour of the Conference because I believe we do have a compelling witness, worthy of our complete devotion.

The genius of the Brethren has always been in action, not in words. Our interest has been in service rather than theology. Here has been our contribution to the church of Jesus Christ and here is our destiny. From the first eight at Schwarzenau to the latest volunteers of 1958, the emphasis has been upon life — "the living of these days."

This is the emphasis, the insight, which we can contribute to the Christian witness. Few would defend the isolation of our fathers. In penitence we acknowledge that often we yielded to the temptation to group pride and institutional permanence. We are sincere in our devotion to the church universal and will struggle under the leadership of the Holy Spirit to find our place in His Kingdom.

The Brethren contribution is not in architecture. We have forsaken the Pennsylvania meetinghouse for a functional structure of varying design but similar to other church buildings. We will not experiment as the Missouri Synod Lutherans do. Our architecture is usually determined by the number of classrooms needed for the church school or the prejudice of a particular member or family.

And I do not believe that the Brethren will be remembered

for their liturgy. Many younger ministers are attracted by a more formal worship. The cross and candles have joined the choir in the sanctuary. We have more responses, increased congregational participation, shorter sermons, and a more formal atmosphere. But there is no disposition to standardize the order of worship, and there is little evidence of creativity in the forms used. This use of form may increase but I see nothing here that is distinctive. The Christian church has never lacked liturgical forms or symbols but always is in danger of worshiping the form instead of God in Jesus Christ.

Again I question whether the Brethren contribution will be in the area of theology. We have not produced outstanding Biblical scholars or students of theology. We are not a creedal denomination which demands special theological study. Brethren are not speculative writers, and the first scholarly journal edited by Brethren is of very recent origin. The Brethren need theological literature and will produce more in the coming years; but I doubt that this will be, or should be, the area of our major concern.

We cannot hope to overtake the large denominations in size but we can have a vital testimony which is respected in the Christian community around the world. Our children may feel impelled to join with other Christians in a larger fellowship, but whether we remain a separate denomination is not as important as whether we maintain our witness. Do not mistake — our witness is not for our glory or pride as Brethren but only for the glory of God.

Our forefathers took the New Testament literally. The Great Commission of Matthew 28, the Sermon on the Mount, and the seventy-times-seven forgiveness of Matthew 18 were more familiar than baseball scores are to us. The vivid pictures of Matthew 25, with the sheep separated from the goats, were burned in our memories.

"'Lord, when did we see thee hungry and feed thee, or thirsty and give thee drink? And when did we see thee a stranger and welcome thee, or naked and clothe thee? And when did we see thee sick or in prison and visit thee?' And the King will answer them, 'Truly, I say to you, as you did it to one of the least of these, my brethren, you did it to me' " (Matthew 25:37-40).

Our fathers preached from the gospels more often than from the letters of the Apostle Paul. And this we understand. However, I believe that the witness of their lives and the burden of their message is beautifully stated by the Apostle in his second letter to the Corinthians (5:17-20): "If any one is in Christ, he is a new creation; the old has passed away, behold, the new has come. All this is from God, who through Christ reconciled us to himself and gave us the ministry of reconciliation; that is, God was in Christ reconciling the world to himself. . . . So we are ambassadors for Christ. . . ."

This then is my faith and my hope — that the destiny of the Brethren will be a ministry of reconciliation. Here is our contribution to the church of Jesus Christ; it is the thread that runs from Schwarzenau to Des Moines and is the Brethren ideal of life regardless of how far short we have fallen in our witness. This ministry of reconciliation has been implicit in all our activities whether explicit in Conference pronouncements or not. Alexander Mack had no intention of founding a new denomination, but, rather, in his own words, "to show forth undaunted godliness by the grace and power of Christ." He thought of himself as re-establishing the "true church of Christ." But we *have* a denomination and the means to make the ideal of reconciliation operative in our lives and communities.

The early Brethren never separated the ministry of the Word from the ministry of service. They took pains to see that those who preached were not removed from the laity. They had no special dress or uniform, no high pulpits, and no salary. Those who ministered the Word were called to preach only after years of faithful service. Today we recognize a specific division of responsibility within the congregation and the special education necessary for a pastor. However, let us not forget that witness and service cannot be separated. Our pastors should always remind us in word and life that service is the true witness. We are "a new creation" in Christ Jesus. And this is our witness.

A ministry of reconciliation involves both word and deed. The word is the word of forgiveness, the good news that "God was in Christ reconciling the world to himself." What God has said to us in the life, acts, death, and resurrection of Jesus Christ has to be spoken. His command is "Preach the gospel to every creature." But our words are only words unless the miracle of the new creation actually takes place. This is God's action of forgiveness and the new life. The word of forgiveness has a logical priority, but the deeds must follow: a new life and character, an act of God in us. Our Lord charged His disciples not only to preach the gospel but also to underline their words with deeds of healing and charity.

In its ministry of reconciliation the church shows its true nature. On the one hand, the church in her preaching points to the coming Kingdom; on the other, in her life the church is the beginning of the Kingdom. A preaching church without lives of love and deeds of mercy has no winning power. She speaks of something she does not have and her only appeal is magic. But it also is impossible to imagine a church which is wholly given over to acts of service; it would not be a church. Our deeds of love are always partial and sinful. Our best efforts can never be the ultimate ground for peace and hope. We cannot save even ourselves — our lives are not sufficient; they only point to God in Jesus Christ, whose love is infinitely greater than ours and who will restore this broken world and make it His Kingdom.

The ministry of reconciliation — the destiny of the Brethren — is more than humanitarian and philanthropic service. We are interested in the helpless, the oppressed, and the refugees, but not simply to improve their physical condition. This is the responsibility of everyone, Christian and non-Christian alike. In more places each year government is assuming responsibilities for these unfortunates; we call it the welfare state. This in no wise changes the burden of the church for the needs of men and women. No welfare state will ever in this sinful world eliminate the oppressed and the helpless. There will always be gaps, and the church must be ready to move into them. However, the church's service must be a witness to her saving Lord. The cup of cold water must be in the name of Christ. All our deeds are a witness to what God has done in Christ.

We might remember that our mission in India began with famine orphans! All of our mission work outside the United States was started among underprivileged people. And this was before Brethren Service was ever thought of. Service has been a part of the Brethren witness from Schwarzenau to Bulsar!

Our service in Europe since the last war has been unique in one respect. We have no congregations in Europe and we did not use our relief activities to establish a new church there. We did not even limit our activities to Protestants, but served men and women wherever they were and whatever their need. This was an unusual example of Christian service — deeds of love and mercy which were not conducted to increase church membership or meant for communicants of a particular faith. Observed from the outside, much Christian service seems selfish because it is directed toward those who are "of the household of faith." These are our first responsibility, but our service dare not stop there.

The Brethren destiny can be a reconciling ministry of service. It would draw its authority from the New Testament and be in harmony with the Christian tradition. Such a ministry would claim nothing for itself save the privilege of witnessing to the power of God in Jesus Christ.

The Brethren were so scared of verbal affirmations that they refused to formulate a creed. To them, deeds were more important than words. We need to remember that the Christian faith is more than a verbal acceptance or an emotional lift. Our commitment to Jesus Christ is a dedication of the entire life. In the words of the Apostle Paul to the Colossians, "whatever you do, in word or deed, do everything in the name of Jesus Christ."

This reconciling ministry must begin with us here tonight. We are representatives of the Church of the Brethren and her future. The great fact about our church is that we belong to the church; it does not belong to us! In spite of all its failures, the church is Christ's body on earth. We cannot condemn and hope to redeem. We recall the word of Albert Schweitzer, who asked simply, "Why should I forgive anyone whom I think to be guilty of hatred, or lovelessness, or arrogance? I must forgive because I know I have been guilty." We must forgive because He first forgave us!

Do we in our homes and our daily activities give a demonstration of reconciliation? Do our friends expect us to bring peace or agitation? Do we try to force our opinions on others? Do we compel such obedience from our children that they anticipate the time when they will be free of our tyranny? Do we expect the congregation to agree with us or else we will not co-operate?

Why should I not state it positively? We are here tonight and can participate in this two-hundred-fiftieth anniversary because men and women were willing to be led by the Spirit of God and gave a demonstration of redeeming love. Some of us are here because our parents gave such a witness that we were drawn to the Lord they served. Some of us are thrilled by the devotion and sacrifice of those who are building the congregations with which we are associated.

In times of great crisis the witness of the world has been: "See how the Christians love each other." Here is the power of the gospel of reconciliation! This is the meaning of the salutations *Brother* and *Sister*. Why must we in the church use the titles of the world? Are we not satisfied to recognize others as our equals before the Lord?

D. J. Niles, the evangelist from Ceylon, reminds us that *fellowship* in the New Testament is always a noun, because it is conceived as God's gift through Jesus Christ, in whom we have a unity more fundamental than any of our divisions. But, he went on to say, in the United States we have made *fellowship* into a verb, emphasizing our preference to associate with one another on the basis of superficial likeness. Is it true that we Brethren limit our fellowship to those whom we like? This is natural but it is not true of the new creation in Christ. In the church we break down the dividing walls of race, color, economic status, and intellectual achievement. We strive to reconcile what appears impossible of unity. But in Christ we are all brought near! Is this too idealistic? No! It is happening, and I see it as our destiny — a ministry of reconciliation!

However, our destiny involves more than our immediate fellowship. The ministry of reconciliation must reach out to our community, our nation, and ultimately to nothing less than the world. It is difficult for some people to realize that the church has never fulfilled her destiny until she has challenged the very premises of the naturalistic society in which she lives. We cannot withdraw from the world. It forces itself upon us, and we have a witness, either for Christ or against Him.

The increasing tensions created by rapid social change give the church its opportunity for a ministry of reconciliation. This is our Brethren opportunity and our destiny. The mobility of people brings new families to our communities. They are not like us, even if they are Brethren, and the temptation is to exclude them, to pass by on the other side. In certain communities we live so close together that different patterns of conduct try our patience and destroy our witness. We cannot go on as we have. We are reaching out to the community and grasping the opportunities God has given us. Greed and selfish hatred are not going unchallenged. We are new persons in Christ and we see all persons, whether we like them or not, as men for whom Christ died.

Our peace testimony in the Second World War gave Brethren youth a new vision of service. They saw an alternative to bearing arms but they also saw many areas of human need and developed a positive witness. Have we understood the significance of this recognition of conscience which the government allows?

It is an alternative granted for religious convictions. Why do we Brethren believe that we cannot participate in war or preparations for war? Our reason is not the superior destructive power of a hydrogen bomb over a rifle. It is not that we fear the end of Western civilization. Our conscientious objection is based on our convictions about God and men. God sent His Son, Jesus Christ, He gave us His Spirit, and He founded His church because men and women are the most important thing in the world. We are God's tools to do His work, and in His sight everyone is important.

Ours is a ministry of reconciliation because we recognize the natural animosity and greed which is in all of us; but we also know the power which is in Christ to change men and women. We have seen the effect of a forgiving, understanding spirit in a mental hospital among those who were afflicted. We have watched a conscientious, intelligent representative of labor gain the trust of his employer because he sought nothing for himself, only the chance to be a vehicle for mediation. We know young men who have found themselves as they spent sleepless hours serving refugees who fled from home in desperation. We saw a missionary who helped Indians to maturity and understanding by acting as a loving older brother sharing their trials and disappointments. We are acquainted with a nurse who is so devoted to the care of her patients that she is a witness to the hundreds of young women who come to her hospital for training. And she is not too busy to participate in the life of her congregation! Hers is a ministry in deeds.

It is my hope that this ministry of reconciliation will be our destiny. May we be known as Brethren with a concern for men and women! Whether we are pastors, teachers, businessmen, mothers, farmers, students, or whatever we are, may we be known as Christians who serve their community in the name of Christ.

The highly complex character of modern society means that most of us serve our Lord in an organizational framework. It is difficult to find the time or the place for individual creative service; but it is possible in every community. And it also is possible to do the Lord's work in a large organization. We Brethren fear organization and large units, but we must remember that certain services can be performed only with designated responsibilities and organization charts. The important thing is not where I serve but how my service appears in the sight of my Lord. The Apostle Paul, writing to the church at Ephesus, says that when each part is working properly the body of Christ is built up in love.

I do not believe that it will be our destiny to establish new churches in other lands. I hope we will work in fellowship with those already established and send our youth to share in their ministry. I hope we will not permit our institutions of service anywhere in the world to take on permanence. I hope, rather, that we will be ready and willing to help in the places of greatest need under whatever Christian auspices. I see in the years ahead a growing ministry of reconciliation in local communities where our congregations are established and where new ones will assemble. We do not claim to have an exclusive message or bishops with apostolic succession; we ask only for an opportunity to serve our Lord and His people.

Our ministry of reconciliation came from God, who through Christ reconciled us to Himself. This is not something for us to enjoy or something of which to be proud. We are no better than anyone else. Our Lord has shown us our true condition, but He has also given us the opportunity for a new life — an eternal life of joy and commitment. This is our destiny as Brethren.

PART FOUR

The European Celebration
(Schwarzenau, Berleburg, Kassel)

27. THE SCHWARZENAU PROGRAM

FORENOON SERVICE
10.00 A. M.

PRESIDING
M. R. Zigler, Director, European Brethren Service Program, Representative to the World Council of Churches

INVOCATION
Freeman Ankrum, Pastor St. James' Brethren Church

ADDRESS
"The Church Facing the Future"
W. A. Visser't Hooft, General Secretary, World Council of Churches

GREETINGS AND PRESENTATIONS
"Welcoming Statements"
The Pastor of Schwarzenau
The Mayor of Schwarzenau
"Response and Presentation of Memorial Volume"
Norman J. Baugher, General Secretary, General Brotherhood Board — Church of the Brethren

ADDRESS
"The Brethren and Schwarzenau"
Desmond W. Bittinger, Moderator Annual Conference, Church of the Brethren

WORSHIP
Kenneth I. Morse, Editor, "The Gospel Messenger," Official Organ Church of the Brethren

BENEDICTION

LUNCH — 12:30 P. M.

ORGAN RECITAL — 2:00-3:00 P. M. (in the Church)
TOURS OF SCHWARZENAU — 2:00-4:00 P. M.

AFTERNOON SERVICE
4:00 P. M.

PRESIDING: *Desmond W. Bittinger*

WORSHIP
  Delbert Flora, Dean, Ashland Seminary

PRESENTATION OF GUESTS AND VISITORS

GREETINGS AND ADDRESS
  "Ecumenical Spirit and Ecumenical Action"
  Ernst Wilm, Bishop Evangelical Church, State Westfalia

ADDRESS
  "Changeless Principles in a Changing World"
  Paul H. Bowman, Chairman 250th Anniversary Planning Committee

BENEDICTORY PRAYER
  S. Loren Bowman, Chairman General Brotherhood Board — Church of the Brethren

SERVICE OF DEDICATION (on the Banks of the Eder River) — 6:45 P. M.

28. EDITORIAL INTRODUCTION

Three communities in Germany are of special interest to the Brethren. The first of these, of course, is the village of Schwarzenau, the place in which the church had its origin. The second is the city of Berleburg, the seat of government for the Wittgenstein district and the residential city of friendly Count Henry, who extended tolerance and protection in the days of Alexander Mack to religious dissenters, including the Brethren. The third is the city of Kassel, which today is the administrative headquarters of Brethren work in Germany.

The anniversary celebration in Europe centered in these three communities, with the Schwarzenau program being of major interest and importance.

The Kassel conference, August 2-5, was considered the regular annual conference of Brethren workers in Europe. The work of the church in Germany, Austria, Greece, and other areas was presented ably and comprehensively by young people who occupy positions of leadership and responsibility. The Kassel conference was inaugurated on Sunday, August 3, by Brethren ministers filling pulpits in more than twenty of the twenty-six churches of Kassel. There followed in the evening a unique and impressive ecumenical service in Martins church, one of the largest and most beautiful churches of the city. The two leading addresses were delivered by Bishop Wuestemann of the area, representing the Protestant churches, and Norman J. Baugher, responding in behalf of the Brethren, who entitled his address "The Church Living Her Lord's Vision."

During the month of August 1958, the city of Berleburg observed the seven-hundredth anniversary of its founding, tolerance and religious freedom being the themes of the celebration. The Brethren were invited to participate in the ceremonies. On August 7, following the Schwarzenau Convocation, the Brethren were received in the city of Berleburg by the mayor and the city council, by His Highness, the Prince of Wittgenstein, and by the religious leaders of the city. Joined by citizens of the community, they filled the Evangelical church of the city to capacity in a service of worship and praise.

The sermon on that occasion was delivered by Landespfarrer Puffert. His message, entitled "Let Brotherly Love Continue," was based on a passage from the thirteenth chapter of Hebrews. Charles Lane, a European worker, served as interpreter and supplied the translation of the sermon which is used in the following pages.

This service was considered the official reception of the Brethren by the church of Berleburg. There were additional receptions at the Berleburg Castle, home of Wittgenstein royalty, and at the Evangelical youth center by the mayor of the city and the city council. — P. H. B.

29. THE CHURCH LIVING HER LORD'S VISION

Norman J. Baugher

General Secretary, General Brotherhood Board; minister; writer; member, General Board of the National Council of Churches. Formerly: pastor, Hershey (Spring Creek), Pennsylvania; pastor, King Ferry, New York; pastor, Monticello, Indiana; pastor, Long Beach, California; member, General Brotherhood Board.

Few greater privileges have come to the Church of the Brethren than to join in this ecumenical service with representative traditions of the church in Germany. We were cradled in this land two hundred fifty years ago. In 1708 our fraternity was born at Schwarzenau, County of Wittgenstein, about sixty miles from Kassel. The founders of our church received their earliest religious nurture in the churches of this and neighboring lands. After the beginning years here they emigrated to the new land across the Atlantic, where our church has grown and served. For over two hundred years our contacts together have been chiefly as citizens of sovereign states. This evening we are meeting together as Christians representing, on the one hand, the several traditions with which we are identified and, on the other hand, something of the unity we find in Jesus Christ, the Lord of the Church and Savior of us all.

The Church of the Brethren is deeply grateful to the churches of the city of Kassel, the surrounding area, and Germany generally for welcoming us as you have to your great country for this celebration of the two-hundred-fiftieth anniversary of the founding of our communion. We pray that the ties of Christian fellowship and brotherhood, broken two and one-half centuries ago and on several occasions of war since then but somewhat re-established during the last decade and a half that our Brethren Service representatives have witnessed in your midst, may not only be furthered now by this ecumenical service but also never again be broken by either international conflict or separation within the body of Christ.

I

I wish to speak briefly on the urgency of the present-day church's living the vision Christ had for His people. When Jesus spoke in Nazareth (Luke 4:18, 19) to inaugurate His active ministry, the urgency of a new revelation and a new strategy for God's people struck with such force that the world has heard only the first rather than the last reverberations of what He said. Probably nowhere in the New Testament does there appear a clearer statement of the objectives and methods — what we call the strategy — of the ministry of Christ and His church. He turned to the scroll of Isaiah and read for His people of all generations to hear:

"The Spirit of the Lord is upon me,
because he has anointed me to preach good news to the poor.
He has sent me to proclaim release to the captives
and recovering of sight to the blind,
to set at liberty those who are oppressed,
to proclaim the acceptable year of the Lord."

Later, in His prayer for the church, Jesus laid this same ministry on His people when He prayed to the Father, saying, "As thou didst send me into the world, so I have sent them into the world" (John 17:18). The Nazareth sermon on the redemptive possibilities of the gospel is something of His vision for His people and His church in which all of us have a common task.

This is what Jesus Christ can do for a man in America, Germany, India, Nigeria, or Ecuador — for the whole world! The purpose of our preaching, our teaching, our missions, our service, our evangelism is that release from things that bind us, freedom from things that enslave us, healing from things that hurt us, may be the joyful, redeeming experiences of life for all men everywhere! What worship in the church must offer, what sacraments and ordinances must make vital and real, what converted living must mean, what a disciple does is to experience and share release, freedom, and healing!

This vision employs a strategy for the Christian in which the methods used are of the very nature and quality of the Kingdom's end which we seek! Here are not only the anointed functions of God's only-begotten Son, but also the commission of all God's children everywhere. Here is not only the vision of a new era for men, but here is also a description of what kind of ministry will usher in such an age: "As thou didst send me into the world, so I have sent them into the world."

II

Review seriatim the aspects of this vision of Christian witness. Sense how immediately relevant to our world situation it is and how straightforwardly it suggests a unique servant role for the church today.

1. First is the concern for the poor — ". . . he has anointed me to preach good news to the poor."

Here is a pattern of pity and passion for people, especially the disadvantaged, which is a dominant quality of the whole ministry of God revealed in His Son. A revolutionary world today challenges the church rather deeply at this precise point. Wherever you travel in the world, the church is challenged to show genuine and energetic interest in the basic elements of good and of earning a livelihood. Very often, in areas where there have been great masses of the earth's poor, the mission of the church has not been identified readily with the plight of the poor or the despair of the disadvantaged. And how tragic that this banner of a "concern for the poor," so native to our Christian gospel, is also the banner under which pagan philosophies spread throughout much of Asia and Africa and America.

2. Next is the mission to the distressed — ". . . he hath sent me to heal the broken-hearted" (K.J.V.).

Walter Russell Bowie observes this about Jesus: "He brought the consciousness of the presence of God not only in the heights but in the valleys also, not only in the lights but in the shadows, not only in those moments when life soars up on wings but in those other moments when it walks with lame and weary feet upon a heavy road."[1] Redemptive suffering is one of the witnesses of the Christian which is of the very nature of the cross itself. To take suffering, brokenheartedness, and sadness and reveal through them a spirit that "transfigures the misfortune with courage and steadies it with trust" is to have that quality of experience and life which is of the very heart of God himself. Around the world dashed dreams, ruined reputations, ill ideals, and separation's sorrow all await the healing and redemptive ministry of the people of God.

3. Then there is a gospel to set life free — ". . . to proclaim release to the captives . . . to set at liberty those who are bruised."

Jesus is sent to free every yoke and bondage of captivity. No fear, no ignorance, no prejudice, no habit, no outer or inner power is so strong but that He can give liberty to the life that is held captive. This is what men must experience in worship, in conversion, in the gradual release from ignorance that comes from study, instruction, meditation, confession, and selfless service in the Kingdom. The church is commissioned to be the agent of release, freedom, and liberty.

But the church does not advocate no captivity, no restraint, no order. She advocates for all men a higher captivity, a commitment of life to God through Jesus Christ, in whom alone life finds the full freedom of the universe. And this freedom cannot be taken away by any tyrant or by any materialism, no matter how many chains be used to bind and enslave the body.

---

[1] Walter Russell Bowie, *The Interpreter's Bible* (Nashville: Abingdon-Cokesbury Press), Volume 8, page 91.

Nor can it be destroyed by any advancement of science which by satellites and other means carries man's experience into the ever-expanding spaces of the universe. This is freedom of life in a Kingdom which blind George Matheson had in mind when he wrote: "Make me a captive, Lord, and then I shall be free." Jesus came preaching release for all whose higher life was imprisoned within them; who were ever in danger of dying with their music still in them; who had not had the image of God in which they were created step forth in life as the statue steps forth from the block of marble at the hand of the master sculptor!

4. Finally, Jesus was concerned about vision — ". . . and recovering of sight to the blind. . . ."

There is a ministry of compassion and concern toward the blind which runs throughout the life of our Lord. The blindness may be physical. It may be a social color blindness or a cultural blindness. It may be a spiritual or moral dullness which does not discern the things of God and of right human relations.

The church is summoned to a great ministry of opening men's eyes to God and to their neighbors! Attitudes toward Him and toward each other are of the very nature of life's meaning. The church must give upward and outward dimensions to life. It is expected to open men's eyes, that in this day of automation, impersonalization, and pre-occupation with things they may recover a perception of God and the values of His Kingdom's coming on earth.

III

All of this consummates in the establishment of a reign on earth important to God — ". . . to proclaim the acceptable year of the Lord." Elsewhere Jesus says it this way: "Thy Kingdom come . . . on earth as it is in heaven."

Across the centuries and even in our time, on many frontiers and in many hearts, this Kingdom is coming! God has ordained its coming! Men are given to its purposes. Life will be laid down for its sake, if need be! And though dark philosophies challenge the Christian faith on every continent of the globe, who can really doubt that we have a Kingdom which is coming and cannot be shaken!

The Spirit of the Lord is upon the church to reign in the hearts of men: showing forth a concern for the poor, carrying forward a ministry to the distressed, setting the imprisoned free and at liberty, and giving vision to the blind. To fulfill such a ministry is the task of the whole church wherever she lives. And the church shall know that she has the blessing of the Spirit of the Lord in so far as she does these things, for the text says:

"The Spirit of the Lord is upon me,
   because he has anointed me . . . and has sent me."

Doing these things is the evidence that we are filled with the Spirit, inspired to live the vision Christ had for His church!

"O church of God triumphant above this world's dark fears,
Wherein our souls seek refuge through all our earthly years,
While in these walls we gather, renew in us God's will.
With prayer and praise we worship; our hearts with courage fill.

"Her task on earth unfinished till wars at last shall cease,
When greed and lust for power give way to paths of peace;
Then brotherhood shall free us from bonds of caste and race;
The church must live the vision that shone in Jesus' face."

— *S. Ralph Harlow*

30. LET BROTHERLY LOVE CONTINUE

Landespfarrer Puffert

> Let brotherly love continue. Do not neglect to show hospitality to strangers, for thereby some have entertained angels unawares. Remember those who are in prison, as though in prison with them; and those who are ill-treated, since you also are in the body (Hebrews 13:1-3).

Brotherly love is the keyword in these days of celebration as you, the members of the Church of the Brethren, acknowledge with grateful praise and devotion the history through which God has led your church for two hundred fifty years.

Brotherly love is the key to what happened two hundred fifty years ago when the first of your forefathers found a haven under the protection of the Prince Regent of Wittgenstein. Now the years of aimless wandering, of being oppressed and persecuted, and the struggle for existence have found an end. Men and women, irrespective of their origins, find a fellowship of brotherhood in the belief that a heavenly Father makes His children brothers. The real bonds of your fellowship were not the common experiences of dispersion, of being refugees, of persecution and travail. Your fellowship was formed under the words "brotherhood in faith."

Brotherhood in faith remained and became ever more the dominating characteristic of the little group, which in 1719 emigrated to America and which today has become a great church.

The memorial celebration at the birthplace in Schwarzenau erects a marker, an "Ebenezer" of gratitude, and testifies that

Christians for the sake of their heavenly Father must be, want to be, and ought to be brothers.

Brotherhood, this self-evident truth of Christian existence, was not only decisive for the little group in Schwarzenau and the great church in America for two hundred fifty years, but also through the message of missionaries and worldwide service, brotherhood has established your church before the world. Therefore, to the first testimony, "Christians must, want, and ought to be brothers because it is God's will," must be added as a witness to such brotherhood: "God has ordained that all men shall live together as brothers." Thus, for two hundred fifty years the Church of the Brethren has received the appeal, "Let brotherly love continue," as a gift and as an obligation.

Brotherhood and brotherly love are actually not self-evident. They were not so two hundred fifty years ago, and they are not so today. They are not the result of the development of the world and mankind. The first members of the Church of the Brethren, who joined together in Schwarzenau, had each one experienced through his harrassed and threatened life just how little self-evident brotherly love, and even its acknowledgement in this world, is. Today, as the world and the church are taken out of the small-town, middle-class situation and thrust into the global expansions of the progress of the world and humanity, brotherhood and brotherly love are no more self-evident than they were two hundred fifty years ago. Our world is quaking with hatred, violence, mistrust, greed, and the self-glorification of individuals, groups, and nations. The sources of and the possibility for brotherly love do not lie in this world.

All the more do we, then, want to listen to God's appeal: "Let brotherly love continue." We need not try to create it; it cannot be our product. But we can remain constant in it as the great gift which God gave to the world, by which He made Himself our brother through Jesus Christ. Brotherhood, brotherly love — these truly make up the full content of the gospel to the world, and, at the same time, the proclamation of His eternal

Lordship. Brotherhood, thereby, is the gospel expressed in the very modern terms of the needs, worries, cares, and difficulties of our present-day world. What greater gift could be given to the world-wide, and yet most personal, needs of life than the gift of the brotherhood of man? However, there is here revealed for us in God's own handiwork the possibility of brotherhood and brotherly love in this world. The cross of Jesus Christ is the indication of just how much God spent and is spending today for the sake of the proclamation of His dominion of love and brotherhood in the world. The risen Prince of Peace is the guarantee that God will bring the dominion of His love to fulfillment.

The call to brotherly love and brotherhood for God's sake is, however, not only a declaration of the dominion of God. This warning is at the same time the authorization of the faithful for doing brotherly deeds and the sharing in the eternal Kingdom. God wants to work through men. Then, we are thus included in the love of God the Father, which overcomes earthly powers, division, and guilt, and which leads us to brotherhood.

Our hearts may well tremble, if we stop to contemplate this great statement. Who, then, is capable of being God's instrument? God's Word alone overcomes our petty faith, our lack of courage; it overcomes the temptations which squeeze our hearts, because we are weak. God's Word alone overcomes the cares which burden our hearts by manifold and unending misery and injustice. God's Word alone overcomes the greed and ingratitude of mankind, which can so easily destroy the efforts toward brotherly love. God's Word overcomes all these outward and inward hindrances because it turns our eyes and hearts away from ourselves and toward others.

Our text cites three ways by which brotherly love is tested:

1. Homelessness: "Do not neglect to show hospitality to strangers."
2. Imprisonment: "Remember those who are in prison, as though in prison with them."

3. Suffering: "Remember those who are ill-treated."

These seemingly haphazard characteristics of the misery of human life receive astonishingly deep and practical significance for the service to which brotherly love is called in this world. Homelessness, imprisonment, and suffering were the identifying marks of those who first united as brothers two hundred fifty years ago. Homelessness, imprisonment, and suffering are the characteristics of the need of our times, against which the Church of the Brethren, heeding God's call, has become active. From the aid which God gave your forefathers has grown the fruit of service and blessing. Those who were led from homelessness to the security of a new homeland now serve in refugee camps for those who have been uprooted by the external, internal, political, and economic confusion of our day. Indeed, they work for integration and re-establishment, as the Heifer Project has manifestly demonstrated.

Those who personally experienced comfort from suffering witness by their extensive service that which Paul from his own experiences in life and faith expresses in 2 Corinthians 1:3-5: "Blessed be the God and Father of our Lord Jesus Christ, . . . who comforts us in all our affliction, so that we may be able to comfort those who are in any affliction, with the comfort with which we ourselves are comforted by God. For as we share abundantly in Christ's sufferings, so through Christ we share abundantly in comfort too."

We in Germany who have experienced the service and witness of the Church of the Brethren in our midst can gratefully say: "Here brotherhood is not just a sentimental feeling, not an idealistic aim, but has become a concrete service, a sharing responsibility, and a warm fellowship."

Brotherhood and brotherly love! The Church of the Brethren has become a devoted witness for this simple and all-including ultimate token of Christian fellowship, which began with the life and works of Jesus, and which, from the days of early

Christianity on, has formed the uniqueness of the Christian community.

God's call to brotherhood and brotherly love, which speaks very directly to us today, we are transmitting through the service and the witness of the Church of the Brethren, so that all Christianity shall not forget, and the whole world shall hear: "Christians must be brothers for God's sake. God wills that all men live together as brothers."

Ultimately brotherhood and brotherly love make up the joyful declaration of the coming of the Kingdom of God. Therefore, the Father wants to perfect His Christianity, so that we as His children will be brothers.

We as members of the German church, which has tasted along with many others the fruits of your brotherly love, join with you in thanking God for all that He has done to you and to your church. We wish to listen with you to this call to brotherly love as the testimony of God's eternal dominion and as the authorization of His believers. He wants to work through us that we may expect the coming of His Kingdom on earth. For the sake of the gift and the obligation of brotherly love we will not cease to praise in word and in deed the love of the eternal Father.

31. THE BRETHREN AND SCHWARZENAU

Desmond W. Bittinger

We are pleased that after two hundred fifty years it is the privilege and the opportunity of the Church of the Brethren officially to return to Schwarzenau. Here in this lovely, quiet valley of the Eder, at the edge of the Black Meadow, we reverently commemorate our anniversary. The multiplied efforts to which you have gone to provide this tent of commemoration and to lodge and feed this multitude of people, who have come from afar, are appreciated by our entire Brotherhood. May God reward you for them.

I. Why We Are Here

Why do we cross an ocean to conduct this pilgrimage?

We have come back to pay our respects to the memories of our forefathers who, in this valley, established themselves into a fellowship and in this river were baptized as the founders and disciples of a new church, the Church of the Brethren. We come, also, to pay our respects to you who have continued to live here, to you whose ancestors made the inception of this church possible, and to you who through two centuries have kindly welcomed those of our people who have visited here.

But even more than for these reasons, we have come back to this valley after two hundred fifty years in order to take stock of ourselves and to reappraise the continuing work which we as a church should undertake to do. We have returned to this valley to seek further guidance from God and to seek for a recommission from Him as we move forward into the unfolding future. The memories and the heritage of this valley are important to us of the Church of the Brethren, both as we look backward and as we face the future. It is our hope to conclude this day with a significant rededication service down by the River Eder.

II. The Significance of Schwarzenau for the Brethren

What happened in this valley that has significance for the Church of the Brethren? Does it have significance also for people other than the Brethren?

Here some earnest seekers after truth found a part of what they sought. Their descendants have sought to conserve and to add to that truth. But of major significance was their attitude toward truth.

Ever since man first trod upon the earth he has been engaged in an unending quest for truth and for the right to live by the truth which his mind could discover. This unending quest has led man to many discoveries and to many conclusions. Usually at some point in these quests the seeker makes a new discovery or grasps a new comprehension. When he does so, too often he stops his quest. He cries out, with pride and satisfaction, "Behold, I have found it!" For him the search for truth has come to an end. He seeks for a way to make his discovery immortal. When he learned to write he set down his "truth" as a creed or a law.

With high fervor he sets out to teach other men of this new truth he has discovered. If they resist his teachings he chides them; they on their part may call him strange, radical, or dangerous. They may even persecute him or slay him.

But truth does not die when its discoverer dies. His followers may carry on his teaching, surrounding themselves with certain distinguishing characteristics and practices.

This fractional approach to truth has given rise to a multitude of religions within our world and to subsequent splintering of these religions into still more orders or denominations. Each of these usually believes that it has the purest knowledge of God and, therefore, feels called upon to proselytize from all others in order to lead men to real truth. Or perhaps it takes an even more militant attitude. This, through the centuries, has led to inquisitions, religious wars, and terrifying suppressions of the free and open mind.

Two hundred fifty years ago, here in this valley, such persecutions were allayed; an unusual freedom was allowed to those who were searching for truth and who sincerely arrived at differing understandings of God.

As a result of this, many who wished to pursue the quest for truth found their way here. Alexander Mack, sacred to the Brethren, was among these. Surrounded by other individuals, he knelt before the open Bible and asked God to give all of them further insights into His truth. Their prayer was for open hearts and minds, which would remain open. Through prayer and searching they came to believe that they had discovered new truths, truths which were not embodied in any other existing denomination as fully as they thought necessary. For this reason they went into the River Eder and by trine immersion established the Church of the Brethren.

III. These Newly Discovered Truths

What were these new truths which they believed they had discovered?

First was the determination to keep open the door through which they had come into existence: the right of a continuing, prayerful, openminded search for truth. In order to assure this they determined from the first that the New Testament would be their perpetual textbook; they would not restrict it with a creed. Discipleship, study, prayer, and growth toward Godlikeness would be their goal. "Knock, and it shall be opened unto you" would be their faith and their prayer.

This was an unusual principle for that day, and it continues to be an unusual principle in the present day. Love, not force;

teaching, not coercion, is to be the way. It has been hard, in each succeeding generation, for the Brethren fully to live up to this striking opportunity and teaching. But they set out to live it and teach it. They desired to broaden the freedom of this valley, to make it as wide as people, to free all minds in a quest for God.

A second aspect of the Brethren findings was that they resolved to follow the ordinances of the Bible as teaching devices. Through such observance the Christian could better grow in grace and in the knowledge of God, they believed.

The Lord's supper is a good example. The Brethren resolved to follow this both literally and in its symbolic teaching. Feet-washing meant that he who would be greatest must serve the most. The fellowship meal, or love feast, meant that Brethren recognized the common brotherhood of all men; their love-feast tables would have no end or barrier; from them no one would be excluded. They would reach around the world. This service symbolized the simple, loving, helpful life to which the Brethren committed themselves.

None of this was entirely new. None was a concept totally different from that held by other churches. But Alexander Mack determined to make the open mind and the simple Christlike life the center of his church. It is reported that after the church was established, when a neighbor asked Mack, "And how shall your believers be recognized?" he replied, "They shall be recognized by the manner of their living."

Mack's teaching was that integrity and honesty should make it unnecessary for Brethren to take the legal oath. Their personal lives were to be lived simply and piously; they were to refrain from the use of alcohols, tobaccos, and luxuries. Their homes would be kept simple; their meeting places would be modest; their dress would not be ornate.

They were not to withdraw themselves into any holy or separate community, but would seek always to be helpful to others. This made it impossible for them to participate in war. Rather, wherever hunger was, they would take food. They would seek out the thirsty with cups of cold water. Wherever discord was, they would seek to bring peace; they could not be a part of conflict which destroys both personality and life.

IV. Subsequent Experiences of the Brethren

What happened to this church subsequently?

It fell under persecution from the very first, particularly by the military, and soon its members left this valley. Presently they were driven from the continent and journeyed to Penn's Woods in America, where notification had been given that the same kind of freedom which they first experienced in this valley would again be accorded to them. There they landed, after a rough ocean crossing, and helped to develop a town which was designated with the name of the country from which they and its Mennonite founders came, Germantown. There, again, they tried to live by the principles of helpfulness and peace.

Once more this led them into persecution, since they could not participate in the wars and conflicts which have plagued and crippled our world throughout much of its history. Christopher Sauer's publishing establishment was destroyed. Other Brethren property similarly was dissipated. The Brethren were willing to pay with suffering for their belief in the way of peace. Consequently, in America, as earlier in Europe, the Church of the Brethren was scattered. From Germantown its members migrated to other parts of the United States, moving with the frontiers as they were opened and new states were formed.

Persecutions followed them, always enhanced when warfare arose. When the War Between the States divided America, the Brethren sought to be helpful to those who suffered in both the North and the South. John Kline, one of their leaders, was shot in carrying out such a ministry. A stone marker erected at the spot where he fell testifies to the continuing desire of the Brethren to be peacemakers, to be helpful instead of hurtful.

Following the Civil War, the Brethren regrouped themselves and undertook once again to widen the freedom of the Eder

Valley to encompass the world. They sent out missionaries to India, China, and Nigeria; some of their teachers came back to Europe.

When World War I encompassed the world, the Brethren, as could be expected, were brought under persecution. Some of them suffered in prison rather than participate in warfare.

Their desire, however, was to find ways to help those who suffered because of war. They wished to go beyond this and to help discover and remove the causes of war; they sought to apply the ways of the free and searching mind to the cause of peace.

The Brethren Service arm of the church was a natural outgrowth of the Brethren belief through the years. The church actively undertook to have recognized and established in America, and later in other nations of the world, if possible, an alternative service to war. The Brethren wished to help others rather than to hurt them. The American government presently accepted an alternative service in lieu of military service. The Brethren and others of like point of view discovered and sponsored ways for young men to serve those who were in need. Some young men did this in lieu of military service. Others did it who were not involved with the military. Young women joined these young men in volunteer and unpaid service.

Thus, the Brethren came back to Europe with goods, cattle, and willing hands. They journeyed to many other parts of the world on the same mission. They entered as helpfully as they could into humanitarian services. Their representatives now encircle the globe. They wish only to give cups of water to the thirsty and to walk helpfully in every dark and lonely valley, under the guidance of Christ, their Example and Teacher.

The Brethren are still searching for the truths of God which will make possible the fulfillment of the ideal of the first Christmas hymn, glory to God on high and on earth peace among men. M. R. Zigler, Dan West, Harold Row, Wilbur Mullen, and many others known in Schwarzenau have been active in giving guidance to this part of the Brethren program. They are still trying to broaden the freedoms, and the sharing, serving spirit of Alexander Mack's beginnings, to encompass the world.

They have become a church of over eleven hundred organized congregations, totaling two hundred thirteen thousand members. Forty of these churches, with a membership of about thirteen thousand, are located outside of the United States in Canada, Ecuador, Puerto Rico, India, and Nigeria. Some of these representatives you have already heard speak here today. Churches also exist inside China, but of these little has been known for the past several years since China has been closed. In addition to these organized churches, a vast number of service workers are, or have been, located throughout Europe and on all the other continents with the exception of Australia. These workers seek to serve needy humanity in any way possible. Thousands of tons of clothing and food have been sent abroad; ten thousand head of cattle under the slogan, "Heifers for Relief," have been sent to thirty-four countries by the Brethren and by others who joined them in this undertaking; six thousand "seagoing" cowboys have transported these cattle to their destinations.

The church maintains six colleges and one seminary. Its headquarters are located at Elgin, Illinois, which is also the site of its publishing plant. The church regularly publishes a half-dozen magazines for various age groups and for the entire church. It also publishes books written by its own members, or by others, thus carrying on the writing and publication interests of its founders.

Each year the church holds an Annual Conference in which delegates from all of these churches around the world meet in inspirational and business meetings. These delegates, usually numbering about one thousand, constitute the governing body of the church. They are drawn without distinction from the laity, from men and from women, thus maintaining the democratic nature of the church.

V. What of the Future?

Where shall the Brethren go from here? What shall be their rededication?

The Brethren have not become a large denomination. They have not turned the world upside down. They have sought with earnestness, however, to give a testimony to simple, openhearted, helpful, Christian living. They have sought to keep their minds and hearts open so that Christ can indeed live, in the fullness of love, within their lives and use them for His Kingdom's purposes.

This should be their commitment for the future. It is a simple commitment: openness to God's increasing indwelling; complete surrender to God's will and to God's use; complete dedication to the Master's prayer for the world, "That they all may be one." This, the Brethren believe, should be their dedication for their future. The Eder River should flow through every valley in the world.

Love is the ultimate weapon against any or all conflict; love alone can cast out fear. God himself is love. The Brethren wish to be wholly dedicated to love.

May God bless this anniversary pilgrimage. May His Spirit bless this valley, and the people who dwell here. May God bless the members of the Church of the Brethren and make of them His servants as He leads us from this valley and from this day into an unfolding and growing future.

32. CHANGELESS PRINCIPLES IN A CHANGING WORLD

PAUL H. BOWMAN

President emeritus of Bridgewater College; minister; lecturer; writer; chairman, 250th Anniversary Committee; compiler and editor of The Adventurous Future; chairman of the committee to plan the new General Offices building; home, Timberville, Virginia. Formerly: pastor, Philadelphia (Bethany), Pennsylvania; president, Blue Ridge College; president, Bridgewater College; member, General Brotherhood Board and earlier boards; moderator, Annual Conference, 1937 and 1949.

The roots of Brethren faith are imbedded in the religious soil of Germany — the country which is our gracious host for these few days.

The kindly and sturdy people of Schwarzenau are in some instances probably our kinsmen by the ties of common ancestry. We might have been brothers also in faith and culture except for the vicissitudes of history and the lapse of the centuries which have separated us.

We are deeply grateful to you, President Wilm, as bishop of Westphalia, and to your associates; to His Highness, the Prince of Wittgenstein; to you, Mayor Gottschalk and the members of the town council of Schwarzenau; and to our friends here and to the citizens of this charming community, for the warmth of your welcome both to your village and to your country.

No more appropriate setting could be found in all the world for the Brethren in which to re-examine our religious heritage and recommit ourselves to the vital and timeless elements of our faith.

I. The World of Absolutes

I do not want to burden you with a multiplicity of texts, but since the Brethren are Trinitarians I assume that it would be in order for me to choose at least three texts for my address.

My first text was found in a very unusual place. It is from a billboard in a large city, the city of Richmond, Virginia, the capital of my home state. That billboard stands at the edge of the campus of a great college. It is also on a busy street where throngs of men and women are continually passing by. It stands also in the shadow of several great public buildings. The state library is close by, as are also the state capitol, the governor's mansion, and other buildings which are centers of government. There at a seat of learning and culture, there in the marts of trade and commerce, there in the confused jungle of politics, this enormous billboard proclaims its message in these vital words: "The changeless laws of God still apply in a changing world."

My second text comes from the New Testament. There is an eloquent passage in the writings of St. Paul in which he mentions One whom "God has highly exalted . . . and bestowed on him the name which is above every name, that at the name of Jesus every knee should bow, in heaven and on earth and under the earth, and every tongue confess that Jesus Christ is Lord, to the glory of God the Father." The writer of Hebrews adds a magnificent stroke to this concept when he refers to the changeless One as "Jesus Christ . . . the same yesterday and today and forever."

My third text is taken from the Annual Conference minutes of 1957. In stating the objectives of the two-hundred-fiftieth anniversary celebration, the Conference said, "We shall seek to conserve for our times the relevant values of our living past."

These texts, drawn from widely different sources, hold in common a single idea. They bear witness to a world in which things are fixed and stable. They disclose those realities of life which do not change with every changing breeze. It is that world of absolutes, a world of changeless principles, the same yesterday and today and forever, which I declare unto you.

It was this changeless world for which our fathers sought two and one-half centuries ago, and for which the spirit of man almost in desperation seeks in our own day.

"Change and decay in all around I see.
O Thou, who changest not, abide with me."

II. Our Changing World

Change is evident everywhere in man's world. Change itself is a changeless law of life which we cannot escape.

Life is full of beginnings and endings. Its processes, irresistible in their force, are in endless movement. Day and night follow each other in rapid succession. No power can halt the rotation of the seasons or arrest the swing of the planets in their orbits. Our world is one of movement and of change.

Even our physical growth is an unending process. The intellectual and spiritual life of man, with its ideas, thoughts, and concepts, is also in constant flux and modification. Our emphases in science, education, government, religion, and all great social movements are revised and modified from generation to generation.

Change is not only the law of life; it is also the law of progress. There are times in history when old ideas must be abandoned and the mind of man emancipated from the past. If new ideas fail to appear and new vision fades, then stagnation and death are inevitable.

It would seem that God loves change, else He would not have made a world like this.

Change is difficult and sometimes revolutionary. Thinking and acting anew is not as simple as we sometimes believe it to be. It is much easier for most of us to go on thinking and acting as we have always done.

What suffering accompanies the abandonment of old prejudices, the setting aside of worn-out dogma, and the freeing of ourselves from the grip of a dead past!

In the midst of our changing order, man is restless. He seeks stability and is constantly in search of solid ground. His spirit demands certitudes which are adequate for the stress and strain of his turbulent life. This deep hunger of the human soul is a common aspiration of Christians everywhere.

III. Christ and Change

Christ, our Lord, was not afraid of change. He sought to conserve the good and the best of the order which was already old in his day. He came "not to destroy but to fulfill." Yet he loosened the shackles of the law which had held the spirits of men in servitude for uncounted centuries. He planted in the minds of a few men some of the most revolutionary ideas of all time. He was the forerunner of a new order. He is always hovering on the edge of today calling His followers to a changing and adventurous tomorrow.

The church of Christ was born in revolution. It has known change and transformation in all the centuries of its history. But through all this it remains unafraid. The church has ridden out storm after storm from Pentecost and Antioch to Rome and Wittenberg, and from the heart of Europe to the shores of America and the jungles of Africa.

The decisive test of Christianity is that in the midst of change and revolution there are elements of faith which remain constant and are continuously relevant to the will of God, to the life of man, and to the problems of complex society.

It was for those principles of faith which defy change and retain their relevancy, that our fathers sought. They struggled, vaguely perhaps, amid the very scenes which here surround us, for those incalculable values of mind and spirit. In study and prayer, and amid misunderstanding and persecution, they sought to separate the permanent and timeless elements of faith from the temporary and transient, and to pass on to us the fruitage of their labors. It is our obligation to keep those principles clear and free them from the hampering accretions of the passing centuries.

IV. Brethren Principles

Our past history, like that of all peoples, has both its charm and its regret. But we are not here to idolize the past or to apologize for the mistakes of our history. Our prime concern is for those living elements of our faith which still apply in our changing world. It is that heritage which we seek to quicken, preserve, and perpetuate for the good of mankind.

Principles are constant and develop along constant lines, whereas the rules of the church are temporary and short lived. The rules may be repealed and superseded, but the order of God rests on moral absolutes which are the enduring substance of the church and of society.

Let us in humility and with a deep sense of inadequacy seek to set forth some of these living and changeless principles.

1. *The principle of the open mind and the open Book.* In the quiet seclusion of this beautiful valley the early Brethren searched the Scriptures, explored history, and sought earnestly for the guidance of the Spirit of God in their struggle to know the mind of Christ.

They rejected the creeds and the dogma of their day not because of disrespect for the church of Christ or failure to appreciate the importance of the doctrinal undergirding of the Christian faith, but because they were convinced of the futility of theological controversy and feared the stultifying effect of creedal pronouncements. Throughout these two and one-half centuries the Brethren have steadfastly refused to subscribe to any formal creed and have with equal steadfastness accepted the New Testament as their sole authority in matters of faith and practice. Our fathers were dedicated to the task of keeping open the channels of truth not only in their time but for all time to come.

We confess our failure to discriminate always between the

rules of the church and the living principles of our faith, and our failure to undergird adequately the doctrinal structure of our faith. We have not always been able to rise above our traditions and prejudices, and we have sometimes closed our minds too quickly. But regardless of our proneness to forget, we consider the principle of the open mind and the free search of the Scriptures relevant to truth and progress and vital to the Christian order in our own times.

2. *The principle of freedom in religion.* The principle of religious freedom undergirds our protest against compulsion in religion and sustains our insistence that dominance over the conscience of man may be exercised by no authority on earth, either ecclesiastical or political. In the light of this position, our fathers admitted into the fellowship of the church only those who were able to "count the cost" and were prepared by confession, penitence, and faith to commit themselves to the duties and responsibilities of the Christian life.

The Brethren have not claimed the right of conscience for themselves alone. What we seek for ourselves in this respect we seek for every honest soul in all the world. We appeal to all statesmen, governments, and political parties in all nations of the world to recognize the right of man to freedom of worship and to the free exercise of faith and conscience. That principle we consider universally relevant to the dignity and the happiness of man, and to the fulfillment of human life. We pray and strive continually that the blessing of this freedom may come to all people everywhere.

3. *The principle of love and universal goodwill.* Our fathers were committed to the principle of brotherly love and goodwill in all human relationships. This they considered Biblical and Christian, morally right and politically practical. It was for them a bond of fellowship in the church and the basis of harmony, stability, and security in society.

As corollaries of this principle, the Brethren advocated nonviolence, nonlitigation, and the adjustment of disagreements and differences by deliberation and reason in the spirit of reconciliation and forgiveness.

They could allow no dominance of one man over another in servitude. They could not condone the practice of racism with its withering effects on life and personality. Nor could they accumulate wealth, demand for themselves unlimited luxury, or claim excessive benefits when those benefits were assessed against others in terms of want, hunger, disease, and suffering. They could not consider themselves irresponsible for those who are unable to stand alone against those forces in society which make for repression, corruption, and disintegration of human life and personality.

On this principle rests the Brethren ministry of relief, rehabilitation, and two hundred fifty years of continuous advocacy of peace and reconciliation.

Another major and inevitable corollary of this principle is our incessant movement for peace and goodwill among the nations of the world. The church, true to its Christ and under His Lordship, must in our concept speak its message of peace to the world on this desperate issue. Brethren can never assent to the military madness of mankind, nor yield to the callousness of the age which coldly condones the staggering burden of war. It is our role, even if we must stand alone, to help create a climate of trust and goodwill in which peace may have a positive promise of success. We consider it our duty as Christians, and as children of our Brethren ancestors, to call upon the nations to seek security, not on the basis of fear and preponderance of arms, but on the basis of love, reason, understanding, and goodwill.

As Christians and as Brethren we have no choice — we must to our utmost refuse to engage in war.

4. *The principle of creative citizenship.* Our fathers regarded religious duty as entirely compatible with civil duty but not subservient to it.

The Brethren recognize the validity of civil government and have generally included in their prayers and supplications all "kings and rulers and those in authority." But they established a boundary between civil and religious duty at the point where the two became irreconcilable. At that point they obey the voice of God rather than the voice of man.

The Brethren seek to be creative citizens. They are not anarchists. They support their government in loyalty but refuse to violate the commands of conscience and of religious faith at the behest of civil, political, or military power. They obey the law, they pay their taxes, they exercise the right of suffrage, and they otherwise take a constructive attitude toward government.

But in times of war Brethren seek to be removed as far as possible from violence and bloodshed. They want to serve only in those enterprises which are dedicated to the relief of suffering and which are calculated to allay the hatred and bitterness engendered by war. They are devoted to a ministry of reconciliation, believing it to be the way of Christ.

5. *The principle of demonstrative Christianity*. Our fathers were devoted to the belief that our profession of faith must offer in everyday life a practical demonstration of its claims.

We confess in humility and penitence our sometimes timid and weak witness for Christ in our own day. Our message to the world, sometimes dull and unconvincing, has often concerned itself with matters of small meaning. We do not waver, however, in our conviction that what we proclaim from pulpit and sanctuary must be verified in our dealings with our fellow men. The tone and quality of our declaration of faith must be reflected in the pattern of life which issues in deeds and actions.

This principle, applied in life, means accuracy and veracity in speech, and honesty in our dealing with one another. It means no false testimony, no short change, no cheap service, no shabby product, no winning by foul means, no compromise with evil. It means a life of humility, of meekness, of simplicity, of purity, of mercy, of justice, and of devotion to all righteousness.

It means a life of peace and harmony, and of love for God and neighbor. Faith, we believe, without verification and demonstration in the crowded laboratory of life is in process of disintegration and decay.

6. *The principle of the simple life.* The doctrine of the simple life has a new relevancy in our day. Our fathers sometimes employed drastic measures in their eagerness to keep themselves disentangled from the world. Their emphasis upon the "other world" may on occasion have limited their awareness of the world in which their daily lives were cast, and may have blinded them to their current responsibilities and opportunities. But their struggle to avoid deflection from spiritual values by the appeal and the insistent demands of the immediate and the temporary confronts us even today with desperate urgency.

The tyranny of things in our Western civilization challenges our highest culture and our deepest spirituality. Our fathers dealt with the problem in terms of dress, amusements, sports, comforts, and the waste of resources in useless expense, extravagant living, and carnal indulgences. But for us the chief concerns of life easily degenerate into the pursuit of happiness based on convenience, comfort, and security. We subordinate the meaning of life to physical and, therefore, to transient ends. Our treasures are those which moth and rust readily corrupt. We labor and earn, we fret and spend for the things we do not need and often do not want, all in order to keep up with the procession, or to hold our party in power, or to prevent our industrial machine from stalling.

Our amazing advances in science and invention, and all the wonders of modern technology, have not modified human frailty, offered relief from encroaching senility, provided an answer to the brevity of human existence on earth or offered a refuge from the terrors of life which haunt us both day and night.

The meaning and significance of human life, trust in the kindly providence of the Almighty who is our refuge and fortress, and loyalty and devotion to spiritual values as against the secular and material, have bounded into new relevance in our day.

7. *The principle of the dominance of Christ.* Our fathers, nurtured in the atmosphere of devotion and prayer at Schwarzenau, in 1708 accepted Christ as their supreme Lord and their only Savior. His name to them was above every name and they bowed the knee to no other. The mysteries of His origin, of His personality, of His sinlessness, of His power, and of His oneness with the Father were above debate and beyond the realm of question and controversy. He was their Lord, yesterday, today, and forever. His will, His teaching, and His comradeship held for them a continuing relevancy to man's spiritual poverty in the midst of his little systems and the shifting sands of his changing world.

When we Brethren are true to our heritage, Christ is Lord of our personal lives. His ideals, and teachings, and example, and spirit, are for us the finalities of faith. Christ is also, for us, Lord of the church which is His body, knit together in love and unity. He is also Lord of history, guiding and directing human affairs to the consummation of that Kingdom which is everlasting.

Brethren have no exclusive claim to the Lordship of Christ. He is the Lord of the whole church, which includes diverse types of worship and great varieties of interpretation, activity, and forms of helpful service.

The dividedness of the modern church must mean agony to the Spirit of our Lord and is a hampering impediment to the effectiveness of His church. Acceptance of the Lordship of Christ implies responsibility for helping heal the breaches of His church in our day.

We must seek unity in diversity and learn that in the midst of conflicting opinion we may still find unity in our common love and loyalty for Christ, who is Lord and Savior of men and women of every race and tongue.

V. Conclusion

These principles we believe to be universally relevant. They witness to ultimate values and are limited neither by time nor by geography. Our fathers believed them to be valid in 1708 and we believe them to be valid still.

Christ our Lord is always going on before. He is always inspiring new ventures of faith and imparting to us new insights. He is forever breaking new ground and calling us to new areas of service.

To our Lord, who is the same yesterday, today, and forever, to the living elements of our faith which we believe to be changeless and yet relevant to a changing world, and to the Lordship of Christ transcendent of both time and space, we dedicate ourselves in penitence, humility, and gratitude. We face the adventurous future with a firm resolve that the living elements of our faith shall, under Christ, continue to live in us and apply in our changing world.

33. THE LITANY OF DEDICATION

On the banks of the Eder, as the evening sun tinted the hills of Wittgenstein with its fading rays, several hundred Brethren gathered at the traditional site of the first baptisms of Brethren in a service of solemn dedication. Moderator Desmond W. Bittinger led this impressive service in conclusion of the Schwarzenau convocation.

HYMN: *Breathe Upon Us, Holy Spirit*

Breathe upon us, Holy Spirit,
As adoringly we bow
At these altars, pure and sacred,
Paying Thee our solemn vow;
All our feeble graces quicken
With the streams of Thy sweet grace,
And make glorious with Thy presence
This Thy holy dwelling place.

Thou art pure and Thou art holy;
Jesus, make us more like Thee.
Thou art meek and Thou art lowly;
So may we, Thy children, be.
Shed abroad Thy love within us;
Fill our souls with light divine;
Holy Spirit, seal, anoint us,
And our earthliness refine.

LEADER: Look down upon us kindly, our Father, as we are assembled reverently before Thee. May our spirits be bowed in thanksgiving and respect for our forefathers who here, in this river, through holy baptism, under Thy blessing brought into being our beloved fellowship, the Church of the Brethren. May our hearts be readied for a rededication in this hour. May we be open to receive whatever blessing and guidance Thou, in Thy mercy, art ready to bestow upon us.

HYMN:
Now receive us as repentant
To Thy heart of love we fly;
Pardon all our sin and folly,
Lead us to Thyself on high.
O these hearts need Thy refining,
And the cleansing of Thy blood!
Consecrate and make us holy,
Through redemption's crimson flood.

Here shall love, like sacred incense,
Upward mount to Thy great throne,
From the cleansed heart and conscience
Of a people all Thine own.
Humble are the gifts we bring Thee,
And upon Thine altar lay,
Yet be gracious to Thy children
As they worship Thee today.

LEADER AND PEOPLE: At that time the disciples came to Jesus, saying, "Who is the greatest in the kingdom of heaven?" And calling to him a little child, he put him in the midst of them and said, "Truly, I say unto you, unless you turn and become like children, you will never enter the kingdom of heaven.

"If your brother sins against you, go and tell him his fault, between you and him alone. If he listens to you, you have gained your brother."

LITANY OF REPENTANCE

LEADER: Almighty God, Spirit of Love and Grace, whose dwelling is with the humble and those of contrite heart, hear Thy children's confession of sin and grant us Thy mercy. For all that has been evil in our lives, for every unholy thought and every impure motive, for all of our failures to give always of our best to Thee, for any

	trifling with truth, or failure to comprehend Thy will, for being petty when we should have been gracious and growing;
People:	Forgive us, O Lord.
Leader:	For every failure to manifest our love toward Thee whose love has never faltered toward us, for every doubt of Thy power and of Thy providence, for every ingratitude, for every act of selfishness, for every unwillingness to share freely with others that which Thou hast so freely given to us, for any dullness of insight which has kept us unaware of Thy goodness and glory, and for every failure fully to do Thy will;
People:	Forgive us, O Lord, and may we henceforth love Thee and serve Thee as we ought.
Leader:	For all the wrong we have done to our fellow men; for hatred and anger and warfare, for waste in wars and preparations for wars, of the products Thou hast given to us; for failures in justice; for arrogant pride and any contempt of the lowly; for forgetfulness of others' pain and advantage taken of others' weakness; for whatever any person may rightfully hold against us;
People:	Forgive us, O Lord, and help us to learn how to love our neighbors as ourselves.
Leader:	For our many failures to live faithfully the principles of our faith as Thou didst reveal them to our founders, for our obsession with the lesser matters of the Kingdom when Thou dost even now press upon us so patiently the weightier matters;
People:	Forgive us, O Lord, and continually teach us.
Leader:	For our faulty following of Thy Son, our Lord and Master; for our hesitant answers to His call for service; for our lack of sensitivity to the full meaning of the cross; for all that mars our best discipleship;
People:	Forgive us, O Lord, and give us grace to follow our Lord and Master as we ought.

Leader
and People: Amen.

LITANY OF SCRIPTURE READING

Leader: And He opened His mouth and taught them, saying, Blessed are the poor in spirit;

People: For theirs is the kingdom of heaven.

Leader: Blessed are those who mourn;

People: For they shall be comforted.

Leader: Blessed are the meek;

People: For they shall inherit the earth.

Leader: Blessed are those who hunger and thirst for righteousness;

People: For they shall be satisfied.

Leader: Blessed are the merciful;

People: For they shall obtain mercy.

Leader: Blessed are the pure in heart;

People: For they shall see God.

Leader: Blessed are the peacemakers;

People: For they shall be called the sons of God.

Leader: Blessed are those who are persecuted for righteousness' sake;

People: For theirs is the kingdom of heaven.

Leader: Blessed are you when men revile you and persecute you and utter all kinds of evil against you falsely, on my account.

People: Rejoice, and be glad, for your reward is great in heaven, for so men persecuted the prophets who were before you.

Leader
and People: Ye are the salt of the earth, but if salt has lost its taste, how shall its saltness be restored? It is no longer good for anything, except to be thrown out and trodden underfoot of men. You are the light of the world, a city set on a hill cannot be hid, nor do men light a lamp and put it under a bushel, but on a stand and it gives light

to all in the house. Let your light so shine before men that they may see your good works and give glory to your Father in heaven.

HYMN: *More Love to Thee, O Christ*

More love to Thee, O Christ,
More love to Thee!
Hear Thou the prayer I make
On bended knee;
This is my earnest plea:
More love, O Christ, to Thee,
More love to Thee,
More love to Thee!

LITANY OF PRAYER FOR THE COMING OF CHRIST'S KINGDOM

LEADER: The kingdoms of this world shall become the Kingdom of our Lord and of His Christ, and He shall reign forever and ever.

PEOPLE: O Father of men, who hast promised that all the kingdoms of the world are to become the Kingdom of Thy Son, purge the nations of error and corruption, overthrow the power of sin, and establish justice and righteousness in every land. Incline the hearts of all rulers and peoples to live and to rule uprightly. May righteousness enter into every city, every church, and every home to dwell and to grow. So may justice, mercy, and peace prevail among the nations and may Thy name be glorified; through Christ, our Lord.

LEADER: May the children of our own land and every land grow to understand the awfulness and the sinfulness of war. May they, under Thy blessing, develop a true love of peace; may we and they renounce all self-seeking; may we and they devote our lives to the service of Christ in the building of a just, a righteous, and a peaceful world. Grant to us the continuing gift of Thy Holy Spirit that Thy Kingdom may come in us and in the world.

PEOPLE: Lord, in mercy, hear us and help us and our children so to do. Amen.

LITANY OF THANKSGIVING AND PRAYER FOR OUR CHURCH

LEADER: Father, we give Thee thanks for the founders of our church, for those who in this river, on their knees, were cleansed and born again, that Thy will might be more fully done in their own lives and in those parts of the world which their influence would touch.

PEOPLE: We thank Thee for our founders.

LEADER: For those who came after them, even until now, we give Thee thanks; for their emphasis on the good life, for their openness to growth and their discoveries of new truth, for their eagerness to live honestly, simply, and helpfully, for their reverence for Thy Word and their faithful study of it, for their endeavor to love and serve their fellow men, we give Thee thanks.

PEOPLE: For these, our seeking fathers, we give Thee thanks.

LEADER AND PEOPLE: Strong Father, give us courage and wisdom for the living of these days.
Deepen our humility.
Broaden our minds.
Increase our dedication.
Tie us inseparably to Thee and to Thy Word.
Make more unselfish and more effective the service we seek to render in Thy name.
Renew within us Thy Holy Spirit.
Make us more forgiving, more loving, more serving.
May we follow more fully the selfless life of Thy Son.
May we forever live and serve Thee,
Under the Lordship of Jesus Christ,
Until Thy kingdom is fully come.
For Thy name's sake. Amen.

LEADER AND PEOPLE: Our Father who art in heaven, Hallowed be Thy name. Thy kingdom come, Thy will be done,

On earth as it is in heaven.
Give us this day our daily bread;
And forgive us our debts
As we have forgiven our debtors;
And lead us not into temptation, But deliver us from evil:
For Thine is the kingdom, and the power, and the glory, for ever.
Amen.

HYMN: *God of Grace and God of Glory*
God of grace and God of glory,
On Thy people pour Thy power;
Crown Thine ancient church's story;
Bring her bud to glorious flower.
Grant us wisdom,
Grant us courage,
For the facing of this hour,
For the facing of this hour. Amen.

PART FIVE

Greetings, Resolutions, and Miscellaneous Materials

34. GREETINGS FROM THE PRESIDENT OF THE UNITED STATES

THE WHITE HOUSE
Washington

June 16, 1958

To the members and friends of the Church of the Brethren assembled in their 250th Anniversary Conference, I send greetings.

Inspired by a splendid heritage of faith and work, the Brethren Communion has long served the Nation in a constructive and creative way. I am sure this anniversary will strengthen your dedication to the sacred objectives of peace, justice, truth, and right.

Congratulations and best wishes for a memorable conference.

Signed: Dwight D. Eisenhower

35. GREETINGS FROM THE NATIONAL COUNCIL OF CHURCHES

GREETINGS TO THE GERMANTOWN CONVOCATION

These greetings were presented at the Germantown Convocation by Dr. R. H. Edwin Espy, the Associate General Secretary of the National Council of Churches.

It is a great privilege to bring greetings from the National Council of the Churches of Christ in the U. S. A. as well as from the World Council of Churches and state and local councils to this historic assemblage of the Church of the Brethren. Your sister churches of many denominations and many nations rejoice with you in the two hundred fifty years of your distinctive witness of brotherhood and service in the name of Christ throughout the world. We join with you in gratitude to Almighty God for the guidance and strength which He has given so abundantly to the Church of the Brethren from the time of your inception in Schwarzenau, Germany, in 1708, through the years of emigration, expansion, persecution, separation, consolidation, and growth up to this present hour.

You are gathered at a time of supreme need in the affairs of men. It is a time that calls as perhaps never before in history for the qualities of spirit and living for which Brethren have always stood. What man of goodwill and sound mind can fail to see that we need a new recourse to the elemental teachings and example of Jesus as disclosed in the New Testament; a resolute practice of love, brotherhood, and service in relations with our fellow men; a spiritual alternative to the madness of modern war; a transmutation of doctrine into life; a simplicity of living and humility of spirit that subordinates the superficial to the substantial and meaningful; a fellowship within the church that relies on gentle persuasion, Christian nurture, and the guidance of the Holy Spirit in the hearts of godly men; a missionary zeal to bring the lonely and the lost of the world into the knowledge and love of God through the saving power of Jesus Christ?

The ecumenical movement is indebted to the Brethren for upholding these verities of our Christian faith and for your willingness to share them with your sister churches. In our common effort to make manifest the reality of the universal Church of Christ, we do not seek uniformity. We need the richness of gifts with which God has endowed all the members of the body of Christ. We in the ecumenical movement are not a superchurch, nor do we espouse a single creed. We acknowledge Jesus Christ as divine Lord and Savior. Because He is our only foundation, we are evangelical in belief and purpose. We are responsibly representative of, not parallel to, our participating member communions. We seek through common worship and witness and service and thought and fellowship to exalt the one Lord, remembering His promise: "Where two or three are gathered in my name, there am I in the midst of them."

In this assurance, those of us here from sister communions in the National Council of Churches feel profoundly at one with you in the memorable observances and ordinances of this day. We join with you as fellow members of the ecumenical movement, which is a movement of the spirit, not an organization or institution. We thank you for what you mean to us.

We look forward to an ever-deepening fellowship with you in the ecumenical witness of the Church of Christ. And we join in prayer to the God and Father of us all that He may bless and use the Church of the Brethren in the future as mightily as He has blessed and used you in the past two and a half centuries for the cause of His Kingdom.

Official Greetings From the General Board

Greetings to the Church of the Brethren on its two-hundred-fiftieth anniversary:

On the occasion of this anniversary year, the National Council of the Churches of Christ in the United States of America extends its fraternal greetings.

We note that your anniversary theme is *Brethren Under the Lordship of Christ*. Believing, with you, that there is but one "good and faithful Shepherd" calling us all into the "one flock," we take our place by your side as you reappraise Brethren history with a view of conserving the values of your living past.

The genius of Brethren life and thought, as your anniversary statement affirms, consists "in relating religion to life, belief to action, and theology to ethics." This demonstrative Christianity becomes a living witness to the Lordship of Christ in our time, offering "redemption to sinners, relief to the needy, assurance to the hungry of heart, joy and harmony in home and family, love and brotherhood to the church, and peace, justice, and neighborliness to the world."

We welcome the clarity of your emphasis upon New Testament teaching and witness, with particular Christian insights concerning the life of peace, temperance, integrity, and domestic tranquility. We share your determination to include all racial, economic, social, and cultural groups within the fellowship of ministering congregations, with the goal an integrated church in an integrated community.

The Christian witness begins today, as you affirmed two hundred fifty years ago, with humility and confession of sin. The disciplines of this anniversary year, we trust, will bring "increasing prayer for purity of heart, for clearness of vision, and for grace to subject the human will to the will of God." Thus, may the Church of the Brethren "be strengthened with might through His Spirit in the inner man" to the end that "Christ may dwell in your hearts through faith" as together we strive for a "redeemed world of personal excellence and social righteousness."

36. A STATEMENT FROM CHURCH WORLD SERVICE

This statement of greetings and appreciation was presented to the Central Committee of the World Council of Churches at Nyborg, Denmark, on August 22, 1958, in behalf of Church World Service.

The churches of the United States of America engaged in the ministries of relief and interchurch aid through Church World Service, National Council of Churches of Christ in the U.S.A., owe a deep debt of gratitude to the Church of the Brethren for its distinctive contribution to their common task. We are richly grateful for the graceful and practical spirit with which across the years the members of this church have borne their witness to the lovingkindness of the Lord and so helped us all to participate more usefully and fully in our service to human need.

The occasion of the anniversary of the founding of the Church of the Brethren offers us the opportunity to express our gratitude. We wish to record the fact of the imaginative helpfulness of the Church of the Brethren in this ecumenical task which we have accepted as our common responsibility. Our expression of thanks and affection to our colleagues has been sharply stimulated by the recent tragic deaths of Mrs. Amy Zigler and twenty members of the anniversary deputation. We hope that the Church of the Brethren will accept this expression of our thanks and our deepest sympathy, in token of which the churches of the United States which work together in Church World Service give to the World Council of Churches the sum of $10,000 toward the cost of its new headquarters. Our wish is that this contribution should be regarded as both a memorial to the persons who have been killed and a tangible expression of our affection and gratitude toward the Church of the Brethren for its witness to the gospel of Jesus Christ across the years.

Signed by:
Harper Sibly: President of Church World Service
Paul B. Freeland: Chairman of the Executive Committee
R. Norris Wilson: Executive Director

37. GREETINGS FROM THE EVANGELICAL CHURCH IN AUSTRIA

These greetings were presented by Dr. Georg Traar, the honorary head of the Protestant Relief Agency of Austria and superintendent of the Evangelical Churches of Vienna, to the Brethren representatives at Vienna on July 23, 1958.

It is a special joy for the Evangelical Church in Austria, on the occasion of the two-hundred-fiftieth anniversary of the Church of the Brethren, to greet a deputation of this church in our own country.

The association of the Evangelical Church in Austria with the Church of the Brethren during the past eleven years has been in the area of interchurch aid. The material aid of the Brethren within the Evangelical Church in Austria cannot be valued highly enough. Naturally the World Council of Churches, the Lutheran World Federation, and other ecumenical organizations have brought to Austria much larger amounts of such help. The distinct value of your help lies in the fact that you brought to Austria not just gifts alone, but your members and workers, who were among us to work with us, to think with us and for us.

The material help does not possess the same urgency now as at the beginning of our co-operation. But it is not sufficient yet, nor will it be for a long time. The need among the individual Austrian church members and among the refugees, who during the last years have acquired citizenship, is still so very great that we alone cannot complete the task. We urgently need the help of the World Council of Churches, and of the Lutheran World Federation, and others. So we would be thankful if the Church of the Brethren would also continue its help.

An essential service of the Brethren is that they have made personal friendship so easy. Therefore, Bishop May, when he was in Evanston, and I, when I was in Minneapolis, visited Elgin and quickly felt as though we were at home.

This warm brotherly fellowship was accompanied also, of course, by another fact. The Church of the Brethren has refrained from establishing churches in our country, and, so far as I know, in all Europe. The temptation to do this has certainly existed. It really reveals deeply grounded brotherhood, and, at the same time, clear Christian awareness, that the Church of the Brethren has followed such a policy. It is because of this fact that your witness of deeds has come with greater weight. Christian love cannot be practiced alone. It must, above all, be practiced in deeds. The Church of the Brethren has at no time and in no place sought or advocated her own interests. Her witness is thereby genuine and convincing.

The approach of the Brethren means for our small minority and our dispersed church in Austria the recognition that we, too, in our program are preaching the gospel and building the Church of Jesus Christ.

At the same time, this recognition means for us the ever-stronger and more effective stimulation to take more earnestly even the service of brotherly love and to develop a genuine service program in our church. Alongside the material help, which dare not entirely stop, the Church of the Brethren has still other tasks in our land. She should declare among us, without serving a shallow pacifism, the witness of genuine brotherhood and the true love of peace.

As the encounter with the Church of the Brethren has always raised questions in our circles about the essential Christian fellowship and brotherhood, so ought we to think through and study these questions in the future with one another on the basis of the Holy Scriptures.

Here, above all, through close co-operation with our church, the attempt must be made to free the objection to participation in the military and in war from the political secondary issues and to fill the form of it with real genuine evangelical content. Through this service the emphasis is not on the *no* to military service but on the *yes* to practical and constructive service as a sign of peace.

The work of the Brethren and the Mennonite units in rebuilding the evangelical school on Karlsplatz has made a decided impression and has demonstrated real pioneer work.

The next step would be the creation of a small working committee, composed of members of the Church of the Brethren and the Evangelical Church in Austria, to work on these questions theologically, sociologically, and practically.

38. GREETINGS AND WELCOME FROM SCHWARZENAU

Dear friends of the Church of the Brethren:

By the time you read these lines you will have already started your preparations for your trip to Schwarzenau. You want to look back to the days of the origin of your church and remember the man who founded this church; you also want to see the place where your church started to develop from a small beginning comparable to the grain of mustard seed as mentioned in the New Testament.

The inhabitants of Schwarzenau are happily looking forward with you to this great day in the history of your church. We are also happy because we can avail ourselves of the opportunity to thank you for all the love and kindness which you have shown to the people of Schwarzenau in times of distress, but especially for the generous gift through which you have helped us build the Alexander Mack Schule.

On this schoolyard the tent will be erected in which people from various countries in the world will meet during the celebration of the anniversary.

May God protect you all on your way to our country and guide you safely back to your homeland.

May August 6 be a day of truly Christian fellowship, thus becoming a real Pentecost for all those who will be gathering in the town of Schwarzenau on that occasion.

In the name of our community,
(Signed: Gottschalk)
Mayor of Schwarzenau

Schwarzenau, April 1958

39. THE SCHWARZENAU RESOLUTIONS

These resolutions of gratitude and appreciation were adopted unanimously by the assembly of about four hundred Brethren at the conclusion of the Schwarzenau convocation on August 6, 1958.

The Church of the Brethren on this sixth day of August 1958, assembled in a world convocation of Brethren at Schwarzenau, Germany, in celebration of the two-hundred-fiftieth anniversary of the founding of the church in this beautiful and peaceful village on the Eder, desires:

First: To recognize with praise and gratitude the kindly providence of God our Father, in bringing safely once again to this land of our fathers so many Brethren from the communities of Europe, and from the countries of America, India, Africa, South America, and other parts of the world. We praise God for that blessed fellowship in Christ which knows no bounds of geography, and no partiality of race or color.

Second: To express our profound gratitude and appreciation to the kindly and sturdy people of Schwarzenau, for their tireless effort in preparing for our coming, for the cordial reception which they have extended to us in their homes and community, and for the warmth of their friendship expressed in countless deeds of kindness and helpfulness not only on this occasion but across many years of visitation by our people to this place of our origin.

We especially express our gratitude to the officials of church and government and request that they convey to the people of the Schwarzenau area our warm greetings and deep appreciation.

Third: To pledge the Church of the Brethren, under the

Lordship of Christ our Redeemer, to a renewed ministry of love to all people to the end that peace between man and man, race and race, nation and nation may become a reality on this earth. We reaffirm our faith in the spirit of love and reconciliation as an instrument of harmony among the peoples of the world and implore rulers and statesmen to seek peace and security, not on the basis of violence and preponderance of arms, but upon the principles of brotherhood and goodwill, of reason and understanding, and of freedom and justice to all.

> Signed:
>
> Desmond W. Bittinger, Moderator of the Church of the Brethren
>
> M. R. Zigler, Administrator of Brethren Service in Europe and Representative to the World Council of Churches
>
> S. Loren Bowman, Chairman of the General Brotherhood Board
>
> Paul H. Bowman, Chairman of the 250th Anniversary Committee

40. IN MEMORIAM

The two-hundred-fiftieth anniversary year will certainly be remembered for its inspiration and spiritual uplift. It will also be remembered in history for its tragedy and sorrow. The accident to our brother, M. R. Zigler, on August 16 at Västervik, Sweden, which resulted in serious injury to him and the death of his companion, Amy Arnold Zigler, cast a shadow of grief over the entire Brotherhood and in many areas of the Protestant world.

The air disaster to KLM flight 607E off the western coast of Ireland on August 14, 1958, which took the lives of ninety-nine persons, including passengers and crew, among whom were thirteen Brethren and seven of their friends and companions, spread sorrow to many homes and families throughout the Brotherhood. While none of these were members of the official European delegation, yet their interest, loyalty, and love for the Brotherhood had called them to the scenes of the church's origin and to the celebration in Europe.

We, therefore, dedicate this page to the memory of those who so tragically paid the price so well known to our fathers as they laid the foundations of our heritage two and one-half centuries ago.

Name	Date of Birth	Residence
*Miss Elsie Armstrong	July 30, 1933	Pennsylvania
*Miss Ruthann Armstrong	May 25, 1933	Pennsylvania
*Mrs. Frederick F. (Minerva Marian Mease) Clements	April 5, 1913	Pennsylvania
Eby C. Espenshade	October 21, 1913	Pennsylvania

*Miss Margaret Groh	September 22, 1889	Pennsylvania
*Miss Joy Groff	December 26, 1933	Pennsylvania
*Miss Rose Groff	June 17, 1932	Pennsylvania
Miss Florence Herr	October 16, 1886	Pennsylvania
John C. Hollinger	February 28, 1936	Pennsylvania
Mrs. Alvin Hertzog (Maria Miller Hackman) Hummer	October 4, 1895	Pennsylvania
Reuben H. Hummer	December 18, 1891	Pennsylvania
Mrs. Reuben H. (Fanny Mae Hollinger) Hummer	September 26 1901	Pennsylvania
Miss Audrey Kilhefner	July 31, 1936	Pennsylvania
Mrs. Clyde (Catherine Neff) Kreider	October 4, 1908	Pennsylvania
Max Snider	May 13, 1933	Ohio
Mrs. Max (Joyce Rust) Snider	February 27, 1936	Ohio
Galen Stinebaugh	August 9, 1916	Virginia
Mrs. Galen (Ruth Whitmore) Stinebaugh	July 1, 1916	Virginia
Miss Mary Esther Stoner	November 13, 1917	Pennsylvania
*Mrs. Clayton S. (Nan Tracy) Stoner	April 10, 1888	Georgia

---

* Friends and companions of Church of the Brethren members.

41. GOD OF ALL NATIONS

(The Anniversary Hymn)

Edward K. Ziegler

God of all nations, whose redeeming love
    Has made us free;
For those whose steps, illumined from above,
    Have followed Thee
To this fair land where freedom came to birth —
We thank Thee, Father, Lord of heaven and earth.

As they in faith, obedient, brave and strong,
    Looked up to Thee,
And helped their neighbors, sharing faith and song,
    Lord, now may we
Turn from our feverish, selfish, pagan ways
To serve with gladness in these fateful days.

Grant us the grace to seek Thy sovereign will,
    With one accord;
With holy boldness all our spirits fill,
    We pray Thee, Lord.
Teach us to see half-built against the sky
Thy Kingdom's towers, with faith's discerning eye.

Thou who dost give us bread, our hearts constrain
    With Christlike care,
Thy children's hunger, fear and tragic pain,
    In love to share,
Until Thy gospel's wondrous peace and power
Shall bring at last Thy Kingdom's triumph hour.

42. AT THE END OF OUR TWO-HUNDRED-FIFTIETH YEAR

Desmond W. Bittinger

Now that we are at the end of our two-hundred-fiftieth anniversary year as the Church of the Brethren, it is good to ask these questions: What have we achieved? What have we learned? Where will we go from here?

Writing personally as one upon whom was placed heavy responsibilities through the year, I would like to share a few impressions.

I. Some Impressions

1. My respect for "diese Jünger" — these young ones — increased.

Two vivid impressions grew out of our experiences in Europe. These were pinpointed in the little "House of Friendship," in Kassel, Germany. This *Friedenhorst* seemed smaller than it really was because it stood in the midst of large churches which had been bombed and blasted in the war. Their steeple towers, though twisted and broken, still stood, pointing like crippled fingers toward the sky. In this "House of Friendship," at the base of these upwardpointing fingers, young people from various parts of the world met together with German and American parents of exchange students, government and church officials, and others who came to talk about the work of God's Kingdom.

The German people told us that when the war was over and we of the American churches sent young people to help them instead of our bishops, our college professors, and our highly trained technicians, they at first were alarmed, almost insulted. What could these youth do for broken cities and destroyed homes? What did they know about the church? Did they have any knowledge of ecclesiasticism and theology?

They soon learned, the Germans continued, that these Christian youth were not as deeply interested in theology as they were in helping people who suffered. They were not as much concerned about rebuilding the broken cathedral walls as they were about helping the people who had worshiped within these walls. These youth came to Europe with willing hands, with clothing, with food.

The European church began to see that we of the American churches were sending to them the most precious thing we had — our youth. They learned that we were willing to entrust our children to those who formerly had been our enemies, because we loved our enemies. As this realization grew, their respect for the American church grew. Their understanding of the place of youth in the life of the church broadened, they told us. They saw that youth might be able to rebuild the concept of the Christian church as a serving, loving, forgiving body of Christ's children. The German people testified over and over to us of their high regard for the significant work of these young people. The Germans thanked the American church for their youth; they thanked the youth for helping them with their hands and teaching them with their deeds.

2. I saw more clearly a church with hands and feet.

Tied immediately to this increasing respect for youth in the life of the church, the German people told us, was a growing understanding of the demanding necessity to bring religion out of the cathedrals, where it often gets musty and cold, and to give it hands and feet. That is what these youth had done. The Europeans did not believe that theology is any less important today than formerly or that ecclesiastical organization is no longer necessary. But they were led to discover that ecclesiasticism and theology without a program of loving, helpful service are insufficient and incomplete. They testified that these young people helped them to discover that. European churchmen and government officials went so far as to suggest that the contribution of the Church of the Brethren to Europe, larger even than its cattle and its material goods, was this demonstration of a religion which has at its center the loving heart of Christ, but which also has hands and feet, a program of loving service.

They and we discussed this together throughout the summer, all over Europe. It was our common agreement, growing out of these experiences and discussions that the churches of Europe and the churches of America can help one another to a more complete understanding of the Kingdom of God, for which Christ both lived and died. For this reason they believe that the Church of the Brethren should not withdraw from Europe, even though much of the material-aid work is done. We, as churches and as Christians together, should keep on discovering things about our Christ.

3. The Spirit of God can come close to us if we will let Him.

I think that this was demonstrated in many ways during the year. The experiences at the Germantown love feast and at the grave of Alexander Mack set the tone for a deeply spiritual year.

The church faced business items at Annual Conference over which there was a wide divergence of opinion. One thing which all of us had in common, however, was that we wanted to be led by the Holy Spirit to discover God's will. A remarkable spirit of Christian courtesy, of prayerful searching, of highly regarding the other person's personality and opinion, and of waiting for God's leading was manifested. Many said that because of this the business sessions were among the high spiritual points of the Conference. The final session, during which we asked God to commission us to go out and live like Christians in our homes, our communities, and wherever God would lead us, was helpful particularly to those who have gone across the seas. Letters which have come back from them since have indicated that the memory of that night is sustaining them in hard places.

God came especially close also when several hundred of us stood beside the River Eder in Schwarzenau, near the picturesque bridge, surrounded by the memories of Alexander Mack, and rededicated ourselves to the service of the Lord as He would direct us.

Even tragedy brought us close to God as a mutual family feeling of sorrow was felt all across our Brotherhood when some of our number were lost in accidents at sea or upon the land. We can thank God that the thousands of miles of travel which were entailed in attending Annual Conference and journeying to Europe did not result in more accidents. God's protecting hand must have been close to us. For those families which did suffer losses we are still united in prayer. This sorrow has brought us all nearer to each other and nearer to God.

4. We examined ourselves in order that we may serve others.

We spent a great deal of time analyzing what it is we as Brethren believe. This was good for us. We tried to lift our specific teachings out of their long backgrounds of history and to discover how they can be most helpful in furthering God's Kingdom in the present world. There was some praising of ourselves. The effort, however, was to steer clear of self-praise, and to concentrate on what we as individuals and as a church are called of God to do now and in the future. This is a quest which we should forever pursue.

II. What of the Goals Ahead?

The Church of the Brethren has set some great goals during its two-hundred-fiftieth year. It is interesting that the culminating and climaxing emphasis of the year centers upon evangelism. Foundational preparation has been made for this by the earlier emphases of the year: repentance, prayer, a clearer knowledge of what it is we believe, a deepened stewardship. Now all of this should culminate and continue in an explosive evangelism. But none of these emphases should ever cease.

This has been a great anniversary year. But its real success will be determined by how we live next year, and the next!

The Spirit of God should abound more fully within us.

Our wills should have more completely become His will.

Our total stewardship should have been enhanced.

Our hearts should be more loving toward all others.

Our Christian beliefs and message should be clearer to us.

We should feel compelled to proclaim and to teach the message more urgently to others.

This has happened to some. Has it happened to you?